Revisioning
the Civil War

Revisioning the Civil War

Historians on Counter-Factual Scenarios

Edited by JAMES C. BRESNAHAN

Foreword by Keith E. Gibson

McFarland & Company, Inc., Publishers
Jefferson, North Carolina, and London

Library
University of Texas
at San Antonio

LIBRARY OF CONGRESS CATALOGUING-IN-PUBLICATION DATA

Revisioning the Civil War : historians on counter-factual scenarios /
edited by James C. Bresnahan ; foreword by Keith E. Gibson.
 p.   cm.
Includes bibliographical references and index.

ISBN 0-7864-2392-7 (softcover : 50# alkaline paper) ∞

1. United States—History—Civil War, 1861–1865.   2. United
States—History—Civil War, 1861–1865—Campaigns.   I. Bresnahan,
James C., 1958–
 E468.R465 2006
 973.7—dc22
                                        2005029559

British Library cataloguing data are available

©2006 James C. Bresnahan. All rights reserved

Cover photograph ©2005 Corbis Images

Manufactured in the United States of America

McFarland & Company, Inc., Publishers
 Box 611, Jefferson, North Carolina 28640
 www.mcfarlandpub.com

To the parents who shaped me,
the siblings who support me,
the wife who puts up with me
and the family who loves me.

Contents

Foreword
by Keith E. Gibson

It's right up there near the top of the list of things historians are warned — indeed, trained — not to do: Do not engage in "what if" history. The logic for this admonition is clear enough. History, after all, is supposed to be what happened — not what almost happened or what might have happened. Yet for most of us history consumers, the most intriguing part of the story is often what might have been, if only ...

It is human nature, not academic discipline, which stirs thoughts of the might-have-beens or the almosts of the past. We want to know the critical moment, the pivotal decision that started the cascade to failure or the rise to victory. In the study of socio-economic history, "the moment" might be a generation or two, that is, a series of events intertwined over distance and time. Only when such historical evolution is viewed from a distance can we begin to see the cause and effect of decision-making.

There is one branch of historical study, however, that is particularly well suited for trading in the "what if" taboo. Military historians, amateur and professional, are encouraged to speculate — and for good reason: *survival*. It is often declared that warfare is the extension of political will. Unlike cultural, socio-economic history, the study of military history quite often revolves around "the moment." Once soldiers take to the field, history becomes a series of moment by moment decisions with immediate life and death impact. What order resulted in soldiers being needlessly sent into a firestorm? What different decision could have avoided disaster? Future success may be revealed in the study of past action.

George Santayana was not specifically speaking of military history when he declared, "Those who cannot remember the past are condemned to repeat it," but those who study military conflict keenly understand his warning. It is the reason those who pursue the profession of arms are so

1

interested in the exploits of their spiritual ancestors. Survival on some future battlefield may very well be influenced by how much time the future decision-maker spent reflecting on the actions of his predecessors. "Stonewall" Jackson was a student of Napoleon's campaigns. The circumstances under which the Confederate general found himself at the southern base of the Massanutten Mountain in June 1862, and Jackson's approach to those circumstances, were curiously similar to those facing Napoleon at the 1797 Battle of Rivoli in his Italian Campaign.

What if Lincoln had not been elected, or for that matter, assassinated five years later? What if Hood had stopped Sherman's relentless march through Tennessee and Georgia? Suppose Lee had remained in the Federal Army? If only "Stonewall" had been at Gettysburg! Wondering does not change history, but it can change the way we think about the past and what we can learn from it.

Jim Bresnahan has come up with an effective three-part approach to examining the "what ifs" of the American Civil War. A brief introduction to each topic establishes the facts. Next, the views of several leading scholars are presented in their own words. Lastly, the often-divergent opinions are summarized. In this way we are presented several intriguing alternatives to the historical facts.

In addition, questions are posed to the scholars exploring the impact of pivotal non-military decisions. How did the Emancipation Proclamation really affect the North, South and foreign reaction to the war effort? Should the South have recruited African Americans for combat roles? What brought the nation to armed conflict — slavery, economics, states' rights? The responses to these questions allow us to join in the ongoing debate. Monday morning quarterbacking? Maybe, but with a purpose. The debate allows us to better comprehend events virtually inconceivable to us today. Monday morning quarterbacking doesn't change the score, but it might change the way the game is played in the future.

The result is that we are left with a better understanding, not of what we might have been, but of what we have in fact become in the intervening 140 years.

Colonel Gibson is director of the Virginia Military Institute Museum, Lexington, Virginia

Acknowledgments

As editor of this counter-factual book, I recognize that this project could not have succeeded without the assistance of some of the nation's top Civil War experts. Whether leading battlefield tours, instructing students or writing books and articles, these folks educate people of all ages about Civil War history, ensuring that the sacrifice of the soldiers will never be forgotten.

The panel's commentary was gathered through both written submissions and telephone interviews. I am much obliged to each participant for taking time to tell us how events *could* have transpired. A hearty thanks goes out to all. I sincerely hope they continue to educate us about the American Civil War because we are the richer for it.

This was my first venture into the literary world, and I need to thank those responsible for lighting the way, including Dick Halseth, Richard Lewis, John Heatwole, Dolores Kostelni and Keith Gibson.

I'd also like to thank the National Park Service for its assistance and cooperation, particularly in providing the maps used in this book.

Finally, I received outstanding support on the home front, from my brothers Tim and Chris, my sister Belinda and my mom and dad. My loving wife, Mercy, and my two dogs, Bailey and K.C., never complained about my long hours at the computer screen. Without the encouragement of family members, I never would have been able to complete this venture.

The Panel of
Civil War Experts

Matt Atkinson is a native of Houston, Mississippi. He received his B.A. and a B.B.A. from the University of Mississippi. He and his wife are employed by the National Park Service and currently reside in Vicksburg, Mississippi. Matt has served in the past at Petersburg National Battlefield, Natchez National Historical Park, Manassas National Battlefield and Gettysburg National Military Park.

Ed Bearss, an independent scholar and historian whose public career started with the National Park Service in 1955, became the service's chief historian in 1981. He continues to serve as a Civil War consultant and stays extremely busy conducting detailed battlefield site tours and speaking on history and preservation-related subjects. Ed is on the road more than 270 days each year.

Richard Beringer received his Ph.D. in 1966 from Northwestern University. He chaired the University of North Dakota's history department from 1993 through 1997. Richard is the author of several Civil War books including *Why the South Lost*, jointly authored with Herman Hattaway, Archer Jones and William Still, Jr., and *Jefferson Davis: Confederate President*, co-authored with Herman Hattaway.

Chris Calkins has been with the National Park Service for nearly three decades. He is currently chief of interpretation at the Petersburg National

Battlefield. Active in battlefield preservation efforts, Chris has authored eight publications, numerous articles and the highly acclaimed "Lee's Retreat" driving tour.

Peter Carmichael received his Ph.D. in history from Pennsylvania State University. He was an assistant professor of history at UNC-Greensboro before taking the director's position at the Lincoln Cottage. Peter is the author of several books on the Civil War including *The Last Generation: Slaveholders' Sons and the Creation of a Southern Identity, 1850–1865* and *Lee's Young Artillerist: William R. J. Pegram.*

Larry Daniel is the author of six books on the Western theater of the Civil War. Larry won the Fletcher Pratt Award of the New York Civil War Round-table and the Mrs. Simon Baruch University Press Award for *Cannoneers in Gray.* He holds a Master of Divinity degree from Emory University in Atlanta and is a Methodist minister in Memphis, Tennessee.

Keith Dickson, a VMI graduate with a Ph.D. in history from the University of Virginia, serves as professor of military studies for the Joint and Combined Warfighting School, Joint Forces Staff College with the National Defense University. He's the author of *Civil War for Dummies* and *World War II for Dummies.*

Brad Gottfried holds a Ph.D. in zoology from Miami University. For over two decades, he has been a full-time faculty member and college administrator and is currently president of Sussex County Community College. He has authored several books on the Civil War including *Roads to Gettysburg* and *Brigades of Gettysburg.*

Mark Grimsley is an associate professor of history at Ohio State University. He received his B.A. and Ph.D. in history from Ohio State and is the author or co-author of several books on the Civil War including *The Collapse of the Confederacy.*

Scott Hartwig is the supervisory park historian at the Gettysburg National Military Park. He is the author of a number of articles and books including *A Killer Angels Companion* and *The Complete Pictorial of Battlefield Monuments and Markers.*

John Heatwole writes about the social history of the Shenandoah Valley and the Civil War in northwestern Virginia. He's the author of *Chrisman's*

Boy Company and *The Burning*. John was appointed by the secretary of the interior to the board of the Shenandoah Valley Battlefields Commission in 1997. He has also served as a consultant to Time/Life Books and Virginia Civil War Trails.

John Hennessy has written two books on the Manassas campaigns including *Return to Bull Run: The Campaign and Battle of Second Manassas*. He is currently the chief historian at Fredericksburg and Spotsylvania National Military Park.

Clint Johnson is a Winston-Salem, North Carolina–based Civil War writer who specializes in showing travelers where they can find Civil War and other historical sites. He also makes it a point to uncover stories that involve lesser-known historical figures. Clint is the author of several books including *Touring Virginia's and West Virginia's Civil War Sites* and *Touring the Carolinas' Civil War Sites*.

Robert E.L. Krick has lived or worked on Civil War battlefields almost continuously since 1972. He graduated from Mary Washington College with a degree in history. Since 1991, he has been an historian on the staff of the Richmond National Battlefield Park. His first book was a unit history on the 40th Virginia Infantry. The University of North Carolina Press published his biographical register of the Army of Northern Virginia's staff officers, *Staff Officers in Gray*, in 2003.

Richard McMurry, a native of Atlanta, received a B.A. in history from the Virginia Military Institute and an M.A. and Ph.D. from Emory University. He's the author of *John Bell Hood and the War for Southern Independence*, which received both the Mrs. Simon Baruch University Press Award and the Fletcher Pratt Award. He is also the author of *The Fourth Battle of Winchester: Toward a New Civil War Paradigm*.

Kenneth Noe, a native of Virginia, is Draughon Professor of Southern History at Auburn University. He received degrees from Emory & Henry University, Virginia Tech, the University of Kentucky and the University of Illinois. He is the author of *Southwest Virginia's Railroad* and *Perryville*.

Donald Pfanz is a native of Gettysburg and has served for over two decades with the National Park Service. He is currently staff historian at the Fredericksburg and Spotsylvania National Military Park. Donald has written several books on the Civil War including books on Confederate general Richard Ewell and the Battle of Fredericksburg.

Gerald Prokopowicz received his J.D. from the University of Michigan and a Ph.D. in history from Harvard. He spent nine years as the Lincoln scholar and director of public programs at the Lincoln Museum in Fort Wayne, Indiana. He is the author of *All for the Regiment: The Army of the Ohio, 1861–1862* and is currently an assistant professor of history at East Carolina University in Greenville, North Carolina.

George Rable received his Ph.D. from Louisiana State University and has been teaching southern history at the University of Alabama since the fall of 1998. He has authored several Civil War books including *The Confederate Republic: A Revolution against Politics* and *Fredericksburg! Fredericksburg!* His current project involves a study of religion during the Civil War.

Gordon Rhea, with a law degree from Stanford, served as special assistant to the chief counsel for the Senate Select Committee on Intelligence Activities. He is the author of several books on the Civil War including *The Battle of the Wilderness* and *To the North Anna River*. He has lectured in the past at the U.S. Army Training and Doctrine Command and has also appeared on Civil War programs on the History Channel, A&E and the Discovery Channel.

Jeff Shaara graduated from Florida State University in 1974 with a degree in criminology. He wrote the prequel and sequel to the classic Civil War novel *The Killer Angels* written by his father, Michael Shaara. The prequel was *Gods and Generals* and the sequel was *The Last Full Measure*.

John Y. Simon received his B.A. from Swarthmore College and a Ph.D. in history from Harvard. He taught at Ohio State University and began editing *The Papers of Ulysses S. Grant* in 1962. In 1964 John moved to Southern Illinois University, where he is professor of history as well as editor of the Grant papers, with 26 published volumes.

Craig Symonds is a professor of history at the U.S. Naval Academy in Annapolis. He has written a number of books on the Civil War as well as several naval histories and historical atlases. His Civil War books include *Joseph E. Johnston: A Civil War Biography* and *Stonewall of the West: Patrick Cleburne and the Civil War*.

John C. (Jack) **Waugh**, a newspaper journalist turned historical reporter, was on the staff of *The Christian Science Monitor* for 17 years as a correspondent and bureau chief. Since 1989, he has been reporting on national affairs in the 19th century. His first book, *The Class of 1846*, won the New York Civil War Roundtable's Fletcher Pratt Award for the best nonfiction book on the Civil War for 1994. He is also the author of *Reelecting Lincoln*.

Jeff Wert is a retired schoolteacher and the author of more than 100 articles, essays and columns in magazines. He is the author of seven books including *Gettysburg— Day Three* and *General James Longstreet*.

Eric Wittenberg is a partner in a law firm in Columbus, Ohio, and received his law degree from the University of Pittsburgh School of Law. He is the author of several books focusing on cavalry actions in the Civil War, including *Gettysburg's Forgotten Cavalry Actions* and *The Union Cavalry Comes of Age: Hartwood Church to Brandy Station*.

Steven Woodworth is an associate professor of history at Texas Christian University. He teaches courses on U.S. history, the Civil War and Reconstruction and the Old South. A two-time winner of the prestigious Fletcher Pratt Award for his books *Davis and Lee at War* and *Jefferson Davis and His Generals*, Steven received his Ph.D. from Rice University.

Preface

Our fascination with the American Civil War knows no bounds. Historians have been writing about it and enthusiasts have been reading about it almost from the opening shots in 1861. A family trip to Gettysburg in 1972 was enough to bewitch a 13-year-old; I've been captivated by the conflict ever since.

We know what happened and we know why it happened. I have long been intrigued with what *could have* happened. This book gives the experts a chance to refight the Civil War, to explore historical alternatives and to voice opinions about not only what *could* have happened but also about what *could not* have happened. Multiple opinions on the same issue should give the reader a broad range of viewpoints to consider.

Speculating about alternative history can be entertaining, educational and also frustrating. No sooner do we answer one question than another one arises. We can learn from history, however, if we focus on the short term and don't overextend. For example, it's fine to say that an attack by Richard Ewell on Cemetery Hill would have driven the Federals off the high ground at Gettysburg on July 1, 1863. It's quite another matter to turn that kind of tactical success into independence for the Confederacy.

If our panelists can get the reader thinking about how Civil War history could have been legitimately different, then this book has done its job. Before we get started, let's take a brief look at what a few of the experts had to say about counter-factual history and the art of being an armchair general.

Is speculating about alternative history a legitimate academic tool?

MARK GRIMSLEY: Even when you are doing straightforward history, you are interpreting the past. You are making explanations, saying this factor or this variable was the most important. For example, when people ask why the Civil War happened, some will say the war occurred because of the disagreement over the issue of slavery. So you can put that statement on its head and say if there had been no slavery, there would have been no Civil War. That's counter-factualism. Either way, you're doing history. It is kind of a thought experiment; most of the time we are doing the thought experiment one way. When we ask "what if?" we are simply doing the same thought experiment, interpreting history, with a different method.

I think it's a valid method, but the problem is that many times people do "what if" history in a beer-and-pretzel type of way. They use very relaxed rules of evidence and logic that are very much in contrast with the rigorous rules that are used in interpreting what actually happened in history.

RICHARD MCMURRY: Counter-factual history is certainly a valid way to go about studying history, but you have to define the parameters of what you're going to do. You have to keep it in the realm of what was actually possible at the time. It has to be technically and logistically possible. If you say X is true but a commander had no way to know that, then is it really valid to fault him for not acting in accordance with it? Take Gettysburg for example. There were literally millions of decisions in that battle with perhaps 2,000 to 3,000 important decisions. Some folks like to change one decision without changing any of the other variables. Say you have a Union sharpshooter and he sees two Confederates, one sitting on a horse talking to the other Confederate on the ground. He says to himself, "Do I shoot the man on the horse or the man on the ground?" He elects to shoot the man on the horse, who turns out to be a private acting as a courier, while the man on the ground turns out to be General Robert E. Lee. If he shoots the man on the ground, the battle and the entire war are changed. So if you change one element, you have to think about how that changes other things.

RICHARD BERINGER: The counter-factual proposition is useful for discussion of future policies and actions. The historical sense may sometimes help us make intelligent decisions about future courses of action. If we know that certain types of actions have usually produced certain kinds of results in the past, we can better judge what to do in the future.

Actually, historians become involved in this more than they are willing to admit, for every time they consider an historical event and its consequences, they imply that there was an alternative. Few things are utterly inevitable. For example, to discuss the Spanish-American War and its consequences automatically questions whether the world after 1898 might have been different without the war, and certainly it would have been.

When folks oversimplify history, then alternative history is dangerous from a policy-making point of view — though it may still be amusing over a glass of beer.

GORDON RHEA: It's easy to sit back 140 years later and use hindsight on battlefield decisions. Our understanding of what happened keeps changing. In the Civil War, commanders only knew about what was happening on their immediate front, and only recently have we been able to pull together diaries, letters and recollections from the folks on all of the fronts to put together the larger picture. There could be holes in even that assessment as some sources survived and others did not, so we could still be missing pieces of the puzzle.

Alternative history can be looked at from the perspective of the common soldier too. My book *Carrying the Flag* is about a 40-year-old private from South Carolina, Charles Wildon, who suffered from epileptic seizures. He was with the 1st South Carolina regiment at the Bloody Angle at Spotsylvania Court House. He carried a flag bravely, and his regiment charged to where it was supposed to go, and the Confederates held a critical part of their lines. It shows that many times a battle or campaign can be decided by one individual or by a number of common soldiers.

1

On the Brink: Secession

The sectional dispute that ripped apart the United States in 1860 had been brewing throughout the 19th century. Northerners and Southerners were divided over several important issues, including states' rights and economic affairs. Another major source of contention was slavery; the two sides were unable to agree on a compromise that would permanently settle the question of whether the national government had the right to stop the extension of slavery into territories.

The national crisis was thrust front and center when Republican Abraham Lincoln, who had vowed to keep slavery out of the territories, captured the presidency in 1860. Recognizing that the North was becoming increasingly dominant economically and politically, and that the election of a Republican could foreshadow the end of their way of life, Southerners chose to form a new nation. South Carolina led the way by seceding in December of 1860, followed by six other states in the opening months of 1861.

A Looming Crisis

By 1860, the North and South had become two vastly different sections of the United States. The industrial North relied heavily on federal protection from foreign imports while the South, an agrarian society, feared national legislation that might damage the Southern economy.[1]

Slavery had existed in America since colonial times and even though it had faded away in the North, slavery received a boost in the South in 1793 with the invention of the cotton gin. Eli Whitney's device greatly increased the demand for cotton and allowed huge quantities of the staple to be raised inexpensively with slave labor. By 1860, cotton exports were worth 191 million dollars; slave property was valued at approximately $2 billion.[2] Due to the economic impact that the elimination of slavery would have, Southerners felt inclined to maintain the institution.

There had also been several unsuccessful attempts, in the first half of the 19th century, to find a permanent solution to the slavery issue. Both the Missouri Compromise of 1820 and the Compromise of 1850 were unable to satisfactorily address the question of what to do with slavery in new states and territories. Then, in 1854, the ill-advised Kansas-Nebraska Act gave citizens of each territory the opportunity to decide whether to permit or ban slavery when the issue of statehood arose. Bloody Kansas became a battleground, with free-soil settlers from the North clashing with pro-slavery settlers from the South.[3]

In the wake of the bloodshed, a new political party emerged. The Republican Party included opponents of slavery as well as business leaders who supported a strong central government that would protect industrial interests.[4] The first Republican presidential candidate, John C. Fremont, turned in a respectable performance in the election of 1856, carrying 11 Northern states while garnering a large popular vote.[5]

In addition to the birth of the Republican Party, the decade of the 1850s brought with it several events that accelerated the movement toward disunion, including John Brown's harebrained scheme in 1859 to launch a slave insurrection in the South by seizing the Federal arsenal at Harpers Ferry, Virginia. U.S. troops quickly thwarted Brown's raid, and Brown was tried, convicted and executed for treason. Before his death, Brown predicted that only bloodshed would purge the guilty land of its crimes. By the time of the presidential election of 1860, relations between the North and the South had become extremely volatile.

Was the Civil War inevitable?

RICHARD BERINGER: Many nations have had a civil war during their history stemming from one issue or another. England, Russia, Spain, China, France and Mexico all have experienced civil wars or revolutions. States' rights, slavery, sectionalism and economics were all issues dividing the United States in 1860. The war could easily have started by 1851 if the Compromise of 1850 had not been passed. The Civil War might have started even without the slavery issue, perhaps over labor and economic issues later in the 19th century. The South felt it was under siege politically as its share of the total population declined relative to that of the North, and the strength of the Northern states grew in the House of Representatives. By 1861, determined leaders on both sides were ready for a fight. The only issue to be settled was who would fire the first shot.

JEFF SHAARA: The Civil War was bound to happen sooner or later. It had been brewing for some time. You can go back to the 1770s, during the American Revolution. There was a lot of disagreement between the different sections of the country over various issues and the 13 colonies came together tentatively. The Southern colonies were nervous about their relationship with the colonies in the North since they were very different cultures. When the Continental Congress came together in 1775, you essentially had representatives from 13 different countries coming together in Philadelphia. So right from the beginning it was a very uneasy relationship. Everything was about compromise and a lot of people had to give quite a lot to bring the nation into existence in the first place. Right from the start, all it took was one incendiary issue to light the fuse and there was no more volatile issue than slavery.

KENNETH NOE: You can trace the causes of the Civil War back to the Missouri Compromise of 1820 and the rise of slavery's expansion as a political issue. Some people will go all the way back to the founding of the colonies. The Kansas-Nebraska Act of 1854 really made the war inevitable. It reopened the issue of expansion of slavery, which had been closed theoretically by the Compromise of 1850. It introduced slavery into an area that had been closed off to slavery due to the Missouri Compromise of 1820. Northerners had come to rely on the Missouri Compromise as the third leg of a stool, along with the Declaration of Independence and the Constitution. Northerners felt betrayed when Northern Democrats joined with Southern politicians to allow slavery into that area north of the old Missouri Compromise line. The Kansas-Nebraska Act destroyed the Whig Party, which was already weak. In its place, you got the Republican Party, a purely sectional party. There were few if any Southern Republicans.

If Fremont had been elected in 1856, as the Republican presidential nominee, the war likely would have started four years earlier. Republicans to Southerners represented the end of slavery, if not immediately. Republicans made it clear that they wanted to put slavery, as Lincoln put it, on its course of ultimate extinction. If Fremont had been elected, it might have been better for the Southern states that would have formed a Confederacy. If you look at Fremont's career in the war, in Missouri and in the East, it's hard to be impressed by Fremont. The Republicans in 1856 realized that

Fremont wasn't particularly bright or adept. He was a macho matinee idol. The Republicans had hopes that Fremont's astute wife, Jessie Benton Fremont, might have a positive effect on him. Fremont proved during the war that he was a poor administrator. He surrounded himself with friends and cut himself off from public opinion. He would have been a poor choice for President when it comes to the Union and that probably would have been better for the Confederacy.

CRAIG SYMONDS: It is hard to argue that anything in history is inevitable but it is hard to see how the Civil War could have been avoided. The central problem of American society in the 19th century, slavery and especially the extension of slavery into the western territories, had defied the best efforts of statesmen to find a compromise. It is very difficult to envision a scenario in which this issue could have been resolved without recourse to arms. Not only had the South grown defensive about the presumed virtues of its labor system, but also the sheer capital investment in slaves was enormous. Eliminating slavery in the middle of the 19th century would be like politicians today declaring that all private property in the stock market was going to be abolished. And for Southerners, the extension of slavery was absolutely essential to its survival. Lincoln's pledge that he would not interfere with slavery where it existed meant nothing. If he prevented its growth, it was the same thing as ensuring its destruction. To be sure, the changing nature of the American economy would have made slavery less profitable over time, but there was not enough money in the country to buy out the slaveholders, and the social commitment to slavery by the South would have made voluntary manumission impossible. In the end, then, I think armed conflict over the future of slavery was inevitable. Lincoln was correct when he noted that "the pinch must come." Another compromise might have delayed the sectional confrontation, but I cannot see how it would have prevented it.

JOHN SIMON: In the 1930s, some historians believed that the Civil War was a needless war. Their belief was that if agitators on both sides had left things as they were, there would be no need for war. The main issue was slavery, and slavery was expected to die a natural death. Many people thought slavery was economically unprofitable. I don't agree. Economic historians have told us that slavery was not on its last legs in 1861. Slavery was actually more profitable than ever. Profits from slavery were higher than or comparable with the best sorts of investments that could be found in the United States. Slavery was something that Southern planters found economically viable.

There was also the question of whether slavery had reached its natural limits. Some argued that slavery could not be extended into the western territories but needed the rich bonanza soil of the South. However, if you look at some fairly recent statistics, the most productive land, when it comes to producing cotton, can be found surrounding Fresno, California, followed closely by a couple of counties in Arizona. With irrigation, these areas can be highly productive.

People also argued that slavery could not be readjusted to industrial production. That belief is belied by the experience of the Nazis in World War II. The idea that slavery was somehow doomed and would fade away was fallacious. In that sense, the war was not unnecessary as older historians made it out to be.

The Republican Threat

The Republican Party's presidential nominee in the 1860 election, Abraham Lincoln of Illinois, was not considered to be a radical opponent of slavery.[6] Republicans also attempted to use moderation in setting up their platform for the election. Even though party members voiced opposition to any plan that would result in the expansion of slavery into new territories, they also promised not to interfere with slavery in states that allowed the institution.[7]

Democrats found themselves divided over the issue of expanding slavery; the result was two Democratic nominees for the 1860 election. The Northern wing of the party, supportive of a popular sovereignty platform, gave its backing to Illinois senator Stephen Douglas. The Southern wing, seeking protection of the rights of slavery in the territories, pledged its support to Kentucky's John C. Breckinridge.[8] A fourth presidential candidate was thrown into the mix when the Constitutional Union party came up with John Bell of Tennessee, in hopes of keeping the nation intact through compromise.

In the end, Lincoln took the election with a solid majority in the Electoral College, although the combined total of the other three contenders outnumbered the Republican by nearly a million votes.[9] Capturing every free state except New Jersey, Lincoln received scant support south of the Mason-Dixon Line. Breckinridge carried most of the South except Kentucky, Tennessee and Virginia, which supported Bell. Douglas grabbed just 12 electoral votes but still wound up second in the popular vote.[10]

South Carolina lawmakers responded quickly to the Republican triumph by calling for a state convention in Charleston, and on December 20 convention members voted to dissolve South Carolina's ties to the

Union. Secession now spread like wildfire; in January and February six additional Southern states voted to join with South Carolina. Lincoln's victory had pushed the nation over the edge of the abyss into disunion.

What if Lincoln had not been elected president in 1860?

GEORGE RABLE: The South certainly felt threatened by the Republican Party. William Seward would have been seen by the South as even more threatening than Lincoln.[11] Lincoln was by no means guaranteed to get the Republican nomination at the party's convention in Chicago in 1860. Lincoln was the second choice among many of the delegates but his campaign managers were extremely skillful.

When you look at the 1860 presidential election returns, the best evidence shows that the two additional candidates, Bell and Breckinridge, did not make much of a difference in the Electoral College. Removing Bell and Breckinridge from the picture might have helped Douglas in several states but the overall picture would have looked the same. There was even a movement in several Northern states to bring together the Bell, Breckinridge and Douglas campaigns. Had Douglas somehow won the election of 1860, the Southern states would not have seceded. One wonders if those voting for Lincoln in 1860 in the North or for Breckinridge in the South would have cast those ballots if they had known about the four bloody years that lay ahead.

JACK WAUGH: It was astounding that Lincoln was even nominated. He was truly a dark horse but he had some shrewd manipulators working for him to win the Republican nomination. Even if Douglas had won the election, the Civil War may have still occurred. Douglas favored popular sovereignty, to allow new territories to decide whether they wanted slavery. However, Douglas and Lincoln had similar views on secession. Once Lincoln had won the election, Douglas told Lincoln that he would do whatever he could to help Lincoln deal with the crisis over secession.

If Seward had been nominated for president in 1860 at the Republican convention, rather than Lincoln, he was much more willing to make an adjustment, when it came to slavery in the territories. In fact, Seward did his best to placate the South while serving as secretary of state. Though he was very much anti-slavery he would have been much more inclined to temporize with the South than Lincoln was in the crunch. Lincoln had told the South that he had no constitutional authority to do away with slavery but he did not want to see it expand. Seward might have waffled on the issue of expansion.[12]

If Breckinridge had won the election, he would have enshrined slav-

Abraham Lincoln. His victory in the 1860 election pushed the Deep South toward secession. LIBRARY OF CONGRESS.

ery forever if he could. Bell, the Constitutional Union candidate, would have done anything necessary to work out an accommodation with the South.

PETER CARMICHAEL: Many people will focus on Lincoln as the instigator of the war. That's not an accurate depiction of events following the 1860 election. Lincoln represented the Republican Party, a sectional based party. The party was committed to stopping the expansion of slavery in the territories. Lincoln had made it clear that he would not touch slavery where it currently existed. Southerners perceived Lincoln and the Republicans as an abolitionist party, an anti-slavery party. With that perception in hand, many white Southerners created a scenario in which they believed they would endure a long, slow death at the hands of the Republicans, due to the party's efforts to stop the spread of slavery. White Southerners thought they had the constitutional right to take slaves to the new territories. They felt if Lincoln succeeded in the push to stop the further spread of slavery, it would be the first step to the dismantling of slavery in the South.

    If someone else had received the Republican nomination, like perhaps William Seward, events would have unfolded in exactly the same manner. The crucial issue here isn't Lincoln but the Republican Party. If the Republicans succeed in the 1860 election, there was probably going to be a civil war. If the Republicans failed in 1860 but won in 1864, we probably would see the war in 1864 because, to the South, the Republican Party represented Northern free labor interests.

Jefferson Davis

    Delegates from the seven states that had voted in favor of secession met in Montgomery, Alabama, in February. The result was a new nation: the Confederate States of America was born, with Jefferson Davis of Mississippi elected president and Alexander Stephens of Georgia named vice-president. Davis had served the United States as a congressman, senator, military officer and secretary of war but appeared surprised by the election results, perhaps preferring a field command instead.[13] Selected over such fire-eaters as Robert Barnwell Rhett, Robert Toombs, William Yancey and Howell Cobb, Davis was viewed as a moderate who would be a more attractive proposition to the Upper South and border states.[14] Over the next four years, Davis would have personal battles with a number of Southern governors and would also be criticized for attempting to exert broad wartime powers.

What if Jefferson Davis had not been elected president of the Confederacy?

JOHN SIMON: My favorite candidate for the president of the C.S.A. was Robert Toombs. He's somebody who drinks too much and is a bit bizarre at times. He's a sound thinker though. He's the person who tells Jefferson Davis not to fire on Fort Sumter. He's the person who, when he learns of the suffering of Union prisoners at Andersonville, says if the South can't take care of the prisoners, the Confederacy shouldn't hold them any longer. It's the kind of statesmanship that the South lacks and counters Davis' pigheadedness, his favoritism with generals, his insistence on being declared right on all occasions and his inability to rally popular support.

GEORGE RABLE: There were a few other candidates considered for the position including a trio of Georgians, Howell Cobb, Alexander Stephens and Robert Toombs.[15] Cobb had Congressional experience as a Democrat and both Stephens and Toombs had been important Whig leaders in Georgia. For various reasons, the Georgia delegation couldn't get together to support one candidate and that opened the door for Davis. Davis may have been the best choice of the four. Stephens' health was always a bit shaky and he wasn't a rabid secessionist. Toombs eliminated himself from consideration due to being publicly drunk on a couple of occasions. Cobb was a competent, colorless politician. Some historians have suggested that Cobb might have been a more effective president than Jefferson Davis. There doesn't appear to be a whole lot of evidence to back up that claim. There really weren't that many choices available and performance in office is very unpredictable. When Lincoln himself was elected in 1860, the expectations probably weren't very high for his presidency. Lincoln had very little administrative experience and there was nothing in his background that would have suggested that he would turn out to be a successful president.

RICHARD BERINGER: The Confederate States of America would have been foolish to elect a different person to the presidency. Robert Barnwell Rhett was too extreme, Alexander Stephens too petulant and Robert Toombs was not always sober. R.M.T. Hunter of Virginia wasn't available because his state had yet to secede. Perhaps the best alternative might have been John C. Breckinridge of Kentucky, but Kentucky was a neutral state and Breckinridge had not yet joined the C.S.A. When Davis was elected, there were only seven states in the Confederacy and he clearly was the most qualified, based on his experience. Perhaps the C.S.A. would have lost sooner, had it not been for Jefferson Davis.

MARK GRIMSLEY: There were very few candidates for the job beyond Jefferson Davis. Southern politicians, by the time, specialized in the politics of opposition and intransigence. The Confederacy simply did not have a lot of presidential candidates who had the capacity for strong, positive leadership, the kind of constructive leadership a new nation required. Only a few individuals were considered beyond Jefferson Davis. Howell Cobb and Alexander Stephens of Georgia were both considered, and Stephens did become vice-president. Robert Toombs was also considered but none of these people would have done a better job than Davis.

JEFF SHAARA: I'm not sure the Confederacy benefited from picking Jefferson Davis. The personality of Davis was important. Davis was the man who organized the Confederacy. Many of the Southern states, like South Carolina, Georgia and Alabama, were very much focused on the issue of states' rights. They felt they had the right to govern themselves as they saw fit within their own borders, and Davis had to overcome that to create the Confederacy. Davis was a powerful philosophical leader; when Davis moved his cabinet to Richmond, one of the things he did was to help the various Southern states see that they really had more in common then some of them might have believed. Texas is a very different place from Virginia, as Florida is different from North Carolina. Yet these states were united in the cause

Jefferson Davis, the Confederacy's first and only president. LIBRARY OF CONGRESS.

of the Confederacy and you can thank Davis for that unity. That was the good news about Davis. The bad news was Davis was very stubborn. Robert E. Lee was very aware in late 1864 that the Confederacy was losing the conflict. Davis, on the other hand, didn't want to hear about that. Davis believed to the bitter end that there was a way the Confederates could still win. In a way, that's a very destructive philosophy and it certainly had a negative impact on the Confederacy.

Summary

Look up the word "inevitable" in the dictionary and you'll see several definitions listed, including unavoidable, irresistible and certain. How could a nation, forged by blood and sacrifice during the American Revolution, be ripped apart less than 80 years later? As panelist Richard Beringer pointed out, there were sharp economic and political differences between the North and South by 1860 and the two sides were ready for a fight. Whether due to pride or a sense of obligation, the North and the South were on a collision course.

The panel members were divided over whether slavery would have continued to thrive without the opportunity to expand into the Western territories. Although another political compromise might have delayed the conflict, most of our experts agreed that it would not have prevented the eventual outbreak of hostilities. Republicans had already taken a stand against the expansion of slavery and, as Craig Symonds asserted, preventing the growth of slavery would ensure its eventual destruction.

Lincoln's election in 1860 has seen plenty of scrutiny over the years; the election of Jefferson Davis in 1861 has received less attention. In Peter Carmichael's judgment, the election of any Republican to the White House in 1860 would have pushed the South toward secession. As for Davis's election, there were only seven states in the Confederacy at the time the selection was made. Choices were limited. Would a different selection in Montgomery have altered the fate of the Confederacy? Most of the panelists agreed that Jefferson Davis was the best option for the South in February 1861.

Perhaps George Rable put it best when he wondered if those who had supported Lincoln and Breckinridge in the presidential election of 1860 would have cast their ballots in the same fashion, had they known about the bloodbath in the offing. Few events in history are inevitable. In this instance, in order to settle the issues of slavery and secession, the American Civil War was unavoidable.

2

The Pinch Comes: Fort Sumter

As Abraham Lincoln prepared to take over as the new leader of what remained of the United States, Confederate president Jefferson Davis affirmed his unrelenting devotion to Southern independence during his inaugural address in Montgomery, Alabama, on February 18, 1861.[1] The time for talk also appeared to be at an end. A last ditch effort by Congressional leaders to find a political solution perished when Lincoln rejected the Crittenden Compromise because it included a clause which allowed slavery in the territories.[2]

Lincoln sent the South a mixed message during his inauguration ceremony in March. Even though he pleaded with the seceded states to return to the Union, the Northern leader also compared secession to anarchy and promised to hold, occupy and possess all federal properties inside the Confederacy.[3]

All eyes then turned to Charleston, South Carolina, where Union troops occupied Fort Sumter, near the mouth of Charleston Harbor. Confederate leaders made it clear that they would not allow a Union stronghold to be maintained in the middle of one of their most important harbors.[4] When it became clear that Lincoln planned to hold the fort indefinitely, Jefferson Davis ordered Confederate military forces in Charleston to open fire, and the Union garrison soon surrendered. Bullets and blood would now settle the issue of secession.

Last Chance to Pause

A last-minute compromise, put forward early in 1861 by Kentucky senator John J. Crittenden, would have allowed citizens of territories to choose whether to enter the Union as a slave state or a free state. Crittenden's proposal would have also re-established the Missouri Compromise line, banning slavery in territories north of the line while protecting the institution south of the line.[5] Hopes for a peaceful solution to the crisis were dashed, however, when Lincoln refused to accept any plan that allowed for the extension of slavery.[6] With the rejection of the Crittenden proposal, both sides edged closer toward an open military confrontation.

What if Lincoln had been more receptive to compromise with the South in the winter and spring of 1861?

KENNETH NOE: The sentiment in the North and the South was that any compromise was impossible in 1861. Many Southerners viewed the Compromise of 1850 as the last great political compromise. The Georgia platform, which many Southern states adopted, stated that the South would not compromise again on the issue of expansion of slavery. The idea of extending the Missouri Compromise line out to the Pacific had been bandied about for years. In the late 1840s, Zachary Taylor had talked about extending the line to the Pacific Ocean, but there was little support for the notion. The idea of extending a dividing line did not interest many people, North or South. There's almost a hint of desperation in it. Don't forget that in 1857, the Supreme Court, in the Dred Scott case, had essentially declared the Missouri Compromise unconstitutional.[7] Crittenden's compromise therefore was going to be unconstitutional and unpopular among many groups. It's hard to imagine the Republicans going along with it because it flew in the face of everything they stood for. The Republican Party originally was devoted to stopping the expansion of slavery. The Crittenden Compromise would have allowed slavery's expansion. Had both sides been willing to go along with it, there's no doubt it would have prevented hostilities in 1861. It may have delayed them forever, but it's hard to imagine it gaining enough support to pass.

STEVEN WOODWORTH: Lincoln had two choices, accept secession or defend the Union. The only way Lincoln could have avoided secession was to use his influence in the Republican Party to persuade the Republicans to essentially abrogate the heart of their platform, the stand against the spread of slavery. If he could have convinced other Republicans to agree to that change, it would have negated the party's entire reason for existence but the South might not have pulled out of the Union. The Republican Party would in all likelihood disintegrated. The anti-slavery movement would have been set back decades and the showdown may have been delayed. Once the South fired on Fort Sumter, Lincoln had no other alternative but war. If Lincoln had not called for volunteers to suppress the rebellion, there would be an independent Confederate States of America today.

PETER CARMICHAEL: The South's course to secession was very uneven. There were profound differences in the way the Southern states responded to Lincoln's election and the idea of secession. Secession fever spread rapidly throughout the Deep South but there was a spirit of moderation in the Upper South, especially in Virginia, North Carolina and Tennessee. Some have criticized Lincoln for not sufficiently nurturing that sentiment in the Upper South. The criticism is that Lincoln's call for troops precipitated the war. Some will argue that if Lincoln had been more patient, a compromise could have been reached. We need to remember that there was a great degree of consensus among all white Southerners about the need to allow for the expansion of slavery into the territories. Any empathetic historian can understand why. The Southerners felt they had a constitutional right to take their property into the territories like any other American citizen. Many will argue that slavery was on the wane and would not have survived in the western territories. That's not the case at all. White Southerners were very creative and innovative in their use and adaptation of slavery, using slaves in mines, railroads and factories. Slavery was changing and was becoming even stronger in the South in the 1850s. The bottom line was white Southerners may have responded differently to secession but they were all ultimately committed to the principle.

No matter what Lincoln did following the firing on Fort Sumter, there simply wasn't any room to compromise with the Upper South. Even the moderates in the Upper South, who wanted to avoid a war, didn't offer Lincoln and the Republicans any room to maneuver. When push came to shove, the moderates in the Upper South insisted they had the right to take slaves into territories. It's difficult to conceive of a scenario where war could be avoided. You had two different societies clashing, free labor in the North and a slave society in the South, and hostilities were bound to happen sooner or later.

CRAIG SYMONDS: Secession was a desperate act, but it was not a frivolous one. The states that seceded were serious about forming a new and separate government. They had decided that the values of a Yankee dominated society were as alien to them as those of China or Japan and they wanted nothing more to do with them. The idea that the South might have returned to the fold if Lincoln had been more conciliatory is simply not realistic. Nor is it conceivable that Lincoln could have acquiesced in secession. If the South had been allowed to establish its independence without Federal interference, it would have sanctified the philosophy of state sovereignty, and the seed would have been planted for any state in the future to leave the union over a real or perceived grievance: income tax, conscription, abortion, etc. It would have meant the end of the United States as a nation. In the end, then, Lincoln's strong stand against secession and his determination to hold the seceding states in the Union by force of arms was essential to the survival of the republic, as he made very clear in his subsequent Gettysburg Address.

Who Fires First?

Lincoln pledged in his inaugural address in March to maintain possession of Federal properties in the South while not initiating aggressive action.[8] Lincoln's promise would now be put to the test. Confederate military forces surrounded Fort Sumter in Charleston Harbor with troops and batteries, in an effort to convince Union leaders to abandon the stronghold.

Confederate batteries had actually fired a few shots in January at *The Star of the West*, a relief ship bringing reinforcements to the Union fortress.[9] Robert Toombs of Georgia warned Jefferson Davis not to fire on the fort itself and risk losing every friend the South had in the North.[10] Toombs's warning fell on deaf ears. Upon learning that Lincoln planned another attempt to send supplies to the fort, Davis gave permission to the Confederate commander of Charleston, P.G.T. Beauregard, to begin offensive operations. Southern batteries opened fire the morning of April 12 and following a bombardment that lasted nearly a day and a half, the Union commander, Major Robert Anderson, surrendered Fort Sumter to the Confederacy.[11]

Events now moved quickly. Lincoln called for 75,000 militia to suppress the rebellion and four additional states, Virginia, North Carolina, Tennessee and Arkansas, responded by leaving the Union and joining the Confederacy.[12] After years of harsh rhetoric, war had finally arrived.

What if Confederate forces don't fire on Fort Sumter?

GEORGE RABLE: There's been plenty of discussion over the years about how Lincoln and his cabinet handled the events at Fort Sumter, but less focus on how the Confederates handled the situation. One wonders what would have happened if Jefferson Davis had decided not to fire on Fort Sumter. Davis was under considerable political pressure to show that the South was a sovereign nation. It was unfortunate for the Confederates that Sumter was located in Charleston Harbor and South Carolina was the most rabid fire-eating state. You had South Carolinians suggesting that if the Confederate government did not take action against Sumter, then South Carolina troops might take action.

In hindsight, it would have been much wiser for Jefferson Davis to hold off on offensive action against the fort because he would have placed Lincoln in a real bind. Lincoln might have had to play a waiting game with the Confederates. There were a number of members of the Republican Party who thought secession was a conspiracy of a small group of politicians. They thought that a majority of Southerners did not strongly support secession and that when tempers cooled, this great reservoir of Unionism could then be tapped. Lincoln and the Republicans overestimated Unionist feelings among the Southern population. If the South hadn't fired on Sumter, Lincoln and the Republicans might have tried to use the approach of masterful inactivity, to wait and see if the South might have come to its senses and return to the Union.

RICHARD BERINGER: If the South had decided to play a waiting game rather than firing on Fort Sumter, its strategy might have confused the North and made things very interesting. We have to remember that it was the South's firing on Sumter that persuaded many Northerners that the war was a just cause. Perhaps by playing the waiting game, the Confederacy might have received recognition by foreign powers, notably Great Britain. Such recognition might have resulted in assistance in case hostilities erupted. There were some in Great Britain who felt it would be to England's advantage if the North and South split into two countries. Some of the British felt the United States would be a weaker potential adversary in the future if the North and South were divided. But it's quite possible that if the clash of arms hadn't occurred at Fort Sumter, the outbreak of hostilities might have happened at another location, like Pensacola.[13] One Confederate, Robert Toombs, had said the decision to fire on Fort Sumter was a fatal mistake for the South. There are those who wonder if Toombs was ever sober enough to come up with that kind of conclusion. If Toombs actually made the statement, he was certainly right!

ED BEARSS: Lincoln's move to hold Sumter forced Jefferson Davis to make some hard decisions. Davis could have allowed Lincoln to send supplies to the fort but that would have resulted in plenty of headaches for Davis in dealing with the South Carolina fire-eaters. Such a move would have also led some to wonder if the Confederacy could be taken seriously as a nation if it allowed U.S. forces to hold one of its forts in a key Confederate harbor. Davis decided he had to take Fort Sumter, by force if necessary.

Some might say Davis and the South made a mistake by firing on Sumter and so giving Lincoln his pretext for calling for volunteers to put down the rebellious Southern states and to coerce those states to return to the Union. You can also argue that if the Confederacy had not fired on Sumter, Virginia, North Carolina, Tennessee and Arkansas would not have joined the Confederacy. Except for Arkansas, those states that joined the South after Sumter were very important to the Confederacy, both in terms of industry and manpower. Without those additional states joining the Confederacy, the new Southern nation may well have faded from the scene. The adding of those four states ensured, for the time being, the Confederacy's survival. It also set both sides on the road that would lead to a war that would kill more than 621,000 people.

The Confederate attack on Sumter also put Northern Democrats in a tough position. They then had to either support the Union or not support it. For example, up until the firing on Fort Sumter, New York's mayor Fernando Wood had been talking about taking New York City out of the Union and making it a free state. So Lincoln made two important decisions regarding Sumter, the decisions to resupply the fort and then to call for 75,000 volunteers to coerce the South back into the Union. It turned a dispute over the possession of the fort into the bloodiest war in U.S. history. Both Lincoln and Davis were in a corner and couldn't show weakness. If Davis had decided not to fire on Sumter or Lincoln had decided to evacuate the fort, those types of decisions would have showed weakness to the rest of the world.

JOHN SIMON: There was a moment in Montgomery when Jefferson Davis had been informed that Lincoln was sending supplies to Fort Sumter and Davis had the decision thrown on his plate whether to take aggressive action at Sumter. He made the kind of decision that was inevitable in his case. Davis was warned by his secretary of state Robert Toombs not to fire the first shot of the conflict, to avoid kicking over a hornet's nest. Davis had been warned of creating a situation whereby a ring of Confederate artillery would be firing on a relatively defenseless fort with a small garrison of some 80 soldiers. The flag of the U.S.A. was flying over the fort. Davis was warned not to fire on the flag. People will be able to understand the indignation felt by Northern citizens about the Confederate firing on the U.S. flag, when they remember the attack of the terrorists on 9–11.

Jefferson Davis. Davis' decision to fire on Fort Sumter enraged the North. VIRGINIA MILITARY INSTITUTE ARCHIVES.

After that attack, Americans broke out their American flags and were reminded of their love for their country and their patriotic feelings. That's exactly what happened in the North as a consequence of the South's decision to fire on Fort Sumter. If there had been a war involving only those people who were pro-slavery and anti-slavery, I suspect those who were pro-slavery would have won. They would have carried 15 slave-holding states and would have had supporters in the North. What Jefferson Davis managed to create at Fort Sumter, in the greatest blunder of the Civil War, was a war for the Union. It was a war that summoned up great patriotic energies and brought together Republicans and Democrats. The Democrats could have easily gloated. Stephen Douglas had warned Lincoln that his policies would bring war. Instead, the Democrats were quick to rally to the defense of the country, and Douglas in particular led the Democratic support for the war, which was absolutely vital.

The amount of opposition to the Union in the North was nothing compared to the opposition to the Confederacy in the South. During the Civil War, an estimated 100,000 white men from the Confederate states fought in Union regiments. The Confederates managed to put about 900,000 men in the field during the war. So one out of every 10 Southerners fought on what might be described from the Confederate standpoint as the wrong side. When we think about how close the Confederacy came to establishing a new nation, this was a very important factor. We're talking not only about 100,000 men who didn't fight for the South, but also about 100,000 men that fought against the Confederacy by joining Union armies.

Lincoln as the Aggressor

Lincoln's response to the firing on Fort Sumter was immediate: 75,000 volunteers were sought for three months of military service and a naval blockade was imposed on Southern ports. Outraged by the attack on the United States flag, enthusiastic recruits responded passionately in the North to Lincoln's call to arms. The Northern leader had hoped to defend Federal possessions in the South without initiating aggressive action; Davis' decision to fire on Fort Sumter relieved Lincoln of the burden of having to make the first offensive move.

What if Lincoln had been forced to fire the opening shot of the war?

RICHARD MCMURRY: The war certainly could have started at Pensacola and would have if not for Fort Sumter. The events at Sumter just happened to come along with a series of coincidences. From the standpoint of pride, it's unrealistic to think that the South would allow Federal possession of Fort Sumter to be maintained. John Simon, editor of the U.S. Grant papers, has compared the situation at Sumter to another situation where the U.S. possessed a military base on the soil of a foreign country against the will of that country. That's Guantánamo in Cuba. Cuba has had the good sense not to attack that base, so the base is still in Cuba and Fidel Castro is still in power in Cuba.

If Lincoln had been forced to fire the first shot, it would have removed the stigma the South received for firing the opening shot at Sumter. Lincoln's options would have been limited for dealing with the South if the Confederates didn't fire on Sumter. The only way Lincoln could have gotten at the Deep South would be to go through two or three slave states that were friendly to the Confederacy. A coastal invasion might have been possible, but it would have been a major undertaking and very difficult to supply the troops once they landed. Theoretically it was possible but it would have been much easier for the Union armies to march across the Potomac or the Ohio River.

JEFF WERT: If the Confederates don't fire on Fort Sumter, Lincoln has no credible basis for attacking the South. A number of border states were still sitting on the fence in the early spring of 1861. These were states critical to the survival of the Union. Had those states sided with the Confederacy, the Union would not have survived. If Lincoln had fired the first shot, he may have wound up driving states like Kentucky into the Confederacy. Firing the opening shot of the war may well have reduced the support for the conflict in some of the states in the Old Northwest. Several of the original settlers in the southern portions of Illinois, Indiana and Ohio came from Southern states like Virginia and Kentucky and had strong Southern sentiments. The sentiments were expressed throughout the conflict, as the Copperhead movement in those areas was very strong. If the South doesn't fire on Sumter, there may not have been as many volunteers from some of those Northern states to join the Union army.

CRAIG SYMONDS: Jefferson Davis made a great blunder when he ordered Beauregard to open fire on Fort Sumter. Without that event, Lincoln would have been hard-pressed to order an "invasion" of the South. In effect, Davis gave up the South's opportunity to pose as the aggrieved victim, and made it possible for Lincoln to rally national support for the war. Lincoln had promised that if local authorities did not resist, he would send only supplies, not reinforcements, into Sumter. If Davis had allowed that, supplies only, the Confederacy would have had to suffer the slight embarrassment of having an alien fort within its territorial waters, but it would have forced Lincoln to deal with the reality of the Confederacy. It would have made it difficult for Lincoln to rally the North around a coercive policy to compel the Southern states back into the Union. Lincoln was terrified that a too-aggressive policy would drive the border states into the arms of the South. He had to have Kentucky, Missouri and Maryland at least as neutrals if not as participants for the Union. He also wanted to keep Virginia if he could. If Davis had not ordered the firing on Fort Sumter, Lincoln might have tried to engineer another confrontation, at Fort Pickens in Florida or at Fort Monroe in Virginia. Somehow Lincoln had to demonstrate his commitment to maintain national control over Federal property. But he had to be subtle. If it became too obvious that he was trying to maneuver the South into a violent confrontation, it would have been more difficult to rally the North, especially the Midwest and the border states to the national cause. Davis helped him out by accepting the role as aggressor. It was a terrible error.

Summary

The road to open warfare was full of miscalculations on both sides. Many Northerners viewed talk of secession as a bluff; a number of Southerners refused to believe the North would fight to maintain the Union.[14] Both opinions were dead wrong.

Fort Sumter was one of the most important events of the Civil War. Lincoln and Davis were boxed into corners: neither man wanted to be the one to fire the opening shot but both men could ill afford to display any sign of weakness. Southern pride and public opinion worldwide were just a few of the issues Jefferson Davis was facing in April of 1861. George Rable stated that the Confederates felt that they could not allow an enemy fort to remain in Charleston Harbor if they had any hopes of being recognized as a legitimate nation.

The decision by the Confederates to open fire on the U.S. flag meant any chance of compromise went right out the window. Ed Bearss stated that the attack on Fort Sumter gained the Confederacy several states that the new nation had to have to ensure its existence. The addition of Virginia, North Carolina, Tennessee and Arkansas came with a hefty price tag, however, as Northerners rallied to the defense of the Stars and Stripes and Lincoln was given the political support he needed to invade the South. As Jeff Wert pointed out, forcing Lincoln to fire the first shot may have resulted in the Upper South joining the Confederates' camp and may have also led to a reduction in Union support for a Federal invasion of the South. The Confederate attack on Fort Sumter transformed a war of words into a fight to preserve the Union for the North, and a fight for survival for the Confederacy.

3

Like a Stone Wall: Bull Run

The first big battle of the Civil War was fought July 21, 1861, near the important railroad junction at Manassas, approximately 25 miles southwest of Washington, along a meandering creek called Bull Run. It was actually more a clash of untrained mobs than a battle between professional, experienced armies. Many of the 35,000 men in Union general Irvin McDowell's army had signed up for just three months of service. With their enlistment terms set to expire, McDowell received orders to move against the 20,000 Confederates under the command of General Pierre G. T. Beauregard.[1]

While Manassas received most of the attention, another important area of operations was the Shenandoah Valley, where Union general Robert Patterson was expected to pin down the Confederates at Winchester under the command of General Joseph E. Johnston. Patterson failed horribly and Johnston slipped away to Manassas to reinforce Beauregard.

Both McDowell and Beauregard had been planning flank attacks for July 21 but the Federals beat the Southerners to the punch, and a large part of McDowell's army smashed into Beauregard's left flank on Matthews Hill. Rebel brigades attempting to make a stand were eventually forced to retreat to Henry House Hill, where Confederate general Thomas Jonathan Jackson had posted his brigade of five Virginia regiments. In one of the key decisions of the battle, Jackson chose to remain on the defensive; his men brought the Union advance to a halt. As more and more Confederates arrived on the field, the advantage swung to the Southerners. McDowell

Irvin McDowell and his staff. Patterson's failure in the Valley may have cost McDowell a victory at Bull Run. NATIONAL ARCHIVES.

was forced to give orders to retreat and an orderly withdrawal soon became a full-scale rout as panicky Union soldiers fled for the safety of the Washington defenses.

Patterson in the Valley

An aging War of 1812 veteran had the responsibility of making sure Confederates in the Shenandoah Valley stayed put. It was up to Major

General Robert Patterson, with 17,000 men at his disposal, to pin down Joseph Johnston's 10,000 Confederates, to prevent them from reinforcing the main Rebel army at Manassas.[2] The ancient Patterson had a chance to deal a serious blow to the rebellion but when the Confederates made threatening moves as if to attack, Patterson cautiously went into a defensive posture, allowing Johnston to place his men on rail cars. Beauregard would get his reinforcements.[3]

What if Patterson had aggressively pursued Johnston?

ED BEARSS: Robert Patterson was a key figure in July of 1861. His job was to stay in contact with Joe Johnston's forces in the Valley so as to prevent Johnston's men from coming to the aid of Beauregard at Manassas. If the Union had a more aggressive commander in the Valley, if they hadn't had an old granny like General Patterson, Beauregard might have met disaster at Bull Run. Undoubtedly, if Johnston had been prevented from leaving the Valley and coming to Beauregard's aid, McDowell would have won a victory at Bull Run.

The South knows the battle as First Manassas and the North refers to it as Bull Run. It might be universally known today as Bull Run if the North had been able to keep Johnston in the Valley. Patterson was assuring Washington that if Johnston was able to leave the Valley, Washington could shoot him. Johnston was able to slip away from Patterson, and the Northern leaders in Washington were much more generous to Patterson than Hitler or Stalin would have been. They simply forced Patterson into retirement.

JOHN HENNESSY: Patterson holds the distinction of being the ONLY man in the Civil War to retreat AWAY from Joseph E. Johnston. Patterson had enough men to accomplish his mission, to keep Johnston pinned down in the Shenandoah Valley. Patterson's failure to keep Johnston in the Valley ranks as one of the great failures of the entire war. Johnston's men will do most of the fighting at Bull Run. Patterson seems to have subscribed to the almost universal Union affliction of worrying far more about what his enemy would do to him rather than what he might do to his enemy. Patterson's performance was the first manifestation in Virginia of the reflexively conservative approach to managing troops that would become entrenched under McClellan.

ROBERT E. L. KRICK: All of our presumptions about how command decisions are made in the war really don't apply to First Manassas. Everyone in July 1861 was unprepared to fight, including the professional soldiers.

Patterson's failure to keep Johnston in the Valley was the key factor in the entire campaign. Patterson had the resources to hold Johnston in place and could have deprived Beauregard of the extra strength he needed to face McDowell. As we saw in Jackson's Valley campaign in 1862, a smaller force could be successful against a larger army by maneuvering. Patterson had the manpower to deal with Johnston. If he had done his job, it's likely the battle on July 21 would have gone McDowell's way. McDowell wouldn't have pursued Beauregard very far south though, with Johnston still on his flank to the west.

CRAIG SYMONDS: Patterson was simply incompetent as a commander and was not capable of pinning down Johnston in the Valley, so in some ways the question is moot. Patterson was one of those officers who simply never should have been given important field responsibilities. He second-guessed himself too much and never made much of an effort to fulfill the letter of his assignment, much less the spirit of it. But it is interesting to speculate what kind of success McDowell might have had at First Bull Run/Manassas, if someone other than Patterson had been in command in the Valley and had kept Johnston's four brigades from the Bull Run battlefield. McDowell was not as incompetent a field commander as many assume. His battle plan for Bull Run was not fundamentally different from the one Lee employed at Chancellorsville. He simply lacked the tools to execute the plan: his army was green, the terrain was unfamiliar and he was unlucky. But even with all that, if Johnston's four brigades, including Jackson's, had not made it to the battlefield, McDowell might very well have succeeded. His flanking movement caught the Confederates by surprise and if Johnston's men had not been on Henry House Hill, Union troops could have swept in around Beauregard's left flank. Moreover, a Union victory at Bull Run would very likely have disorganized the equally green Confederate army and sent it fleeing back toward Richmond.

Standing like a Stone Wall

McDowell's plan to hit the Confederate left flank July 21 got off to a slow start due to a lengthy and confusing march, but Union prospects appeared to be bright when the assault column finally crossed Bull Run at Sudley Church. Sweeping across Matthews Hill, the Federals were initially confronted by Brigadier General Nathan Evans' brigade and then by the brigades of Barnard Bee and Francis Bartow. The Confederates fought hard but faced overwhelming pressure from both front and flank;

the Southerners were sent streaming in retreat toward Henry House Hill.[4]

It was at Henry House Hill where Bee attempted to rally his men with the assistance of a Virginia brigade under the command of Brigadier General Thomas Jonathan Jackson. Jackson, a former Virginia Military Institute professor, had a choice: he could advance and attack the Federals, or remain where he was and fight from a strong defensive position. Jackson decided to stand his ground. His men held their position and, thanks to Barnard Bee, their commander acquired a new nickname, Stonewall.[5] With the help of additional Southerners arriving on the scene, the tide of battle turned in favor of the Confederates. McDowell's men would soon be in full retreat toward Washington.

What if Jackson had led his men to Matthews Hill, rather than remaining on the defensive on Henry House Hill?

ED BEARSS: Stonewall Jackson got his famous nom de guerre by standing fast, like a stone wall, on Henry House Hill while the hard pressed Confederate forces on Matthews Hill were retreating past him. If Jackson had not made the decision to stand fast and defend Henry House Hill, if he had instead decided to immediately move to Matthews Hill to assist the Confederates there, he would have suffered the same fate as Bee's and Bartow's men. Bee and Bartow went to Matthews and they were able to delay the Union forces, coming in on the Confederate left flank, for about two hours. When Jackson arrived on Henry House Hill, Bee's and Bartow's men had been overwhelmed and were retreating. Jackson decided to use the time he had to position his artillery in a sheltered defiladed area of Henry House Hill and positioned his infantry at the edge of the woods. If Jackson had decided to attempt to provide more immediate relief to the retreating Confederates by marching to Matthews Hill to come directly to their aid, the Union forces would have overwhelmed him. It's debatable whether the Confederates could have won the battle.

JOHN HENNESSY: Jackson's greatest contribution at First Manassas was his selection of the line on Henry Hill. It was a critical and contrary decision. First, most commanders would have followed their instincts to lunge forward as far as possible. Jackson did not. By deciding against a move on Matthews Hill, Jackson preserved his command intact. He also bucked most instincts by taking position on the rear of the hill, not the forward slope. Jackson's decision gave the Confederates space to work and recover. It also ensured that Jackson's men would not be swamped by the retreating troops of Bee, Bartow and Evans. By taking position on the rear slope of Henry Hill and breaking off the engagement for the moment, Jackson also bought some time for the Confederates, or perhaps McDowell gave it. Either way, the extra time was critical to the Confederates' turning the tide of battle.

Had Jackson moved directly to Matthews Hill, his men would have been overwhelmed, just as the other Confederate units had been earlier. The Federals had close to 14,000 men moving into the Matthews Hill area by noontime. Under those circumstances, a Union victory seems likely. A victory by McDowell would not have had the decisive effect imagined by so many. No battle of the Civil War had a truly decisive impact. The idea that the conflict would be resolved by a single victory on a battlefield was to be proven time and time again to be outright nonsense.

JEFF WERT: There were about 20,000 Union soldiers milling around Matthews Hill once Bee and Bartow had been forced to retreat. There was also a critical two-hour period where McDowell's men did not aggressively continue to pursue the Confederates. McDowell was on the field and essentially offered no leadership during that time. His performance was never explained, but the key was to organize the raw troops for a coordinated assault on Henry House Hill. It was not an easy task but McDowell had perhaps 20,000 troops on hand and that was a figure the Confederates could not match. The assault on Henry House Hill would have gone forward well before any Southern reserves were able to reach the field to hit the Union right flank. It's difficult to heap too much criticism on McDowell since his officers were so inexperienced this early in the war.

The key is Thomas Jackson. Had Jackson advanced toward the oncoming Federals, his brigade probably would have been overwhelmed A well-trained soldier like Jackson recognized that Henry House Hill dominated the terrain. Jackson also realized that it was much easier for inexperienced troops to fight from a defensive posture this early in the war. If Jackson had led his five regiments to Matthews, he would have faced enemy forces in his front and on his right flank due to Federal troops moving across Bull Run. Jackson's decision to remain at Henry House Hill helped to turn the tide of battle.

ROBERT E. L. KRICK: Jackson made the right decision to remain in a defensive posture on Henry House Hill. At the same time, the Confederates might have been able to reap some benefits had Jackson decided to leave Henry Hill and advance toward Matthews Hill, directly to the assistance of Bee and Bartow. The farther north the battle raged, the more time Beauregard had to move reinforcements from Manassas Junction to the battlefield. If Jackson moved to contest the Union advance, he would have been able to delay the Federal forces long enough for additional Confederate reinforcements to arrive on the scene. Even if McDowell's forces had somehow been able to hold on to Henry House Hill at the end of the day, the Union troops would have been vulnerable to a direct attack on the 22nd, with their backs to Bull Run. Given the topography and the manpower ratio, McDowell's best bet for a meaningful victory was to drive the Confederates decisively from the field.

To Pursue or Not to Pursue

What began as an orderly retreat from the battlefield for the Federals quickly degenerated into a chaotic rout and a potential Union disaster. Would the victorious Southerners press their advantage? Confederate president Jefferson Davis met with Johnston and Beauregard to discuss the possibility of pursuing the retreating Federals toward Washington but finally decided that the Southern army was too disorganized for further action.[6]

In the first big battle of the war, the South had won an impressive victory, inflicting nearly 3,000 casualties on McDowell's army while suffering approximately 2,000 losses.[7] After the battle, several Confederates would speak of missed opportunities, including Stonewall Jackson, who allegedly claimed that he could have destroyed what remained of the Federal army with 5,000 men.[8] Confederate general James Longstreet declared that his brigade could have pursued the retreating Federals all the way to Washington,[9] while Edward Porter Alexander concluded that such an advance might have forced an evacuation of the Union capital.[10]

What if the Confederates had attempted to advance on Washington following their victory at Bull Run?

ED BEARSS: If the Confederates had followed Jackson's advice and pursued the defeated Federals towards Washington, you could argue this was the South's best chance to win the war on a military initiative. I see the Confederates following the fleeing Union soldiers and being able to occupy Arlington Heights. The Confederates didn't necessarily have to directly attack the Union capital. By placing artillery on Arlington Heights, the Confederates could then shell Washington. Many of the retreating Union soldiers were already panic-stricken. By shelling Washington, the Confederates would have been able to place the Lincoln administration in a state of panic. Unlike 1814, when the British burned Washington, the U.S.

government in 1861 was a much larger bureaucratic body, much more centralized. The Confederates would have posed a much more serious long-term threat to the U.S. government's operations than the British did in 1814. The Confederates would still have to cross the Potomac to get into Washington, to get at the U.S. government itself. But my belief is the Northern government would have had to abandon Washington if the Confederates had gained control of Arlington Heights.

KEITH DICKSON: One of the key tenets in military art is exploiting victories. The South should have taken any and all steps to follow up on its victory at Bull Run. If nothing else, a move on Washington would further hamper the Union war effort. Whether the Confederates captured Washington or shelled the city, it would have been a severe psychological blow to the North. It's also possible that a move on Washington that forced Lincoln's cabinet to evacuate to New York or Philadelphia might have led to a negotiated peace. At the very least, it would have given the Confederates control over all of Virginia and southern Maryland. The victorious Confederate army after Bull Run was really just a mob of young boys, filled with adrenaline and terror after the war's first big battle. Disciplined soldiers, such as the Army of Northern Virginia following its victory at Second Manassas, might have had a better chance to capture the Union capital.

JOHN HENNESSY: I have always considered the idea of a Confederate move toward Washington after First Manassas as impractical. The victory at Manassas disorganized the Confederates only marginally less than the defeat discombobulated the Federals. Huge portions of the Union army had not even fired a shot on July 21 and remained largely intact. Those forces would have presented a serious obstacle to the Confederates. The Southern army would have been unprepared to overcome such resistance. If the Confederates had attempted to make a move on Washington, they would have squandered most of the benefits gained by the victory at Manassas.

JEFF WERT: A Confederate advance on Washington was not an option. We tend to think of Civil War soldiers as chess pieces that can be moved easily across the board, or in this case the map. Yes, the Confederate casualty rate was low compared to other battles in the war, but the Southern troops were about as disorganized in victory as the Union troops were in defeat. The letters of Union soldiers make it clear that the Federals were certainly demoralized when they left Bull Run, but they weren't totally beaten and would have made a stand at Washington. The Union Army had artillery in place at Arlington and added tens of thousands in reinforcements in just a few weeks. It would have been a major challenge for the Confederates to advance on Washington and it made no sense to take the risk. Generals by nature are cautious and Lee himself probably wouldn't have attempted a march on Washington in July 1861.

CRAIG SYMONDS: The disorganization and confusion within the victorious army made it impossible for the Confederates to pursue. There was a lot of discussion about a possible pursuit even at the time, and much more discussion later. The night of the battle, there was a conference that included Jefferson Davis, who had ridden out to the battlefield, Johnston, and Beauregard. At that meeting, a report that the Union army was completely shattered and vulnerable to a rapid pursuit led to a brief conversation about how, if at all, this might be undertaken. But then more information arrived that implied the earlier report was unreliable, and that in any case no southern troops were available for such a pursuit, so the idea was dropped. Much later, when the fortunes of war turned against the Confederacy, Southerners looked back to this moment wistfully and many implied that a great opportunity had been squandered. But in fact, the Southern army could not have pursued the Federals even as far as Cub Run, much less into the streets of Washington.[11] The victors were as used up by this first battle between eager and earnest amateurs as the losers were.

Summary

Anyone who thought that the dispute between the North and the South would be settled quickly and painlessly was sorely mistaken. As was the case in many Civil War battles, a thin line often separated victory from defeat. There was no greater example of this than the battle on July 21, 1861.

Bull Run could have been a huge Federal victory, had it not been for Robert Patterson and Thomas J. Jackson. One panelist after another agreed that if Patterson had been able to keep Joseph Johnston in the Shenandoah Valley, McDowell would have won a decisive victory at Manassas, forcing Beauregard to retreat south. Jackson's tactical decision to remain on the defensive on Henry House Hill was another important factor in the Confederate victory. Some brigade commanders might have been tempted to charge into battle to save endangered comrades being overwhelmed by the enemy. Many of our panelists pointed out, however, that it could have been disastrous for the Confederates if Jackson had attempted to attack the Union troops on Matthews Hill. Several of the experts, including Ed

Bearss and John Hennessy, praised Jackson for recognizing the value of defending Henry House Hill.

Time management turned out to be a major factor in deciding the outcome of the battle. Jackson's staunch defense bought the Confederates precious time to bring more troops onto the field and, as Jeff Wert mentioned, McDowell's prospects for victory were dimmed when his army failed to promptly advance on Henry House Hill following the Union success on Matthews Hill.

The most divisive issue among the panelists was whether the Confederates could have reaped more rewards from their success on July 21. Ed Bearss and Keith Dickson both claimed the Confederates could have advanced on Washington and attempted to shell the Union capital. John Hennessy argued that the Southerners were too disorganized to pursue the beaten Federals and that such a move might have actually cost the Confederates the fruits of their victory.

In the long run, the South's stunning triumph at Bull Run may have actually been more beneficial to the Federals than to the Confederates. There were those in the South who felt that the victory at Bull Run guaranteed their independence; Union leaders now recognized the need to better organize their powerful resources for the long, bloody road that lay ahead.

4

Grant's Beginning,
Johnston's End:
Fort Donelson and Shiloh

Bull Run had been a disastrous setback for the Union war effort in the East in 1861; Federal armies in the West, however, were making excellent progress in the opening months of 1862. In February, Union forces captured Fort Henry and Fort Donelson in Tennessee, forcing the overall Confederate commander in the West, Albert Sidney Johnston, to evacuate Nashville while his second in command, P.G.T. Beauregard, gave up the Confederate stronghold of Columbus, Kentucky. With Union armies under Ulysses S. Grant and Don Carlos Buell in pursuit, Johnston chose Corinth, Mississippi, as the spot to reorganize his army of 40,000 men.[1]

By April, Grant's army of 45,000 men was situated on the western bank of the Tennessee River at Pittsburg Landing while Buell's 25,000 soldiers were headed in that direction from Nashville. Johnston decided to assault Grant before Buell could arrive.[2] Scheduled to begin April 4, the attack was delayed nearly two days due to confusion over marching orders and heavy rainfall.[3]

By dawn on April 6, Johnston's men were ready to strike. Initially successful, the Confederate attack soon bogged down as inexperienced units became disorganized, and the retreating Federals occupied a strong defensive position, which came to be known as the Hornet's Nest.[4] Worse yet for the Confederates, Albert Sidney Johnston was mortally wounded.

By the time the Southerners were able to continue their advance toward Pittsburg Landing, Grant had established a strong defensive line, supported by Union gunboats on the Tennessee River.

With reinforcements from Buell and Lew Wallace, Grant turned the tables on the Confederates April 7, attacking and driving Beauregard from the field. Union casualties amounted to more than 13,000 men while the Confederates, forced to withdraw to Corinth, lost nearly 11,000 men.[5]

Unconditional Surrender

Shortages of men and equipment hampered Albert Sidney Johnston's efforts to defend Kentucky and Tennessee early in 1862.[6] To defend against Union forays on the Tennessee and Cumberland Rivers, near the Kentucky-Tennessee line, the Confederates had constructed Fort Henry on the Tennessee and Fort Donelson on the Cumberland. Union general Ulysses S. Grant would use those two forts to make a name for himself.

Outfitted with 17,000 men and a squadron of new ironclad gunboats, Grant captured Fort Henry on February 6 and then prepared to assault Fort Donelson. Although Johnston sent reinforcements to the fort, a divided command structure that featured three brigadier generals, John B. Floyd, Simon Bolivar Buckner and Gideon J. Pillow, spelled disaster for the Confederate garrison.

The Southerners certainly had their chances to escape the doomed fort. Early on February 15, with Grant away at a conference, the Confederates launched a breakout attempt, bending back the Yankee line and temporarily opening the road to Nashville. Buckner favored an evacuation of Fort Donelson but Pillow argued that the Confederates were in no shape for a long march. Floyd sided with Pillow.[7] The unfortunate Confederates were ordered back to their original positions in the fort.[8]

Grant would not waste time in taking advantage of the Confederate mistake. Returning from his conference, Grant immediately launched a successful counterattack that forced Buckner to ask for surrender terms.[9] Grant insisted on immediate and unconditional surrender, forcing Buckner to hand over the fort and 12,000 Confederates and giving the North its biggest victory thus far in the war.[10]

What if Johnston had sent more men to defend Fort Donelson?

JOHN SIMON: Grant was enormously aided by the Confederates in Fort Donelson. Albert Sidney Johnston couldn't decide whether to throw in all his strength, to evacuate the Confederate garrison at Donelson or to leave enough men at Donelson to inflict plenty of casualties on Grant's army. Grant was given the chance to win his first big victory. Gideon J. Pillow managed to create a temporary Confederate victory, a breakthrough at Donelson, and then pulled back to decide what he should do next. Pillow was such an incompetent general that it never occurred to him that he might win. It was a miracle straight from heaven that the Confederates had been as successful as they had been, due partly to Grant's absence on the 15th while he was visiting the Union naval commander in the campaign. The Confederates had won a tremendous victory and while the Confederate commanders were trying to decide what to do next, Grant came back and attacked the fort on the other side. Anyone but Pillow could have achieved more success from his assault on the 15th. Grant had his share of near disasters, at Belmont, at Donelson and at Shiloh. Grant was resilient and he learned his lessons fighting battles.

KENNETH NOE: The Confederates had spread out their troops thinly along their border with the Union. Johnston needed to give more emphasis to those two forts much earlier, placing more troops to defend them. If the Confederates could have somehow held Henry and Donelson, the war in the West would have turned out very differently. After the loss of those two forts, it was just one disaster after another for the Confederates. I always like to compare it to an old-fashioned can opener and using it to punch through the lid. Once you get through the lid, there's not much behind it.

LARRY DANIEL: The important thing about Fort Donelson is to note how Sidney Johnston saw it after the fall of Fort Henry. He did not think the water battery was going to hold and did not think the Union gunboats could be stopped. So the question becomes why did he reinforce Fort Donelson since he openly stated that he did not think the fort would hold. If you send more infantry, that's not going to do anything to stop a fleet of ironclads. Johnston never really wrote an answer to that question. Some people, like Albert Castel and Steven Woodworth, have said Johnston was trying to buy time to get his main army back to Nashville and across the Cumberland River. That's as good an answer as one can expect, although I would never rule out the possibility that Johnston simply was making a show of aggressiveness. Ultimately, the loss of Fort Donelson meant the loss of Nashville.[11] I don't know if Johnston intended to make a stand at Donelson. Donelson essentially was a trap and there have been suggestions that the battle for Fort Donelson should have been fought between Forts Henry and Donelson. If the battle could not have been won there,

Johnston needed to withdraw to Nashville. Johnston never came to that conclusion.

What could have been done at Donelson itself? Nothing, because if you defeat the gunboats, you're still subjected to capture by Union forces on land. It's true the Confederates could have escaped, but the Confederate leaders at the fort were simply incompetent. The Confederates broke out of the fort and then turned around and went right back in the fort. Ultimately Fort Donelson points to the $64,000 question in the West for the first two years of the war. How do you stop the Union gunboats without exposing a land garrison? This happens at Fort Donelson, Island Number Ten, at Arkansas Post, at Port Hudson and at Vicksburg. When you add those up, it comes to roughly nine Confederate divisions that were captured, over 65,000 men who were lost defending the rivers to the last. You could claim that the South attempted to defend too many points, but there's also the political consideration of surrendering territory without a fight. Jefferson Davis realized that if Confederates yielded their rivers and cities, morale would suffer in the South. Joseph Johnston's answer was to fight the Union armies once they got away from the rivers. Beauregard's answer was to keep small garrisons on the river and then rescue them when they got into trouble. Both recognized that the rivers were traps.

RICHARD MCMURRY: The initial Confederate breakout attempt February 15 at Donelson was successful, but the Confederate generals chose to go back in the fort rather than attempt to escape. Some have said the Confederates were exhausted and hungry but I maintain it was better for the Confederates to escape the Union trap. The Confederates could not have held Fort Henry, which was about half under water, or Fort Donelson much longer than they did. What they could have done was avoid the disaster of losing both the forts and their army at Fort Donelson, just as they could have avoided the disasters of losing armies and forts at Island Number Ten, at Arkansas Post, at Vicksburg and at Port Hudson. The strategy should have been to hold the fort for a reasonable time but avoid having the army bottled up in the fort to be battered into surrender.

Loss of a Strong Pillar

The initial Confederate charge at Shiloh took Grant totally by surprise. When the Federals rallied and formed new lines, Albert Sidney Johnston decided to take matters into his own hands by leading troops into battle at a peach orchard near the Hornet's Nest. It was a fatal mistake. A ball struck Johnston's right leg, clipping an artery and the Confederate leader soon bled to death.

Johnston was thought by some to be the most capable of all of the professional soldiers who had cast their lot with the Confederacy.[12] His death may have prevented a Confederate victory at Shiloh and may have also robbed the South of one of its greatest military leaders, although Ulysses Grant would later claim that Johnston was vacillating and undecided in his actions at Shiloh.[13] Jefferson Davis chose to differ: Davis asserted that the Confederacy's strongest pillar had been broken.[14]

What if Albert Sidney Johnston had not been mortally wounded at Shiloh?

RICHARD MCMURRY: Sidney Johnston would have been more desirable as a theatre commander in the West owing to his ability to work with his subordinates and with Jefferson Davis and the Confederate government. No other Confederate commander in the West could claim that ability. That's the real significance of Johnston's death. He wasn't necessarily a great military leader who would have won the war for the Confederacy. With Johnston dead however, the Confederates never had another general trusted by Jefferson Davis, in the West or anywhere else, other than Lee. Davis always felt that Sidney Johnston was his best general. If you could contact Jefferson Davis today and ask him who was his best general, he would tell you Albert Sidney Johnston. Once Johnston was gone, there wasn't a general who had Davis' full trust and confidence. I don't think A.S. Johnston was a brilliant strategist or tactician, but with Sidney Johnston in command the Confederates might have been able to avoid the numerous disasters they suffered in the West, including Vicksburg, Port Hudson and Missionary Ridge.

STEVEN WOODWORTH: The farther down the road we go, the more difficult it is to speculate on Johnston's future and his possible achievements. When Johnston was removed from the scene thanks to his wound at Shiloh, eventually Braxton Bragg was given command of the Confederate armies in the West. Bragg has received more criticism than he deserves over the years. However, Bragg wasn't very skillful when it comes to dealing with subordinates and motivating his officers. Albert Sidney Johnston was the exact opposite. Bragg was also accused of being halting and of losing his nerve at key points in a campaign. Johnston again was the exact opposite type of commander. Albert Sidney Johnston would have offered the Confederates armies in the West great strength and leadership, traits the South missed in its future commanders in the West.

KEITH DICKSON: Johnston was a man of extraordinary courage and capability. There's no question the Confederate assault the first day at Shiloh was disrupted by the loss of Albert Sidney Johnston. Jefferson Davis was a big supporter of Johnston and stated, after the war, that the loss of Johnston was critical to the ultimate defeat of the Confederacy. Grant also displayed personal courage during the battle in trying to rally his forces in the final defensive perimeter near the Tennessee River. Grant was nearly killed by a shell fragment that actually hit the scabbard of his saber. Grant survived and Johnston didn't. It's the pure chance of war and the uncertainty that always accompanies warfare.

KENNETH NOE: Johnston had never really commanded large bodies of men until Shiloh. He had frittered away opportunities in the West and retreated out of Kentucky. Many accounts suggest it was Beauregard and not Johnston who was calling the shots at Shiloh. It's difficult to imagine Johnston ever becoming a great general. A victory at Shiloh certainly would have helped his image. Given time and positive publicity, Johnston might have developed into the kind of general that Jefferson Davis thought he would.

Sometimes I think Davis might have been better off sticking with Beauregard, who was somewhat underrated. Beauregard was fairly aggressive and made good decisions at Shiloh. Davis didn't like Beauregard and was still angry about events at First Manassas. The West became a dumping ground for generals who got on the bad side of Jefferson Davis and Robert E. Lee. Davis and Bragg had feuded in the 1850s but Bragg was able to build a relationship with Davis once the Civil War started. Bragg built that relationship basically by fawning on Davis. Bragg was politically astute enough to know that the president had to be reminded that he was in charge. Lee was pretty good at that. Beauregard was not and Joe Johnston was not.

It was hard to be a successful Confederate general in the West. There were so many factors working against you. You had so much territory to cover and all of the rivers flowed into your territory so the topography was against you. The Confederacy would have had a difficult time winning in the West even with Robert E. Lee in command.

Fatal Delay

Johnston's original battle plan at Shiloh called for the Southerners to turn Grant's left flank, cut off his line of retreat to the Tennessee River and then launch an assault that would push the Yankees back to the Snake Creek area and force the surrender of Grant's army.[15] After being taken off guard by the opening Confederate attack, the Federals soon regained their composure and formed new lines, including a position held by Union general Benjamin Prentiss, who rallied his men on an old wagon road. The sunken road would go down in the history books as the Hornet's Nest.

Johnston's death meant that P.G.T. Beauregard was now the new Confederate commander, and Beauregard chose to smash the Hornet's Nest instead of bypassing it and focusing his attacks on the collapsing Union flanks. The loss of Johnston's leadership also seemed to take some of the steam out of the Confederate attack.[16] Prentiss' men held their position for six hours before finally surrendering.[17] By the time the Rebels were able to move forward again in the early evening hours, Grant had put together a solid defensive line, bolstered by Union gunboats on the Tennessee River and reinforcements from Don Carlos Buell and Lew Wallace. Union troops repulsed Beauregard's final twilight assault.[18]

What if the advancing Confederates had bypassed the Hornet's Nest?

GEORGE RABLE: If Johnston hadn't been wounded and was available to coordinate the Confederate assault throughout the day on April 6, it's possible the South could have registered a major victory at Shiloh. It was difficult, if not impossible, to completely destroy armies during the war. One thing we forget, when we talk about these huge battles, is how difficult it was to handle these large armies and how difficult it was to achieve decisive victories. Let's assume for the moment that Johnston wasn't mortally wounded, that the Confederates were able to successfully bypass the Hornet's Nest and that Grant was shoved back against the Tennessee River. It's debatable whether the Confederates could have destroyed Grant's army. The Confederate battle plan had to be executed to near perfection in order to be successful. Beauregard's marching orders, leading up to the assault, were far too complicated to be carried out by relatively green troops. Speculating that the battle could have turned out differently assumes that the battle plan will be executed flawlessly. That's like expecting to watch a football game without penalties or turnovers. It might happen but it's extremely rare.

MATT ATKINSON: Johnston's goal was to push Grant back, take Pittsburg Landing and force the Union army back across the Tennessee River. The deployment of the four Confederate corps prior to the battle played a crucial role in the outcome of the battle. Johnston positioned his corps one

Albert Sidney Johnston. What if Johnston had survived the first day at Shiloh? VIRGINIA MILITARY INSTITUTE ARCHIVES.

behind the other in line of battle. Units became jumbled as the battle progressed. The only way the Confederate corps commanders could sort out the mess was to take command of the various sectors of the line. Had the Confederate corps been deployed from left to right, the command structure could have been maintained more easily. Nevertheless, command confusion was going to be a problem to contend with no matter kind of deployment Johnston used, because of the terrain. The battle was being fought on a narrow front between Lick and Owl Creeks.

The Hornet's Nest really proved to be the undoing of the Confederate offensive. When the Confederates succeeded in driving back the Federal flanks around the Hornet's Nest, the road to Pittsburg Landing was opened. Instead of bypassing the Federal stronghold, the Confederates elected to assault the position and eventually succeeded in encircling it. These tactics resulted in massive Confederate casualties and, more importantly, the loss of precious daylight. Had Johnston avoided his wound and had the Confederate forces remained organized and bypassed the Hornet's Nest, Johnston's men would have had a good chance to take Pittsburg Landing and Grant's army may well have been forced to retreat.

CRAIG SYMONDS: Albert Sidney Johnston, whatever military genius he might have possessed, had never commanded an army as large as this one. All Civil War generals were going through a learning process in the first few years of the war, trying to educate themselves about how to maneuver such large bodies of men on a battlefield that stretched beyond their own line of sight. At Shiloh, Johnston behaved more like a colonel in command of a regiment, or a brigadier in command of a brigade, than the commanding general of an army. His deployment of troops was awkward, and through much of the battle he was near the front, with his sword out of his scabbard, encouraging his men and directing small-unit assaults on the Hornet's Nest, instead of directing divisions from a headquarters in the rear. Had Johnston deployed his command differently, the momentum of the Confederate assault on April 6 might well have driven Grant's army into the river before reinforcements arrived.

Two things, besides his own difficulties, worked against Johnston: Confederate looting of the Union camps and the difficulties at the Hornet's Nest, both of which slowed the Confederate assault. It is possible to argue that Grant was saved by two Union gunboats, the Tyler and the Lexington, which fired heavy caliber shells over the heads of the Union soldiers along the riverbank and into the onrushing Confederates. Even so, a better disciplined and more adroitly directed Confederate army might have completed the destruction of the Union army on April 6. And if it had, that would not only have changed the momentum in the western theatre but Grant also never would have emerged as the man who later captured Vicksburg, saved Chattanooga and led the Overland Campaign.

ED BEARSS: Albert Sidney Johnston let Beauregard draw up the attack plan for the Confederates. The plan called for an attack along a broad front, over a mile in length, violating a cardinal rule of war, that a general who is strong everywhere is also weak everywhere. Beauregard had read too much about Napoleon. Beauregard was looking for an Austerlitz but the terrain at Shiloh was not similar to Moravia.[19]

When the Confederates were successful early in the day, especially when they routed Prentiss' men from their camping area, the Confederates didn't pursue. They allowed Prentiss to fall back with some of his men and form a defensive line. The Confederates gave the routed Union soldiers a chance to reform and establish a position, which would be known as the Hornet's Nest. The Confederates made a series of piecemeal attacks on the Hornet's Nest. Johnston rode to the extreme Confederate right and left Beauregard in tactical control of the Confederate forces near Shiloh Church. When his troops begin to stall in the move to press on to Pittsburg Landing, Johnston tried to use his personal leadership to help break a stalemate. Johnston was wounded and bled to death. The loss of Johnston further stalled the Confederate offensive and gave the Union forces additional time to prepare defensive positions farther back from the front line.

The Confederate plan was to use their right to drive the Union army back into a cul de sac between Snake Creek and the Tennessee River, to force Grant's army to surrender. The problem was the Confederates never really effectively used their right until too late in the day. If they had been able to push Grant back into that cul de sac, Buell would not have been able to reinforce Grant because Buell had to be moved across the Tennessee River. He would not have been able to reinforce Grant in significant numbers.

It was about 5:30 P.M. when the Confederates finally broke the Union lines at the Hornet's Nest. I used to think, until I walked the battlefield, that the death of Albert Sidney Johnston robbed the Confederates of a victory at Shiloh. However, if you walk the battlefield and notice the terrain between where Johnston died and another water obstacle the Confederates would be facing, Dill Branch, you realize it would have taken a superman to get across Dill Branch. The real problem was the Confederates' failure to address the problem of the Hornet's Nest, which should have been addressed earlier in the day rather than at 5:30 in the afternoon.

Grant Counterattacks

With reinforcements, Grant was ready to launch his own assault on April 7. Despite being surprised tactically the day before, Grant never lost his confidence; his men recaptured much of the ground they had lost April 6 and Beauregard was forced to withdraw. Instead of being a disastrous

Ulysses S. Grant. A loss at Shiloh might have ended Grant's military career. LIBRARY OF CONGRESS.

Union defeat, Shiloh merely delayed the Federal advance on the important rail junction at Corinth, Mississippi.

What if Grant's army had been forced to withdraw from Shiloh on April 6?

CRAIG SYMONDS: A Confederate victory at Shiloh doesn't end the war. What ends the war for either side is losing the political support at home necessary to sustain the conflict. For the Confederates to win the war, Lincoln has to be driven from office, either by failure in the election of 1864 or by impeachment, perhaps by the Radicals and Copperheads combining forces. It's the same story on the Confederate side. The loss of the Army of Northern Virginia and Richmond would be terrible blows but the war continues as long as the rank and file of the army and the civilian population sustain the war policy. That's why the war ended in April of 1865. It ended partly because Lee surrendered but mainly because the civilians in the South recognized defeat.

RICHARD MCMURRY: If the Confederates had won at Shiloh on April 6 and A.S. Johnston had survived, it would have made no great difference in the immediate military situation because there were enough Union forces nearby, under Buell, Wallace and Pope, to stop Johnston. I don't think the Confederates could have used a victory at Shiloh to undo all the damage they had suffered in January and February in Kentucky and West Tennessee.

MATT ATKINSON: Even if the Confederates were able to defeat Grant's army, we wouldn't have seen mass surrenders on the part of Grant's men. Even so, Grant's army certainly would have been forced to retreat to reorganize. The Confederates then would hold the initiative and have several options, including heading south to defend New Orleans or heading north. A move south doesn't seem likely. Without a navy, the Confederates would have been hard pressed to hang on to New Orleans.[20] The Confederates instead would have headed north, in an effort to regain Nashville. The Union army in the West might have been in disarray and it certainly would have taken the Union commanders time to recover.

Replacing Grant

Even with his victory on April 7, Grant was roundly criticized for being surprised by Johnston's initial assault on the 6th. When urged to

relieve the Union general, Lincoln made a decision with far-reaching consequences: He threw his support to Grant, explaining that he couldn't spare
a man who fights.[21]

Grant's career would eventually skyrocket. After capturing Vicksburg
in 1863 and receiving command of all of the Union armies in 1864, Grant
would be the one to accept Lee's surrender at Appomattox in 1865.

What if Grant had been removed from command following a Union defeat at Shiloh?

KEITH DICKSON: Henry Halleck would have demoted Grant, if Grant had
lost at Shiloh, due to the politics of the time. Grant may well have been
cashiered for the Union defeat and faded from the scene. The shell fragment that wound up hitting the scabbard of his sword April 6 could have
easily killed Grant. Without Grant at the helm, it would have been difficult
to find a replacement to lead the Union army to victory in the West. One
person who comes to mind, down the road, is James McPherson, a well-
respected Union commander who eventually was killed in the battle for
Atlanta. It also would have been difficult to find a general who could lead
the Army of the Potomac to a long-term strategic victory. One possibility
may have been Winfield Hancock.

Grant's career hinged on Shiloh, surviving the first day and winning
on the second day. His ability to hang on, organize his men and successfully counterattack on April 7 transformed his career. Grant was able to
see the war clearly and tie political goals with military tasks. The Civil
War was essentially a stalemate until Grant found a way to carry out political goals and military operations simultaneously. We don't see that kind
of achievement when it comes to the Confederates. Jefferson Davis directed
overall operations while Robert E. Lee handled military operations strictly
in the East. Lee eventually was made commander-in-chief to handle all
military operations but it was far too late to make a difference.

RICHARD MCMURRY: If Grant had lost that first day at Shiloh, his Civil
War career would have been finished because he had been surprised at
Fort Donelson and at Shiloh. Grant was in the doghouse before the battle
at Shiloh. He was in command only because the former commander,
Charles F. Smith, had been seriously injured in an accident a week or two
earlier when he hurt his leg getting out of a boat. It would not be easy to
replace Grant and his accomplishments in the West. I don't think Sherman could have functioned without Grant as kind of a mentor, a post to
which he could hitch himself. George Thomas probably never would have
gotten much of a chance. Thomas was a Virginian and didn't have the

political connections that a successful general must have. I don't really see an alternative to Grant. It may not have made much of a difference in Virginia but it would have made a big difference in the West.

CLINT JOHNSON: A loss at Shiloh means Grant's career is finished. Grant and Sherman were both taken by surprise by the Confederate attack April 6. Sherman himself actually chastised Union officers for talking about picket activity and for reporting that they saw Confederates in the woods. Grant and Sherman were generals who did not know where their enemy was. If Grant had suffered a defeat at Shiloh, his reputation would have been ruined. If Grant and Sherman are removed from the picture, who does the Union turn to for future victories? One possibility down the road might have been James McPherson, but he would have been too low on the totem pole after Shiloh to be noticed by Henry Halleck. Buell may not have been the choice because there were those in the North who viewed Buell as a southern sympathizer. Buell would have been the ranking general on hand, though, so perhaps his career may have turned out differently. It always struck me that Buell wasn't given important duties following Shiloh, although he had a good career in the Army.

MATT ATKINSON: Grant is sacked if the Confederates win at Shiloh. Think of the domino effect from the loss of Grant in both the East and the West. It's doubtful a Union commander could have been found in the West who could have come up with the strategy Grant did for taking Vicksburg. You also have to wonder if the Union could have found a commander with the strength and persistence in the East to pursue Lee's army as Grant did in 1864 and 1865. William T. Sherman certainly could have by 1864, but he may been let go as a result of a Union loss at Shiloh as well. Meade in the East and Rosecrans in the West could not have matched Grant's accomplishments 1863–1865.

Summary

Just as several factors conspired to deprive the North of a triumph at Bull Run, the Confederates also narrowly missed out on a potential victory at Shiloh. The loss of Albert Sidney Johnston and the decision by the Confederates not to bypass the Hornet's Nest may have saved Federal forces from an overwhelming defeat and Ulysses S. Grant from an early exit from the war.

Our experts generally agreed that the loss of Albert Sidney Johnston disrupted the Confederate offensive on April 6; there was less of a consensus about Johnston's long-term value. Steven Woodworth praised Johnston's strength, leadership skills and ability to deal with subordinates. A future Confederate commander in the West, Braxton Bragg, had anything but a smooth rapport with the generals under his command. A. S. Johnston was also very friendly with Confederate president Jefferson Davis. The relationship between Davis and another future Confederate commander in the West, Joseph Johnston, was often full of animosity.

The one to two day delay in launching the attack on Grant's army, the looting of overrun Yankee camps and the decision to crush the Hornet's Nest cost the Confederates a possible victory at Shiloh. There's no question that Civil War armies were nearly impossible to destroy, but several of the panel members agreed that the Confederates had a chance to either isolate Grant along the Tennessee River or to force his retreat. Perhaps it's unrealistic to seek perfection from an inexperienced army such as Johnston's. As panelist George Rable remarked, battle plans are rarely executed flawlessly.

Grant's storybook military career nearly came to an abrupt end at Shiloh. Keith Dickson pointed out that Grant was nearly killed by a Rebel shell on the first day of battle and was sharply criticized afterwards for being surprised at Shiloh. Several of the experts agreed that a Confederate victory on April 6 would have resulted in Grant's dismissal. The question then becomes who would emerge to lead Union forces to victory at Vicksburg in the West and to defeat Robert E. Lee and the Army of Northern Virginia in the East. The list of viable candidates is indeed a short one.

A victory at Shiloh might have allowed the Confederates to reclaim a portion of Tennessee and could have also placed Ulysses S. Grant on the shelf for the remainder of the war. Grant's dogged determination, however, spurred the Federals to a convincing victory on April 7 and left the South to lament the loss of one of its potential top theatre commanders, Albert Sidney Johnston.

5

Saving Richmond:
The Peninsula, the Valley
and the Seven Days

George B. McClellan was the officer called upon by Lincoln to save the Union, in the wake of McDowell's embarrassing loss at Bull Run. Dubbed the "Young Napoleon" by Northern newspapers, the Army of the Potomac's new commander had won a few minor victories in western Virginia in the summer of 1861. Now McClellan immediately set out to build a national army, although his critics charged him with being excessively cautious to the point of outright timidity.[1] McClellan would also develop the bad habit of overestimating the strength of his opponent, thanks in part to the famous detective Allen Pinkerton who served as McClellan's chief of military intelligence.[2]

By the spring of 1862, McClellan was finally ready to move on Richmond. Rather than approaching the Confederate capital from the north, he decided to land his massive army at Fort Monroe and advance up the Virginia Peninsula, albeit with fewer men than anticipated.[3] To protect Washington from an unexpected Confederate advance, Lincoln and his secretary of war, Edwin Stanton, removed Irvin McDowell's 38,000-man I Corps from McClellan's command and ordered it to cover the area between Washington and Fredericksburg.[4] McClellan would start his campaign against Richmond and Joseph Johnston's Confederate army with 90,000 men, rather than the 130,000 men he expected to have.[5]

McClellan's advance up the Virginia Peninsula inched forward in April. McClellan wasted several weeks preparing to lay siege to the Confederates defending Yorktown, only to have his prey suddenly vanish. The heavily outnumbered Confederates evacuated the city and withdrew toward Richmond, just as McClellan was ready to employ his heavy artillery.

Other Union generals in Virginia tried to lend McClellan a hand that spring. A political appointee from Massachusetts, Major General Nathaniel Banks, led a Federal army in the Shenandoah Valley while John C. Fremont commanded another Union force in western Virginia. Banks and Fremont were hopelessly outclassed though by their Confederate counterpart Stonewall Jackson, who stunned Union leaders in Washington with a series of victories in the Valley, helping to deprive McClellan of potential reinforcements.

With McClellan moving along the Chickahominy River and drawing ever closer to Richmond, Joseph Johnston decided to attack a portion of the mighty Yankee army on May 31. Tactically indecisive, the two-day battle of Seven Pines and Fair Oaks yielded one important result: Johnston was seriously wounded and replaced by Robert E. Lee.

Unwilling to allow McClellan to lay siege to Richmond, and with the Union army situated on both sides of the Chickahominy, the aggressive Lee dispatched most of his troops to the north bank of the river to tear into McClellan's exposed right flank.[6] After nearly a week of hard fighting in the Seven Days battles, McClellan had retreated to the James River, Richmond was saved and the Confederates had seized the initiative.

Duel of Iron

The first naval battle in history involving armored warships occurred on the open waters of Hampton Roads when the *Virginia* and the *Monitor* clashed on March 9, 1862. In seizing the Gosport Navy Yard in Norfolk in April of 1861, the Confederates had also grabbed the scuttled *Merrimac*, one of the Federal navy's powerful steam frigates. The inventive Confederates gave the newly re-christened *Virginia* iron covering four inches thick and a four-foot iron beak attached to the bow.[7] At the same time the *Virginia* was being readied, Swedish-American inventor John Ericsson was producing the *Monitor*, the Union's first ironclad, which featured a revolving iron turret with two 11-inch guns and was said to look like a tin can on a shingle.[8]

The *Virginia* went into action on March 8 and immediately produced results, sinking two wooden warships, the *Congress* and the *Cumberland*, and driving the steam frigate *Minnesota* aground. The *Monitor* arrived on the scene late in the day and the stage was set for the epic battle of ironclads the following day. Each ship pounded the other without inflicting any serious damage and, even though the battle was tactically a draw, the *Monitor* had won a strategic victory by preventing the further destruction of the Union navy's wooden ships at Hampton Roads.[9] Forced to retire to the safe haven of the Elizabeth River, the *Virginia* had to be scuttled by the Confederates when Federal troops re-occupied Norfolk.

What if the Virginia had defeated the Monitor in the first battle of ironclads?

CLINT JOHNSON: The *Monitor-Virginia* battle at Hampton Roads was a momentous clash, not just because it was the first battle of ironclads. This was a battle that could have brought McClellan's Peninsula campaign to a quick halt and could have had larger ramifications for the Confederate navy. One of the designers of the *Virginia* was John Mercer Brooke, who also designed the Brooke rifled cannon. The *Virginia* had four Brooke cannon on board, one forward, one aft and one in the center on each side. The cannon fired armor-piercing rounds called bolt shot. They look like dumbbells you might pick up at a gymnasium.

When they first took the *Virginia* out into Hampton Roads, they expected to be facing only wooden ships. The goal was to set the Union ships afire, so the Confederates only took explosive shells and solid shot for the first day. When the *Virginia* was going out the following day, the Confederates lacked the intelligence that the *Monitor* had arrived the night before. Thus the Confederates reloaded only explosive shells and solid shot. As we know, the fight that day between the *Virginia* and *Monitor* was essentially a draw. The Confederates had previously tested the effectiveness of Brooke cannon firing bolt shot and found that it could penetrate up to eight or nine inches of armor. The *Monitor* was armored with eight one-inch layers of iron around its turret. So the chances were pretty good that a bolt shot could have penetrated the *Monitor's* turret. A couple of good shots could have killed the turret gun crew. Even a glancing blow on the deck of the *Monitor* by a bolt shot could have penetrated the armored deck, which featured only one inch of iron. The result would have been that every wave would have brought water into the *Monitor*. I think it was a distinct possibility that had the Confederates had bolt shot on board, the *Virginia* could have sunk the *Monitor*. It may well have taken the Union navy some time to recover. The next two designs for ironclads were less than stellar. One was the new *Ironsides*, which turned out to be kind of a forerunner to the battleship. The other was the *Galena*, which turned out to be a terrible idea for an ironclad. The *Virginia* would then have been able to wreak havoc on local Union forces, and the Confederates might have been able to hang on to Norfolk and the Gosport Navy Yard.

When the Union forces captured Gosport eventually, they found drawings for several ironclads that the Confederates could have completed had they held on to the Gosport Navy Yard. The fellow who helped to build the *Virginia*, John Luke Porter, had on the drawing board small lightly armored ships that would use limited crews and would operate against Union blockade vessels at night. It was the forerunner of the PT boats we saw in World War II. You can imagine the problems the Union would have faced had the Confederates been allowed to hang onto the Gosport Navy Yard and mass produce these vessels. The Confederates could have built them at Gosport, loaded them onto rail cars and shipped them to every southern city, where they would have been operating against the wooden blockade ships used by the Union. They would have operated at night, using hit and run tactics as were used by the U.S. PT boats against the Japanese in World War II. It's conceivable that the Confederates could have broken the Union blockade.

By the way, the Confederates realized their mistake; on the *Virginia's* third trip out into Hampton Roads, the Confederates loaded bolt shot on board the *Virginia* to use against the *Monitor*. The Confederates cruised back and forth, trying to get the *Monitor* to come out and fight. The crew of the *Monitor* refused to give battle so we never saw a second battle of the *Virginia* and the *Monitor*. The Confederates had an investigation into who was responsible for forgetting to load the bolt shot onboard the *Virginia* before the battle with the *Monitor*. Both Porter and Brooke denied that it was their responsibility to make sure the bolt shot was loaded. I tend to blame Josiah Gorgas for his failure to issue orders to have the bolt shot onboard the *Virginia*.[10]

ROBERT E. L. KRICK: The first battle of ironclads could have had a big impact on McClellan's Peninsula campaign had the *Monitor* not been ready or had the *Virginia* wound up winning the engagement. The potential of an unopposed C.S.S. *Virginia* is fascinating to contemplate. Presumably it would have ruined the waterborne aspect of McClellan's campaign and perhaps forced him to take the overland route. For the *Virginia* to continue to operate though, the Confederates had to maintain possession of Norfolk, of the Gosport Navy Yard. The *Virginia* could not really go out into open sea and couldn't go up the James to Richmond. The ironclad could essentially operate only in the Norfolk and Hampton Roads area. Even without the *Monitor*, Union authorities could have offset the *Virginia* by destroying its base and forcing it to make for Richmond, where presumably it would have run aground on a sandbar on its way north.

CRAIG SYMONDS: The story of the *Monitor*'s fight with the *Virginia* is so dramatic that if it had been a movie script, the critics would complain that it was too contrived. The *Monitor* arrived in Hampton Roads in literally the nick of time. If it had come a week later, the *Virginia* might easily have destroyed the rest of the Union fleet in the roadstead. Under those circumstances it is hard to see how McClellan could have continued with his Peninsula Campaign.

But even without the *Monitor*, the *Virginia* could not have extended its influence beyond Hampton Roads. It had a top speed of five knots, consumed coal profligately, and had a very deep draft. It couldn't go up the James River, and it couldn't go out into open water. Its commander, Franklin Buchanan, didn't think it could survive even in the relatively protected waters of the Chesapeake Bay. So the notion that the *Virginia* could somehow have spread terror along the Atlantic seaboard was simply a fantasy.

Of course that did not prevent the Union's secretary of war, Edwin Stanton, from worrying about it. At a cabinet meeting held the day after the first Battle of Hampton Roads, when the Virginia destroyed the *Cumberland* and the *Congress*, Lincoln called a cabinet meeting. Stanton was so nervous about the *Virginia* that he kept getting up from his seat and going over to the window to look downriver to see if, even then, the *Virginia* was on its way to shell the White House.

Winning by Marching

In the spring of 1862, Stonewall Jackson was given the dual responsibility of controlling the agriculturally important Shenandoah Valley and tying up Union manpower. Despite being outnumbered by Union forces in the region, Jackson marched his men swiftly from one end of the Valley to the other, defeating one Federal army after another and depriving McClellan of much needed reinforcements.

Jackson actually lost the opening battle of the Valley Campaign in March at Kernstown but then received additional troops, swelling his ranks to roughly 14,000.[11] Even with the reinforcements, Jackson faced a difficult task in trying to defend Staunton, his base of operations, from Nathaniel

Banks's army at Harrisonburg and John C. Fremont's army approaching from the west. Taking full advantage of the Valley's unique geographical features and relying on rapid movements to keep Banks and Fremont apart, Jackson beat each Union commander in detail. After halting Fremont's advance with a victory at McDowell on May 8, Jackson swept down the Valley, overwhelmed a Federal contingent at Front Royal on May 23 and then defeated Banks at Winchester two days later.

There was still a chance for approximately 35,000 Federals to seal off Jackson's line of retreat to the south, if the Union commanders moved quickly.[12] Fremont was concentrated at Franklin, 50 miles closer to Harrisonburg than Jackson was, while troops under James Shields were situated to the east. Lincoln ordered Fremont and Shields to move quickly to crush Jackson between the two Union jaws, but once again the ability of Jackson's foot soldiers to move great distances in a short amount of time came into play.[13] By the time Fremont and Shields converged at Strasburg, Jackson had escaped the trap and was 12 miles to the south at Woodstock.[14]

Stonewall kept on moving south and east, taking his army to Port Republic, southeast of Harrisonburg, in an effort to remain between Fremont and Shields. It was at that point that Jackson almost became a Union prisoner. Federal cavalry nearly bagged the Confederate commander with a surprise raid on June 8 but Jackson and most of his staff narrowly escaped on horseback.[15] Stonewall then brought his Valley Campaign to a successful conclusion by defeating Fremont at Cross Keys on June 8 and by turning back Shields's advance guard at Port Republic the following day.

With just 17,000 men, Jackson had immobilized more than 50,000 Federals, troops that McClellan could have used in his campaign against Richmond.[16] Ulysses S. Grant would later question whether Jackson's campaigns in Virginia justified his reputation as a great commander, and whether Jackson would have been able to achieve similar victories later in the war against the likes of Phil Sheridan, William T. Sherman and George Thomas.[17]

What if Stonewall Jackson had faced better Union generals during the Valley Campaign?

CRAIG SYMONDS: Stonewall Jackson was, and remains, something of an enigma. He was brilliant in the Shenandoah Valley in 1862, but a disaster on the Virginia Peninsula during the Seven Days campaign. Indeed, Jackson had a more uneven record of battlefield success than his champions often admit. I caution my students at the Naval Academy against choosing Jackson as a role model. He was secretive with his subordinates, refusing to share his plans with them; he was demanding of his soldiers, which worked well with eager volunteers in 1862 but might not have been as successful with the conscripts and tired veterans that made up the army in 1864; and he was coldly and utterly unforgiving when his subordinates failed to live up to his expectations.

It may well be that much of Jackson's reputation derives from his dramatic death at the moment of his greatest triumph. Because he never had to serve in the grinding Overland Campaign of 1864, or the bitter siege of 1865, his Civil War career is associated with the glory days of the Army of Northern Virginia. I'm not sure his historical reputation would have been as glittering had he lived. One

Stonewall Jackson. Jackson's success in the Shenandoah Valley deprived McClellan of reinforcements. NATIONAL ARCHIVES.

wonders, for example, if he would have fared as well against Phil Sheridan in the Valley in 1864 as he did against Fremont, Shields and Banks in 1862; or if he could have bamboozled Grant the way he did John Pope or Joe Hooker.

JEFF WERT: There's no question that the Union commanders in the valley, Banks and Fremont, left a lot to be desired. On the other hand, even if the Union forces had been lead by a more capable commander, you have to wonder if Jackson still wouldn't have been able to outmaneuver them. The Valley Campaign certainly established Jackson's reputation but it also showcased his talents. He had the uncanny ability to impose his will on events. Jackson wasn't necessarily a great tactician, but he was able to get his men to do things other generals couldn't get their men to do. He certainly was helped a great deal by facing opponents like Fremont and Banks. Neither one was much of a general. Both were more politicians than military leaders.

JOHN HEATWOLE: The Lincoln administration was still fixated on Richmond in the spring of 1862. It took until nearly the end of Jackson's Valley Campaign for Northern authorities to understand clearly how much of a potential threat the Valley would be in the future. In early 1862, they were wearing blinders to everything except Richmond, so they would not have sent a commander to the Shenandoah that they thought could be better used in breaking down the gates of Richmond. The Lincoln administration was also still trying to evaluate the strengths of their general officers, and the officers themselves were trying to learn the ropes of commanding large forces. Anyone sent besides Banks, Shields and Fremont might have had more success but then again, they might have fared worse.

What if Fremont had sealed off Jackson's escape route to the south, after Jackson's victory at Winchester?

JEFF WERT: There was a chance for Fremont and Shields to seal off Jackson's escape route to the south. Fremont was the key man in this scenario. Shields was under McDowell so he couldn't really move until McDowell released him. Had Fremont pushed his troops at all, he could have cut off Jackson's line of retreat. Jackson would have then been in plenty of trouble. Communication and coordination between the different Union armies in the Valley was difficult, to say the least. There were few generals in the war who were able to match Jackson's men in marching great distances in a day. The Stonewall Brigade's march south from Harpers Ferry to escape the clutches of the Union army was a remarkable feat. In my mind, if Jackson's line of retreat south had been blocked, his only alternative would have been to stand and fight. This would have been a battle where Jackson would have been hard pressed. Jackson's men were simply exhausted from the weeks of constant fighting and marching. Jackson's men would have been severely fatigued in any battle at that point with Fremont's men.

ROBERT E. L. KRICK: Shields and Fremont had a chance to seal off Stonewall Jackson's escape route to the south, following Jackson's victory over Banks at Winchester in May of 1862. If the Union forces had blocked Jackson's escape avenue to the south, I'm not sure if Jackson would have been forced to fight or could have possibly escaped to the east.

The Union could have employed better concentration of forces against Jackson in the Valley Campaign. In my mind, the Union decision to use three separate armies to chase down Jackson was probably the wiser course, considering the geography and the terrain.

Using separate armies at a venue where maneuver and strategy were especially important seems like a significant advantage for the Federals. The problem for the Union wasn't splitting their forces. The Union commanders simply didn't coordinate their armies very well. We now know that strategy, operations and secrecy were the strengths of Jackson's generalship. Three able foes might have been able to suppress Jackson in the Valley, but certainly not one and probably not two.

JOHN HEATWOLE: Fremont and Shields were closing in on Jackson after First Winchester but Jackson could still be active. If Jackson had attacked Fremont at Strasburg, Jackson knew the lay of the land and probably would have tried to flank Fremont. That would have been enough to send Fremont into a host of doubts. The other scenario is that Jackson would have gone by way of Cedarville and would have taken the high ground north of Front Royal. He had plenty of artillery ammunition to soften up Shields, whose force was not in good shape. Shields had an entire regiment without shoes and another without pants. He was also worried about the possibility of a Confederate force coming into the Valley from the east, further up the Valley near Luray. Shields had nothing to be worried about; it was all in his head, but he would have been very tentative fearing for his rear.

If Jackson had been cut off in the main Valley from moving south, the chances were good that he still could have beaten or sidestepped one force and then taken up a position of his own choosing to deal with either Fremont or Shields on his own terms.

KEITH DICKSON: Fremont could have been quicker to seal off Jackson's escape route to the south after Jackson's victory at Winchester. That's not to say Jackson would have been necessarily placed in a terrible position. It's Jackson and Fremont after all. Jackson always wins in that confrontation. Fremont had no business running an army. Naturally, after the Valley campaign is over, Fremont disappears. Jackson would have been willing to give battle to Fremont even though Jackson's men were very tired. His men were willing to go wherever Jackson told them to go because they believed in him.

The big question would have been whether Jackson's superiority over Fremont as a commander took precedence over the Union's advantage in numbers. Fremont wouldn't necessarily have to fight an offensive battle with Shields's men approaching from the east and Banks's army to the north. Jackson though had the advantage of knowledge of the terrain, and his army was flexible and able to march quickly. Jackson also had a gift to inspire his men to do magnificent things.

What if Jackson had been taken prisoner by Union cavalry at Port Republic June 8?

DONALD PFANZ: Jackson was nearly captured at Port Republic and it was Jackson's own fault. He failed to post his troops properly and he placed himself in a very perilous position, with him on one side of a river and most of his army on the other side. It's interesting to speculate how the Confederates might have fared in 1862 and beyond in Virginia if Stonewall was sitting out the war in a Northern prison camp. There wasn't anyone on the Confederate side, at that point in the war, with Jackson's confidence and boldness. If Jackson had been taken out of the picture, command of his forces would have probably fallen to Ewell. Ewell would have done a tolerable job but not up to Stonewall's standards.

ROBERT E. L. KRICK: Would Jackson have been exchanged if he had been taken prisoner? I think so. I think he would have been exchanged for a Union general of similar rank or equal value. We saw major generals traded for each other a few times during the war. In the short term though, the Confederates would have had problems in the Valley and also in the fight near Richmond against McClellan. If Jackson had been captured at Port Republic, Ewell probably would have assumed command in the Valley. My guess is that Ewell, lacking knowledge of Jackson's plans, probably would have decided to play it safe and retreat into the mountains, perhaps retreating through Brown's Gap. This would have paralyzed Lee's plans for an offensive against McClellan to save Richmond.

JOHN HEATWOLE: If Jackson had been captured at the North Bridge at Port Republic June 8, the Union cavalrymen might have been able to hang onto Jackson if they realized how important their prize was. However, if the bridge remained intact, Confederate troops would be able to pursue and might have been able to retake Jackson.

Taking Jackson into captivity presents a problem. If the Port Republic battle had never been fought or won by the Southerners, would Jackson be considered as important a figure or would he have been just another major general waiting to be exchanged for someone of equal rank? Jackson had not yet worked in the field with Lee. His reputation would have been flawed by his capture when the incident was dissected and it was discovered that he had placed himself in a precarious position. Jackson would have been exchanged, and by the time of his release someone else might have risen to the top in Lee's estimation. Jackson's absence from the Seven Days should not have a made a difference. Ewell would not have made a more lackluster showing in eastern Virginia than did Jackson.

The Numbers Game

In his advance up the Virginia Peninsula, George McClellan frittered away several opportunities to crush his outmanned opponent. For instance, McClellan faced just 11,000 Confederates when he arrived in front of the Rebel fortifications at Yorktown in early April. The Confederate commander, the theatrical Major General John Bankhead Magruder, put on quite a show for McClellan by firing his artillery on a regular basis and parading several hundred Confederates in and out of a thicket. McClellan had no way of knowing that it was the same small body of men marching around in a circle.[18] Falling for the ruse and deciding that the Confederate line was too strong for a direct assault, McClellan wasted precious time preparing for a siege before the outnumbered and outgunned Confederates decided to evacuate Yorktown.[19] By the end of May, McClellan's army was within 10 miles of Richmond, with three corps located on the north bank of the Chickahominy River and two corps situated on the south bank.[20]

What if McClellan had been more aggressive during the Peninsula Campaign in April and May?

ED BEARSS: George McClellan was an enigma. He was a wonderful organizer and organized a magnificent army but due to his innate caution, he was unable to use the Army of the Potomac to gain a decisive victory over the Confederates. There were several occasions when McClellan had opportunities to gain those decisive victories, including his Peninsula Campaign in 1862. As the British describe it, McClellan's movement transporting his army from Alexandria to the Peninsula was the stride of a giant. However, from early April until early May, the giant's pace became glacial as McClellan's progress up the Peninsula inched along. McClellan certainly missed opportunities at Yorktown against Magruder. McClellan had this habit of overestimating Confederate numbers, giving the Southern forces numbers that defy the imagination. If McClellan had looked at all of the intelligence sources that were available or even read the census, he should have realized the kind of huge numerical advantage he had.

CLINT JOHNSON: McClellan was the victim of poor intelligence during the Peninsula Campaign. He was using Allen Pinkerton to tell him what kind of Confederate forces he was facing. He trusted Pinkerton implicitly, but Pinkerton would just make up numbers out of thin air. Had Pinkerton given McClellan the real numbers and had McClellan believed those numbers, we might have seen a different outcome in his campaign for

Richmond. It's certainly conceivable that McClellan might have decided to march all the way to Richmond in April of 1862. Had McClellan done that, the Confederates would have been in a bad situation, similar to the situation the North would have been in had Washington been lost following Bull Run. If McClellan had captured Richmond, the North might have called for peace negotiations in an effort to have the Confederates return to the Union. McClellan may well have advanced aggressively on Richmond had he received good intelligence on Confederate strength or intentions.

GEORGE RABLE: McClellan clearly had an opportunity to inflict a major defeat on the Confederacy. The Confederates were on the defensive and Joe Johnston had not shown any willingness to go on the tactical offensive. There was a chance for the North to end the war in the summer of 1862 without the Emancipation Proclamation having been issued. If McClellan had captured Richmond and taken the Confederate army guarding Richmond out of the picture, the end of the war was a distinct possibility. McClellan though was militarily cautious and politically conservative.

What would the peace have looked like before the Emancipation was issued? It would have been a Northern victory that may well have been an incomplete victory in many respects because the source of all of the difficulty, slavery, may still have been intact. In fact, there were some abolitionists in the North who worried the war would end too soon. The northern public wasn't committed to an emancipation policy and Lincoln issued it in the fall of 1862 essentially as a war measure. If the South had returned to the Union in the summer of 1862, the only way to eliminate slavery would have been with a constitutional amendment.

McClellan's army was certainly superior in manpower to the Confederate army. We know that numbers don't always dictate how a battle will play out and we know it was difficult to destroy Civil War armies. Even so, if McClellan had inflicted a serious defeat on Johnston's army outside Richmond, the war could have come to an end. There was dissatisfaction in the South about the way the war going. The Confederates had suffered several setbacks in the West, including the losses of Fort Donelson and Fort Henry and the heavy losses suffered at Shiloh. If you read the deliberations of the Confederate cabinet in the first half of 1862 and the accounts in Confederate newspapers, you get the impression that Confederate morale was sagging at this point in the war. So a large Union victory on the steps of the capitol in Richmond may well have finished off the Confederacy.

JEFF WERT: McClellan was an engineer at heart and personally cautious. There's an argument that engineer-trained officers tended to be more cautious, but then again Lee was also an engineer-trained officer. McClellan saw hordes of Confederates that didn't exist and he wanted to believe the inflated intelligence figures given to him by Pinkerton. Pinkerton was shrewd enough to realize those were the kinds of numbers that McClellan wanted from him. McClellan had said at one time that if his army was lost, then the country is lost and the cause is lost. No one could question McClellan's patriotism. Certainly if you read his letters you get the feeling that McClellan was almost paranoid about the Lincoln administration.

McClellan had the opportunity on several different occasions to capture the Confederate capital of Richmond. Great commanders in military history possess boldness when it's called for and rise to the occasion. McClellan's will was put to the test and he failed badly. McClellan always wrote how he loved his men and I think he viewed the Army of the Potomac as his wonderful creation. He underestimated what his men could do and was unwilling to unsheathe the sword that he had created.

Lee Takes Command

Joseph Johnston's retreat across the Virginia Peninsula in April and May had allowed McClellan's army to take up position just a few miles from Richmond. With the safety of the Confederate capital at stake, Johnston attempted to carry out a complicated maneuver aimed at destroying two Union divisions near Seven Pines, approximately 10 miles east of Richmond. The subsequent two-day fight left both sides essentially where they were at the beginning of the battle; Johnston himself was incapacitated after being struck by a bullet in the shoulder and a spent shell fragment in the chest.[21]

The wounding of Johnston would be one of the most pivotal events of the entire war. Jefferson Davis selected Robert E. Lee to be Johnston's replacement, an appointment that did not impress George B. McClellan, who described Lee as being weak under grave responsibility, wanting in moral firmness and timid and irresolute in action.[22] Lee would soon produce dividends for the Confederacy and McClellan would have plenty of chances to reconsider his opinions.

What if Joseph Johnston had not been wounded May 31, 1862?

ROBERT E. L. KRICK: I don't see anything in Johnston's record, before or after May 31, 1862, that would lead me to believe that Johnston could have saved Richmond from falling, as Lee did when he took over for the wounded Johnston. If Johnston had not been wounded, he would have continued to shrink his defensive perimeter around the Southern capital. Eventually Union mortar shells would have been landing in the streets of Richmond, killing civilians. The question would then become whether Jefferson Davis would have sacked Johnston in time to save Richmond. Before May 31, 1862, Johnston had a very solid reputation thanks to the victory at Bull Run and was popular with his men and in the Confederacy. Meanwhile Lee had no experience commanding a huge army, so I don't think it was feasible that Lee could have replaced Johnston before Johnston suffered his wound at Seven Pines. So if Johnston wasn't wounded and wasn't sacked by Davis, McClellan would have captured Richmond by mid-July and essentially ended the war. I don't see how the Confederates could have continued to operate militarily in the East. The Confederates could not have operated in the Richmond area without access to Richmond's hospital facilities, rail yards, munitions and governmental offices. Certainly some of these facilities could have been rebuilt elsewhere in the South, but that would have taken time and it wouldn't have been easy. The fall of Richmond would have ruined the Confederates in 1862. I can't say whether reunion in the summer of 1862 would have brought an immediate end to slavery, since the Emancipation Proclamation had not been issued yet. As things turned out, McClellan's inability to capture Richmond and bring the war to a quick end in 1862 resulted in a prolonged war, during which the Union's war aims changed and were expanded to include emancipation.

JEFF WERT: Joe Johnston essentially fought only one offensive battle in his career during the Civil War and that was at Seven Pines. The war turned on the day Johnston was wounded, allowing Lee to rise to command the army defending Richmond. The only way the Confederacy could win the war was to get some sort of political settlement brought about by a series of battlefield victories. They only had that opportunity in the East, although I agree they lost the war in the West. Had Johnston not been wounded, Davis would have fired Johnston in mid to late June. If he didn't fire Johnston, we would have seen the siege of Richmond. McClellan would have captured Richmond and that would have ended the war.

What happens to slavery if the war ends in June or July of 1862 when the Emancipation wasn't issued until the fall of 1862? Lincoln himself was not an abolitionist. I know Lincoln offered compensation to the Border States, including Delaware, in return for an end to slavery. It's possible the South might have been able to return to the Union in the summer of 1862 with their slaves, at least in the short term. It's hard to imagine the Repub-

Robert E. Lee, who would seize the initiative to save Richmond. VIRGINIA MILITARY INSTITUTE ARCHIVES.

licans would have allowed that to take place. They might have insisted on a plan for gradual emancipation in the Southern states. The federal government was going to compensate Delaware to get rid of slaves in that state. McClellan wasn't fighting the war to end slavery, so it's ironic that his failure to capture Richmond lengthened the war and ensured slavery would be outlawed by the Emancipation Proclamation. McClellan was adamantly opposed to emancipation.

ED BEARSS: If Johnston had not been wounded May 31 and had maintained command of the Confederate forces around Richmond, McClellan would have continued to inch forward toward Richmond. He would have maneuvered for position against Johnston and I believe he would have been successful in his campaign to capture the Confederate capital. Johnston would have given up Richmond without a fight just as he essentially gave up Atlanta without a fight. If McClellan had captured Richmond in June of 1862, the Union position in the war would have looked promising. The Confederates would have lost, at that point, Richmond, Corinth in the West and a good portion of the Mississippi River. The Confederacy's chances of still being in existence by January 1, 1863, would have been slim and none. I also believe there was a good chance, under that timetable, that there may not have been an Emancipation Proclamation issued freeing the slaves. Even if the Emancipation Proclamation had been issued and the end of the war followed soon thereafter, I don't believe the 13th Amendment would have been approved, at least not at that time.

Richmond Saved, McClellan Escapes

Robert E. Lee wasted no time displaying the daring and audacity he would be known for throughout the war. By late June, McClellan's army was positioned on both sides of the Chickahominy River, with 30,000 men of the Union V Corps on the north bank of the river. Leaving just a few divisions to keep McClellan out of Richmond, Lee moved 65,000 men north of the Chickahominy to assail McClellan's exposed right flank.[23]

Lee and his subordinates agreed to begin the offensive June 26.[24] The opening assault on Fitz John Porter's V Corps at Mechanicsville resulted in severe losses for the Confederates, while Stonewall Jackson's troops bivouacked for the evening just a few miles away without seeing action.[25] A furious Confederate attack the following day drove Porter's Corps from the field at Gaines's Mill. Lee's troops suffered nearly 8,000 casualties; Jackson's men were delayed taking part in the assault due to poor staff work and a misdirected march.[26]

Lee's aggressiveness had shaken McClellan, prompting the Union commander to order a change of base from White House Landing on the Pamunkey River to the James River, and the Confederates searched for an opportunity to strike the fleeing Federals. June 30 at Glendale may have been Lee's best chance to split the retreating Union column and destroy segments of McClellan's army in detail.[27] Two Confederate divisions under James Longstreet and A.P. Hill hit the Federal line, but an assault by

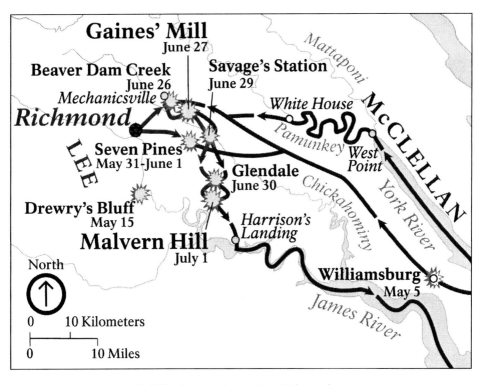

McClellan's campaign against Richmond

Stonewall Jackson on William Franklin's Corps at White Oak Swamp never materialized. While Jackson's men repaired the burned White Oak Bridge, their commander lay down under a tree and went to sleep.[28] Jackson made no effort to find a potential crossing, even though one of his cavalry officers reported the discovery of a useable ford about a quarter of a mile upstream.[29] William Franklin said the Federal army would have suffered a defeat at Glendale had Jackson attacked at Brackett's Ford and the White Oak Bridge, and he also claimed a defeat at Glendale would have reduced McClellan's army to a disorganized mob by the time it reached the James River.[30] McClellan's men, however, were able to escape to Malvern Hill, a strong defensive position within range of Union gunboats on the James River, and massed Yankee artillery proceeded to blast Lee's men apart on July 1 after a series of ill-advised Confederate assaults.[31] Despite his victory at Malvern Hill, McClellan continued with his retreat to Harrison's Landing on the James River.

The Seven Days had been bloody, resulting in nearly 16,000 Federal casualties and costing the Confederates over 20,000 men, losses the South could ill afford.[32] Confederate Edward Porter Alexander would later claim that had Stonewall Jackson marched and fought during the Seven Days as he had marched and fought in the Shenandoah Valley, McClellan's huge army may have been largely destroyed.[33]

What if Stonewall Jackson had performed better during the Seven Days?

KEITH DICKSON: June 30, 1862, was a perfect situation for the Confederates to do serious damage to at least a portion of McClellan's army. With Longstreet and Hill attacking at Frayser's Farm and Jackson moving from the other direction, from White Oak Swamp, the Confederates could have inflicted a serious defeat on the Army of the Potomac. Jackson was at the right place at the right time with the right force and yet he was sleeping under a tree. Everyone was waiting for the order to move forward, and Jackson was lethargic and seemed almost comatose due to fatigue. I think he heard his orders but perhaps didn't fully understand the implied tasks that Lee had in mind. In Jackson's report after the battle June 30, he made it clear that he would remain at White Oak Swamp until he was ordered to move elsewhere. Jackson had always followed the exact letter of his instructions. Eventually Jackson moved away from that in his relationship with Lee, so that Lee gave him very general instructions and then Jackson followed through as he saw fit. The Seven Days, however, was really the first time Jackson and Lee had fought together. Jackson was still in the mode of following his orders to the exact letter, nothing more and nothing less. So another reason Jackson may have remained at White Oak Swamp and did not take part in the fighting June 30 was that he wasn't specifically ordered to move forward and launch an assault.

ROBERT E. L. KRICK: In hindsight, it would have been better for the Confederates to delay the attack on McClellan a few days. There is conflicting testimony as to when Jackson wanted to launch the assault on McClellan's right flank. Longstreet claimed after the war that at the meeting of the Confederate commanders June 23 he talked Jackson into delaying for a day the start of the attack. Perhaps that's true, maybe not. I'm sure if Jackson knew his march to the battlefield was going to be delayed and was going to run into so many unforeseen obstacles, then without question it would have been better to start the assault on McClellan on June 28 rather than June 26. I don't believe that by waiting a few more days there was an increased risk of McClellan attacking Lee's thin line guarding Richmond. An aggressive push by McClellan toward Richmond would have created unwelcome problems for both commanders. A truly vigorous attack by the

Federals might have caved in the Confederate defenses east of the city, but then Lee would have been on McClellan's flank, and McClellan would have held Richmond without any line of supply. On a map, this series of moves would have looked like a revolving door and probably would not have helped either army. McClellan needed to beat Lee on the battlefield and Lee needed to compromise McClellan's supply line to win this campaign.

Had Jackson arrived above Beaver Dam Creek earlier on June 26 as planned, his presence would have forced the Union V Corps away from the creek defenses, and Lee's campaign would have commenced with a virtually bloodless victory as designed. In the long run, the events of June 26 did not greatly influence the development of the campaign. Jackson was not terribly late June 27 for Gaines's Mill. Had the Union V Corps been aligned as Lee and Jackson supposed, then Jackson's difficult march to the battlefield might have been more important. As it was, his minor tardiness was not much of an issue.

There was the chance at Glendale June 30 to catch McClellan's army in mid-stride at it was approaching the James River. There were seven Federal divisions from four different corps with no coordinated leader on the field June 30. Lee had a good portion of his army at hand and certainly had the chance to inflict a serious tactical defeat on the Army of the Potomac. Jackson's lethargy at White Oak Swamp, whether from fatigue or from misunderstanding his orders, hurt Lee's plans for the day at Glendale. Jackson lost an opportunity to maneuver two of the seven defending Union divisions away from a strong point while he punched in one shoulder of the Union perimeter. If Jackson had moved with his usual alacrity, the Federal lines west of the Riddell's Shop intersection probably would have collapsed earlier, thus increasing the degree of the Union defeat there. But even with Jackson at full throttle on June 30, the Confederates stood no chance of inflicting the sort of catastrophic defeat on McClellan's army that some historians and veterans have suggested.

CRAIG SYMONDS: Scholars often chalk up Jackson's poor performance in the Seven Days Campaign to physical exhaustion. According to this view, he simply drove himself to the point where he literally could not pick himself up off the ground. Another factor was that, unlike his exploits in the Shenandoah Valley, he was operating in unknown terrain. Whatever the cause of it, there is little doubt that his failure on the Peninsula constituted a missed opportunity for the Confederate army during McClellan's retreat. By day three of the Seven Days, McClellan had lost his nerve, and although his army was in a controlled retreat, McClellan himself was on the edge of panic. A successfully executed double envelopment by

Jackson on the one hand, and Longstreet and Hill on the other, might well have sent McClellan over the edge. He might have tried a desperate Dunkirk-like evacuation from Harrison's Landing that would have allowed Lee a chance to apply the coup de grace. So to be sure, Jackson's uncharacteristic lethargy during the Seven Days marked a lost opportunity for Lee and the Confederacy.

One of the most interesting things about this episode, however, is Lee's willingness to overlook it. As a rule, Lee was unforgiving with failed officers who put his plans at risk. When officers failed to produce, Lee generally sent them West or off to some other command. But he forgave Jackson's performance on the Peninsula and almost immediately afterward sent him off on an independent command to turn back Pope's Army of Virginia. So Lee, at least, thought Jackson's odd behavior during the Seven Days was an aberration.

JEFF WERT: The renowned Confederate artillery commander Edward Porter Alexander claimed the critical day in the history of the Confederacy was June 30, 1862, at Glendale. Alexander was the finest historian of the Army of Northern Virginia who was actually a member of that army. Jackson failed to take part in the attack at Frayser's Farm that day; Jackson simply had reached his physical limit. His conduct was certainly baffling when you compare the Seven Days to Jackson's other efforts during the war, both before and after the Seven Days. Had Jackson crossed White Oak Swamp and pressed Franklin's Union VI Corps, it's quite possible Jackson could have broken Franklin's lines. If that happened while Hill and Longstreet were attacking toward the crossroads at Glendale, the Army of the Potomac would have been staring at a decisive defeat. A defeat of that nature could have eliminated the entire army from active operations for a period of time and possibly even brought about a settlement between the North and South. Lee was most upset at the end of the day about the failure of his plans to be carried out.

Summary

When studying the Union campaign against Richmond in the spring and summer of 1862, the focus rests squarely on three men: George B. McClellan, Robert E. Lee and Stonewall Jackson.

Ed Bearss described McClellan as being an enigma. McClellan certainly had the resources to capture the Confederate capital if he had been willing to use those resources. McClellan had a chance to attack Lee's thin lines in front of Richmond June 25, and could have continued to battle Lee's army after Gaines's Mill rather than retreating to the James River.[34] Jeff Wert concluded that McClellan's will was put to the test and he failed badly.

May 31 was truly one of the most important days of the Civil War. It was on that day that Joseph Johnston was wounded and Robert E. Lee was named the Army of Northern Virginia's new commander. Several of the experts agreed that a healthy Johnston would have remained in command, resulting in McClellan's taking of Richmond and the demise of the Confederacy. Robert E. L. Krick stated that the fall of Richmond would have ruined the Confederates in 1862.

Then there's the mystery of Stonewall Jackson. Whether we chalk it up to fatigue, poor staff work or miscommunication, there's no getting around the fact that the Jackson of the Seven Days was not the Jackson of the Valley. Nearly all of the panelists agreed that had Jackson energetically attacked the Union rear guard at White Oak Swamp on June 30, Lee's Seven Days offensive might have reaped greater rewards. The degree of the Confederate victory is another matter entirely. Robert E. L. Krick declared that the Confederates had no chance to inflict a catastrophic defeat on McClellan's army, although Jeff Wert claimed that the Confederates had the opportunity to register a victory that might have prevented the Army of the Potomac from undertaking active operations for quite some time.

Both sides had reasons to smile and to be upset after the Seven Days. McClellan had failed to take Richmond but his army had escaped to the James River. Lee had saved Richmond but had failed to wreck the Army of the Potomac. There was no escaping the fact, however, that the strategic picture in the East had been radically altered in a matter of days. On June 25, McClellan had been threatening Richmond. One week later, the Army of the Potomac was licking its wounds along the James and Robert E. Lee had been established as the savior of the Confederacy. Lee and McClellan would meet again in less than three months; this time the fight would be north of the Potomac.

6

Rebels on the Move:
Second Manassas,
Antietam and Perryville

A betting man might have put his money on the Union to win in the spring of 1862. Albert Sidney Johnston was gone, the Federals had captured New Orleans and McClellan appeared to be on the verge of taking Richmond. Southern independence seemed to be a forlorn hope but by late summer, in a stunning turnaround, the Confederates had seized the initiative and had launched raids into both Kentucky and Maryland.

Robert E. Lee had blunted McClellan's campaign for Richmond at the Seven Days and now faced a new threat in John Pope. A blustery and pompous general who had registered several small victories in the West, Pope received command of the Army of Virginia, a new force consisting of 50,000 Union soldiers.[1] The Confederates would be vastly outnumbered if Pope and McClellan were allowed to combine their armies so Lee detached Stonewall Jackson, who registered a hard fought victory on August 9 over a segment of Pope's army under Nathaniel Banks at Cedar Mountain. Always the gambler, Lee then sent Jackson on a long march into Pope's rear, in an effort to suppress Pope before the bulk of McClellan's army arrived on the scene. Jackson moved his troops to an unfinished railroad grade near the Bull Run battlefield and beat back several attacks by Pope on August 29. Longstreet's men then arrived on the field, and when Pope attempted to break Jackson's line on August 30, Longstreet delivered a crushing flank attack, sending the Yankees fleeing for the safety of the Washington defenses.

Lee's sensational victory at Second Manassas forced Lincoln to turn to George McClellan to pick up the broken pieces of the Federal armies. That would take time, however, and Lee would continue to keep his army active, receiving approval to take the Army of Northern Virginia into Maryland, on a raid aimed at encouraging foreign intervention.[2]

The gods of war now smiled on McClellan. A Confederate courier lost a copy of the orders detailing the Army of Northern Virginia's movements and when Union soldiers discovered the plans, McClellan had the information he needed to crush Lee. His chance came September 17 at Sharpsburg. In the bloodiest single day of fighting in the entire war, McClellan launched a series of uncoordinated attacks while the heavily outnumbered Rebels bravely held their ground. Tactically a draw, the battle was a strategic victory for the North. Lincoln used the opportunity to issue the Emancipation Proclamation, which declared that all slaves held in a state or part of a state, which was in rebellion, would be free as of January 1, 1863.

Robert E. Lee wasn't the only Confederate commander taking the war to the Union that summer. In the West, the Army of Tennessee's new leader, Braxton Bragg, attempted to reoccupy Tennessee and move into Kentucky.[3] Federal forces under General Don Carlos Buell caught up with Bragg at Perryville, Kentucky, in October; after an inconclusive battle, Bragg chose to withdraw into Tennessee. Another Confederate raid had been stymied.[4] The Confederates would never again be in a position to launch simultaneous offensives in both the East and the West.

Bagging the Crowd

With Pope's army situated on the north bank of the Rappahannock River, Robert E. Lee took bold steps to forestall a junction between McClellan and Pope. Rolling the dice, Lee split his army. Stonewall Jackson's half marched deep into Pope's rear, destroyed the Federal supply base at Manassas on August 27, and then took up a position on an unfinished railroad line at Groveton. Jackson aggressively attacked Union general John Gibbon's brigade as it marched eastward from Gainesville on August 28. In a fierce stand-up fight at Brawner's Farm, the opposing lines slugged it out a mere 75 yards apart, with each side suffering about 1,300 casualties.[5]

At this point, Pope could have moved northeast to link up with McClellan. Pope chose to stay and fight, promising to bag the whole crowd of Rebels if his men moved quickly.[6] Pope certainly outnumbered Jackson, by nearly a three-to-one margin, but his advantage was wasted due to piecemeal attacks on Jackson's line on August 29.[7] With dreams of a major victory dancing in his head, the sorely misguided Pope sent reports to Washington that the Confederates were retreating toward the mountains.[8]

Fixated with the idea of destroying Jackson's wing, Pope ignored reports that Longstreet's men had taken up a position on the Union left.[9] When Pope blindly renewed his offensive against Jackson on August 30, Longstreet struck the undermanned Union left flank and, with Jackson's help, drove the Yankees from the field.

It was as close as Lee would ever come to destroying an entire Union army.[10] The Federals lost over 14,000 men at Second Manassas, compared to nearly 9,500 casualties for the Confederates.[11] Pope was transferred to Minnesota to deal with an uprising of Sioux warriors and Robert E. Lee was given the opportunity to cross the Potomac and carry the war into Maryland.[12]

What if Pope had properly coordinated his attacks on Jackson's line at Second Manassas?

ROBERT E. L. KRICK: Almost any analysis or critique of the Second Manassas campaign has to begin with the understanding that the Union commander John Pope was simply overmatched. The Confederates did a lot of good things but all of the Confederate success was greatly increased by Pope's incompetence. I really do believe Pope was the worst major figure who commanded an army in Virginia during the war.

If Jackson had not taken the offensive against Banks and Pope in early August, the Army of Northern Virginia conceivably might not have won the juggling game between the James River front and the north-central Virginia front. Lassitude by Lee and Jackson perhaps would have permitted a more rapid and powerful concentration of Federal forces in Fauquier County. While that might not have mattered for Cedar Mountain, it would have made the subsequent Confederate victory at Second Manassas more difficult.

The three-day battle at Manassas opened August 28 with Jackson's assault on a portion of Pope's army at Brawner's Farm. Jackson knew, thanks to couriers, that Lee and Longstreet were within range. Jackson's assault on Pope makes sense when we realize that Jackson knew he had help on the way. Even so, I'm not too sure Jackson was wise to launch the attack at Brawner's Farm. Jackson was unaware of the Union deployment

John Pope. Should Pope have bagged Jackson at Second Manassas? LIBRARY OF CONGRESS.

on August 28 and he had little business in unveiling his position to what might have been a powerful Union response. I don't see that the reward was worth the risk at Brawner's Farm.

Lee and Longstreet arrived on the battlefield on the 29th but much of the fighting between Pope and Jackson occurred before Longstreet was in position to make a difference. Pope waffled and wasted time on the 29th. Pope had the chance to concentrate his forces and with a direct assault he could have seriously hurt Jackson's force. Pope and his subordinates inexcusably squandered the greatest advantage they had, which was their superior strength against a divided Confederate army. You always hear bad things about frontal attacks during the Civil War but, in this case, it was the way to go for Pope. A frontal assault, on that terrain, would have reaped greater dividends than piecemeal dithering. Pope simply wasn't capable of bringing off a concentrated, large-scale frontal assault on Jackson's line.

JOHN HENNESSY: It seems clear to me that Pope was bent on finding Jackson and fighting him, before getting back into the Washington defenses (and back into McClellan's world). Had Jackson not elected to be found by Pope at Brawner Farm, Pope would have thrashed around until he found Jackson. It would have been logical and easy for Pope to simply withdraw into the Washington defenses. He had ample opportunity to do so; his orders clearly gave him that option. But his aggressive instincts and his desire to perform in a theatre where McClellan had failed drove him to be needlessly aggressive. How could he follow up his bombastic verbiage of the summer with a simple retreat in the face of Lee?

Pope was not well positioned to fight a defensive battle. I have found no indication that the thought entered his mind. Too, it's clear that Lee did not intend to fight an offensive battle unless immense opportunity came into his lap, as in fact it did. Had Pope not attacked August 29 and August 30, there would have been no significant battle along the banks of Bull Run. Lee would have maneuvered Pope farther east and the campaign would have been but a component of the Maryland Campaign.

As for McClellan, he had ample reason to be careful in his advance to aid Pope. He had seen Taylor's brigade mauled on August 27, and that was reason enough not to be more impetuous than usual.[13] The fact is, enough of McClellan's troops had already arrived with Pope, notably the V Corps under Porter and the III Corps under Heintzelman, to swing matters in favor of the Union. Pope had more than enough men and resources to defeat Robert E. Lee.

Plugging the Gaps

With Pope's attention focused squarely on Jackson, Lee and Longstreet marched to rejoin Stonewall before Pope could overwhelm Jackson's half of the army. To get to the battlefield, Longstreet's men would have to cross the Bull Run Mountains at Thoroughfare Gap. With a proper defense of the mountain passes, Pope could have delayed and possibly even prevented the two Confederate wings from coming together.

Consumed with the idea of destroying Jackson, Pope simply didn't allocate enough men to plug the mountain gaps and keep Longstreet at bay, leaving only James Ricketts' 5,000-man division to contest the advance of Longstreet's 25,000 men through Thoroughfare Gap on August 28.[14] The Confederates flanked Ricketts' position and also sent additional troops through Hopewell Gap six miles to the north, forcing Ricketts to retreat.[15] As a result, Longstreet rejoined Jackson on August 29, extending the Confederate battle line south across the Warrenton Turnpike, in position to launch a brutal flank attack against Pope on the 30th.

What if Pope had delayed Longstreet's arrival at Second Manassas?

JEFF WERT: If John Pope had concentrated his attacks on Jackson's line and had taken steps to either prevent or delay Lee and Longstreet from getting to the battlefield, he had a chance to register a decisive defeat on Jackson. Jackson probably could have escaped west but he would have escaped with a lot fewer men.

Pope was a miserable failure. Pope conducted his entire campaign in August of 1862 based on what he thought Lee would do. You can't base your plans for a campaign on what you think your opponent will do. Pope almost suffered from myopia in a sense of seeing what wasn't there. Pope certainly had the chance to delay Longstreet from getting to the field by a stout defense at Thoroughfare Gap. By August 30, Pope had consolidated most of the elements of his army at Manassas; Jackson's troops would have been facing overwhelming numbers on the 30th if Pope had delayed Longstreet's arrival. I hesitate to say Jackson's army would have been destroyed. I do believe Jackson's wing of the army could have been wrecked at Second Manassas, had Pope done a better job concentrating his attacks on Jackson's line and kept Longstreet from arriving on the 29th.

ROBERT E. L. KRICK: Pope failed to appreciate the full significance of plugging Thoroughfare Gap to prevent Lee and Longstreet from reaching the field. Pope made no significant effort to block the gap. Had Pope been able to block the pass, the Confederates would have been able to use other gaps in the mountains, to the north and the south, to get to Manassas. Even so, it would have been a tremendous impediment and Longstreet would have been further delayed from arriving on the field. There are only two ways in which a stout defense of Thoroughfare Gap would have been meaningful. If the Confederates elected to storm the pass and waste their offensive firepower on a fight for the gap, that might have helped Pope defeat Jackson. Or, presuming that Pope had a full grasp of his surroundings, and of Jackson's situation, the Federals might have delayed Longstreet sufficiently to allow Pope to overwhelm Jackson. This latter alternative required a level of generalship seemingly out of Pope's reach that August.

The Lost Orders

Second Manassas put the ball in the Confederates' court. Robert E. Lee expressed to Jefferson Davis his desire to take the war into Maryland, in hopes that an invasion of the North might improve the South's chances to extend a peace offering to Lincoln.[16] Crossing the Potomac in early September, Lee split the Army of Northern Virginia into several parts, in the belief that the overly cautious McClellan, lacking information about the whereabouts of the Confederate army, would move slowly. Stonewall Jackson led several divisions back across the Potomac to capture the Union garrison at Harpers Ferry, while a single division under D.H. Hill was left to hold the critical passes of South Mountain.[17]

Fate stepped in and provided McClellan with an intelligence gold mine. A Confederate courier lost a copy of Special Orders No. 191, the orders outlining the Army of Northern Virginia's movements. When Union soldiers discovered the paper wrapped around three cigars on September 13, McClellan was handed the opportunity to gobble up at least a portion of Lee's scattered army.[18] The Army of the Potomac's pursuit led to fighting at the South Mountain passes on September 14, at Turner's Gap, Fox's Gap and Crampton's Gap, and forced the Confederates to withdraw to Sharpsburg, a tiny Maryland town just a couple of miles from the Potomac. The fate of Lee's Maryland Campaign would be decided along the banks of Antietam Creek.

What if Union soldiers hadn't found Special Orders No. 191?

KEITH DICKSON: Every general would like to fight George B. McClellan. Lee was not afraid of McClellan. He knew McClellan would move slowly, would be very cautious and would be befuddled when the initiative was taken away from him. That's essentially what happened to McClellan at every battle. The only time McClellan made any type of energetic movement was after he was given Lee's battle plan in September 1862 and made aggressive moves resulting in the battle of South Mountain. Even with the information, McClellan couldn't use it to defeat Lee because, as a general, McClellan was simply not capable of fighting a major battle to a successful conclusion. McClellan had all of the advantages in September of 1862. He outnumbered Lee and he knew essentially where Lee's forces were. It really came down to the personality, the will and ability of the commanding generals and Lee was superior to McClellan. A commander has to be able to apply the right amount of force at the right time and McClellan just did not have that ability.

If McClellan had not found Lee's lost orders, he would have slowly moved north after Lee, into northern Maryland. Lee would have been threatening Baltimore and Pennsylvania and this campaign may have looked a lot like the moves made before the battle of Gettysburg. Lee may well have headed into Pennsylvania, threatened Philadelphia and then swung back to the south to make a move on Washington. The difference between 1862 and 1863 was that Meade was an energetic commander and fully understood what was riding on the campaign. McClellan was going to let Lee set the tempo of the campaign. Lee would have had the initiative and could have picked his field of battle. Lee would have defeated McClellan somewhere north of the Potomac and that would have ended the Civil War. Lee would need to defeat McClellan decisively and would then be in a position to directly threaten Washington. Remember the political situation in the fall of 1862. The South was victorious in several battles between June and September and there was a lot of discussion about the possibility of foreign intervention. Lincoln was in a desperate political situation and was under pressure to change the war from a conflict to save the Union to a war for emancipation. He needed Antietam to take place to make the switch in the North's war aims. So if McClellan had lost a decisive battle to Lee north of the Potomac, Lincoln's administration may have been forced to evacuate the Union capital. Foreign intervention or mediation would have become a real possibility, as would the close of hostilities.

SCOTT HARTWIG: If Lee's orders weren't lost, Lee would have captured Harpers Ferry and had the time to re-concentrate his army in Western Maryland. Lee had wanted to concentrate in Hagerstown and he may have been able to do that given the cautious pace of McClellan's advance. McClellan had quite a bit of intelligence about the Confederates, but it was very conflicting and it left him confused and uncertain about Confederate intentions. This changed when he found Special Orders No. 191. Confederate movements that had previously baffled him began to make sense.

Without the discovery of those orders, McClellan would have kept his army well concentrated and advanced slowly to South Mountain. Once he seized the mountain passes his movements would have been dictated by where he thought the Confederate main body had gone. If they had invaded Pennsylvania he may have tried to operate against their communications. If Lee concentrated at Hagerstown, McClellan almost certainly would have approached this position as cautiously as he did Frederick.

Invading Pennsylvania was a risky option for Lee because McClellan was so close to his communications. Given the dispositions of the two armies on September 13, I don't think Lee could have effected a concentration of the army any farther north than Hagerstown.

Lee's army was probably in worse physical condition that September than at any other time during the entire war. His logistics had failed and his men were subsisting largely off apples and green corn in Maryland, a diet that caused quite a few to break down, and contributed in no small measure to the massive straggling the army experienced in Maryland. The physical drain on Lee's men decreased the army's offensive capabilities as well as its ability to maneuver.

The newspapers had built up the threat Lee posed to Northern cities like Washington, Baltimore and Philadelphia. Lee was perfectly happy to have people believe the threat was plausible. Lee had as much intention of attacking or laying siege to those cities as he did of sending his army to the moon. Logistically he couldn't have supplied his army to attempt it. Lee had no siege artillery and lacked the logistical tail for such an operation. You need railroads to supply this type of operation. Lee also didn't have the strength to do it. The only city Lee might reasonably have been able to threaten was Pennsylvania's capital, Harrisburg. There's one account given by one of Lee's subordinate officers, who claimed to have an interview with Lee on September 10 in which Lee told him that Harrisburg, and the Pennsylvania Railroad bridge over the Susquehanna, was his objective. Historians have largely discounted this account because Lee himself, in some interviews he gave after the war, said his objective was to enter Maryland to give battle to the Union army. Lee was looking to take on the Union army and defeat it north of the Potomac in hopes that such a victory might influence the fall elections in the North.[19] Lee underestimated Northern will and support for the war. He believed that if his battlefield successes could convince enough of the Northern population that the war would be long and expensive, that they would vote out the Republicans and elect a Congress more sympathetic to negotiating an end to hostilities and granting the Confederacy its independence. But while many Northern Democrats were vocal against Lincoln's prosecution of the war, and were opposed to making the destruction of slavery a war aim, a majority supported the war to preserve the Union.

JEFF WERT: McClellan was already starting to pursue Lee and head north when he discovered Special Orders 191. The Army of the Potomac arrived in Frederick on September 13. With Longstreet at Hagerstown, Lee was making plans to go into Pennsylvania to reconsolidate. However, when McClellan reached Frederick, even before the special orders were found by Union soldiers, the initiative had been handed over to McClellan; he was in a position to thwart any plans by Lee to enter Pennsylvania. Finding Special Orders 191 gave McClellan a jolt of confidence that he probably needed. McClellan did not go forward for another 18 hours, and he can be criticized for that failure to move promptly and for failing to attack perhaps on the 13th. He should also have had more men in the Middletown and Pleasant Valley areas, just east of South Mountain, by the 14th. The battle for the South Mountain gaps ended up being an all-day fight on the 14th because the Federals moved slowly getting ready for the fight. Finding Special Orders 191 was a great intelligence coup for McClellan. In my mind though, once the Federals got to Frederick, any plans by Lee to head into Pennsylvania probably had to be put on the shelf, especially when it took longer than anticipated to capture Harpers Ferry.

Surrounding the Ferry

To protect his lines of communication with Virginia during the raid into Maryland, Lee dispatched Stonewall Jackson and a large portion of the Army of Northern Virginia to swallow up the Union garrison at Harpers Ferry. Located at the confluence of the Potomac and Shenandoah rivers, Harpers Ferry was dominated on three sides by Maryland Heights, Loudon Heights and Bolivar Heights. The Federal commander on the scene, Colonel Dixon Miles, failed to properly defend the high ground, allowing Jackson to rain artillery shells on the hapless Federals on September 14.[20] Recognizing that the situation was hopeless, Miles surrendered his 12,000 men the following day, the largest capture of U.S. forces until World War II.[21]

What if the Union garrison at Harpers Ferry had attempted to hold out longer?

SCOTT HARTWIG: The Union commander at Harpers Ferry, Dixon Miles, wasn't the best choice for that position. Miles didn't handle his troops as well as he might have. More skillful handling of his forces might have enabled him to hold out another day or two. Many of his men were new troops who lacked even rudimentary training. He was facing crack troops led by Stonewall Jackson. Once the Confederates captured Maryland Heights, the gig was up, as Miles's troops simply were outmatched and out-gunned by the Confederates. Miles's only alternative to surrender was a useless slaughter of his men. I don't fault him for surrendering; his error lay in his ineptly conducted defense that enabled Jackson to place him in an indefensible position before help could arrive.[22]

The other problem was that McClellan did not dedicate enough forces to try to relieve Harpers Ferry. He allotted one army corps to try to break though to Harpers Ferry. It wasn't enough men to get the job done, given the enemy forces they had to fight through to bring relief to the Union garrison. The blame for the Harpers Ferry debacle can be split equally between McClellan and Dixon Miles. If McClellan had broken through or the Harpers Ferry garrison had been able to hold out longer, Lee simply would have withdrawn his entire army back into Virginia. Part of his army might have been damaged badly because he had some troops that were isolated. His Maryland campaign would have failed because the Confederates would not have been able to attain any of their objectives, but Lee's army would have remained largely intact. We also would not have seen the battle at Antietam.

CLINT JOHNSON: The real Union hero in September of 1862 was General John Wool. He was in command of the Union forces in eastern Maryland. It was standard procedure in those days to pull out an outpost if it was in the way of an invading army. So normally Wool would have evacuated the Union garrison at Harpers Ferry while Lee's forces were heading north from Virginia into Maryland. Instead, Wool sent three different telegrams to the Harpers Ferry garrison, ordering those men to remain in Harpers Ferry and maintain the defense of the town. It was against military protocol but Wool knew that Lee could not leave the Union garrison at Harpers Ferry in his rear along his lines of communication with Virginia. So Wool was willing to bet that Lee would halt his invasion of the North in order to take care of the Union troops at Harpers Ferry. Harpers Ferry wound up slowing Lee down for three full days.

The actual Union commander at Harpers Ferry, Colonel Dixon Miles, wasn't very capable. He was rumored to be an alcoholic and he actually violated Wool's orders by surrendering the garrison and the town to Stonewall Jackson. Had Miles tried to hold out longer, his troops might have had a much greater loss of life before the Confederates were able to capture the town. Miles decided, for humanitarian purposes, to surrender the garrison.

The Deadliest Day

The fate of Lee's Maryland raid was decided on September 17 at Sharpsburg in a battle that was a huge gamble for Lee, since his army would fight with its back to the Potomac with only one river crossing shallow enough to be used as a possible escape route.[23]

The Army of the Potomac would do most of the attacking that day but very few of the attacks would be properly coordinated. McClellan began his assault at dawn, sending Joseph Hooker's I Corps against the Confederate left flank under the command of Stonewall Jackson. After bitter fighting in the Miller Cornfield, Major General Joseph Mansfield brought his Union XII Corps into the fight; Mansfield was mortally wounded in the East Woods while his men drove as far as the Dunker Church before being repulsed. Then it was Major General Edwin Sumner's turn. His division from the II Corps pushed into the West Woods and was mangled after blindly colliding with Confederate reinforcements.

The focus then shifted to a sunken country lane in the Confederate center as Federal troops breached the Rebel line along Bloody Lane. With 8,000 men from William Franklin's VI Corps and Fitz John Porter's V Corps standing by to deliver a potential death blow to Lee's shattered center, McClellan erred on the side of caution, deciding not to send reinforcements. The breakthrough was contained.[24]

Finally it was Major General Ambrose Burnside's turn. Burnside had wasted several hours on the Union left trying to find a way to get his IX Corps across the Rohrbach Bridge, a narrow stone bridge across Antietam Creek that would in the future forever be known as Burnside's Bridge. Federal troops finally took the bridge late in the day, and the Army of the Potomac appeared to be ready to drive into Sharpsburg and wreck Lee's right flank when A.P. Hill came to the rescue. A forced march from Harpers Ferry brought Hill's men onto the battlefield in the nick of time to repulse the final Union attack.[25]

McClellan's army had suffered over 12,000 casualties; Lee's army had lost more than 10,000 men in the bloodiest single day of fighting during the entire war.[26] Confederate Edward Porter Alexander would later conclude that McClellan's habit of making partial attacks allowed the outnumbered Confederates to concentrate defenders at the point of attack.[27]

What if McClellan had properly coordinated his assaults on Lee's line at Antietam?

STEVEN WOODWORTH: McClellan had about 75,000 men waiting to fight and about 46,000 actually fought at Antietam. Had McClellan committed

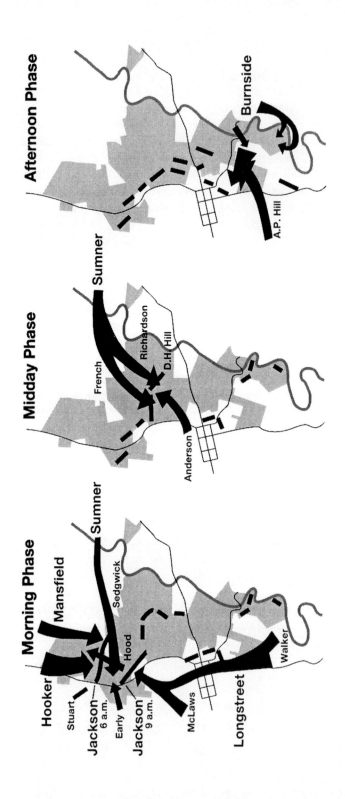

The Battle of Antietam, September 17, 1862

all of his troops, I don't think there's any way in the world Lee could have survived. The Army of Northern Virginia would have been destroyed. Lee would have been killed or captured. That may not have ended the war right then and there. There were other Confederate armies in the field. A big victory at Antietam certainly would have shortened the war considerably.

It's wise to put in a caveat with respect to McClellan. He was the general who could win the war during any afternoon, but he was also the general who could lose the war in any afternoon. He was intensely aware of that fact. On the other hand, it's fair to criticize McClellan by comparing him to other generals like Grant. Grant wasn't successful all the time but if Grant had been given McClellan's opportunity at Antietam, Grant would have pushed on aggressively and possibly would have won the campaign and the war.

PETER CARMICHAEL: Lee's army was on the brink of collapse and was ripe for the taking. Lee's army was having a number of problems supplying itself and that was going to reduce its efficiency, its morale and its ability to fight. I can recall Daniel Harvey Hill's comments about the condition of Lee's army following Antietam. Hill stated that Lee was considering recrossing the Potomac and attacking McClellan's army, which is simply amazing to me. I can't believe Lee was so disconnected from the reality of his army. Hill allegedly told Lee that the army was on the brink of collapse and was in no condition to fight another battle.

If McClellan had attacked with all of his men at the same time, I just don't see how Lee could have withstood that assault. McClellan launched three major assaults on different portions of the field, but not in unison. They occurred at different times during the day. McClellan watched these assaults unfold in front of him. It seems as if McClellan had very little control over these individual assaults. Any type of combined simultaneous assault would have resulted in a major victory for McClellan.

CRAIG SYMONDS: If McClellan had employed all his forces at Antietam, including Porter's huge corps, which he kept in reserve, and attacked all along the line at the same time, I cannot see how Lee could possibly have withstood the onslaught. Outnumbered, with his back to the swollen Potomac River, Lee might well have suffered annihilation with most of his army captured and Lee himself taken prisoner. Even if McClellan had renewed the battle on September 18, he might still have grasped a decisive victory. He had more fresh men on hand — men who had not fought on the 17th — than Lee had in his whole army. But of course McClellan was constitutionally incapable of risking his entire army in a single battle. To paraphrase a line Lincoln used later, McClellan held Lee's army in the palm of his hand. He had only to close his fingers to crush it, and he could not bring himself to do it.

ED BEARSS: McClellan's basic battle plan wasn't too bad; his mistake was not committing his reserve. McClellan had Lee on the ropes by 9 A.M. on the Union right. The Confederate left was wavering but McClellan didn't continue the attack. He had the Confederates on the ropes when Union forces broke through at the Bloody Lane in the center but didn't pursue the advantage. When Burnside's men on the Union left, late in the day, hammered the Confederate right, McClellan had the V Corps available as a reserve to use as support for Burnside's attack but he didn't employ them. The V Corps certainly had more men to offer than A.P. Hill did when he arrived from Harpers Ferry to provide reinforcements for Lee. So McClellan showed his flaws of military character.

Lee, at Antietam, was seen all over the battlefield; McClellan only crossed the Antietam once during the battle. There was a time during the battle when it appeared McClellan had gathered his nerve and was about to send in Franklin's men as reinforcements. A slightly wounded General Sumner had witnessed the disaster that befell Sedgwick's men in the West Woods, however, and urged McClellan to be cautious. Perhaps the best break that the Union could have had on the 17th would be to have Sumner either badly wounded or killed. McClellan did a good job reorganizing two disorganized armies following Second Manassas but he simply lacked the killer instinct on the battlefield. One big push by McClellan on any part of the line, at the right time on the 17th, would have made the difference. If Grant had been in command of the Army of the Potomac, we would have seen an all out attack on the morning of the 18th and that would have been the end of the Army of Northern Virginia.

September 18

Lee's tired, battered army remained defiantly in place following the slaughter on the 17th. With the Potomac at his back, Lee gambled and remained on the defensive, holding his position even though McClellan still had enough troops on hand to attack again on the 18th. Confederate officer Edward Porter Alexander claimed McClellan had Porter's V Corps and other units that could have been used to attack the exhausted Confederates.[28] When McClellan chose instead to wait for reinforcements from Maryland Heights and Frederick, Lee's men were able to slip away and return to Virginia to fight another day.[29]

Abraham Lincoln and George B. McClellan meeting a couple of weeks after Antietam. LIBRARY OF CONGRESS.

What if McClellan had renewed the battle on September 18?

PETER CARMICHAEL: McClellan had enough reserves on hand September 18 to pursue Lee. Lee's decision to stay at Sharpsburg September 18 was incredibly audacious, to the point of being reckless. I have no idea what Lee was hoping to gain by staying put except to buy his army some time to get the wounded and wagons across the Potomac.

Lincoln realized following both Antietam and Gettysburg that he needed his generals to pursue the Confederate army. He knew battlefield victories were not enough to bring the war to an end. When it came to logistics and discipline, McClellan was one of the best generals in the history of the war. When it came to the tactical management of an army, McClellan was probably one of the worst generals in the entire war. He was the polar opposite of Lee when it came to managing a battle. I can't think of another general, compared to Lee, who had better control of his army and still allowed his subordinates to make important decisions. Lee knew his subordinates had information he didn't always possess, so he allowed them to fight their own fight. Lee made it possible for his subordinates to achieve impressive tactical victories such as Longstreet at Second Manassas and Jackson at Chancellorsville. Lee put everything in place for his subordinates to succeed.

SCOTT HARTWIG: Following the savage battle on the 17th, McClellan's subordinates overwhelmingly supported his decision not to renew the battle on the 18th. Almost all of the Union generals overestimated the strength of Lee's army. A common figure given for the Confederates at Antietam was 100,000. We know Lee only had about 40,000 men, which reveals how hard the Confederates fought on the 17th. McClellan was not the type of general who had the fiber to endure something as terrible as the fight on the 17th and then continue the battle the next day, like a U.S. Grant might do. There were very few men who possessed the grit of a Grant or a Lee, and who could endure the kind of carnage that occurred at Antietam and realize there was a need to continue the offensive.

Had McClellan decided to attack again on the 18th with Porter's Corps, the end result probably would have been the same as we saw on the 17th, a stalemate with heavy losses. Lee would have still held his position and been in a position to withdraw. Porter's Corps essentially consisted of two unused divisions, Morrell's division and Humphrey's division. Humphrey's division contained some 6,000 men, all brand new Pennsylvania regiments with little training and no combat experience. Morrell's division was composed of veterans, but putting the two divisions together, McClellan had about 10,000 men to work with. Those were the only fresh unused troops McClellan did not have on line on the morning of September 18. The VI Corps was fresh, but had McClellan pulled them off line for offensive operations, he had to replace them with beat up units from the

I, II or XII Corps. Given the overestimate of Confederate strength, this was unlikely. On the other hand, thousands of stragglers had rejoined their units in Lee's army. For example, Lafayette McLaws would write on the 18th that his division was as strong on the 18th as it was on the 17th, despite losing about 1,000 men on the 17th.

ED BEARSS: Perhaps McClellan's greatest missed opportunity was September 18 at Antietam. McClellan had two corps that essentially went unused the day before and had also been reinforced by two divisions that made good the Union losses on the 17th. Rather than launching an attack, McClellan dawdled until he knew Lee had departed the field. There never was a more striking personality difference, in the way the Union's battles were conducted, than between McClellan and Grant. Grant, after the first day's fight at Shiloh, was anxious to strike the following day; McClellan, after the fight on September 17, decided on a delay, allowing Lee to escape.

Could Lincoln have gone with a different army commander following Second Manassas? Lincoln made the right move when he decided to retain McClellan after Pope's loss, when Pope was sent West to battle Indians. McClellan was able to successfully reorganize the army following Seven Days and Second Manassas; he simply couldn't make use of it. In hindsight, Lincoln made a bad decision when he decided to let McClellan go, due to the lack of pursuit following Antietam.[30] A Union staff officer was quoted as saying that the darkest day in the history of the Army of the Potomac was when Ambrose Burnside was named the army's new commanding general.

The Kentucky Raid

After Federal forces captured Corinth, Mississippi, at the end of May, the overall Union commander in the West, Henry Halleck, shifted his focus from crushing Rebel armies to occupying Confederate territory. Ulysses S. Grant was given the task of holding Memphis and western Tennessee while Don Carlos Buell's Army of the Ohio was sent eastward to rebuild railway lines and occupy Chattanooga, as the Union war effort grew stagnant.[31]

Meanwhile a stern and rigid disciplinarian, General Braxton Bragg, now led the Army of Tennessee. Bragg and fellow Confederate general Kirby Smith decided to take advantage of Halleck's strategic changes by moving their separate commands northward to reoccupy much of Tennessee and liberate Kentucky. Confederate expectations that large numbers of Kentuckians would flock to the Southern army were bitterly dashed however, when a mere 2,500 came forward to volunteer for service.[32] Many Kentuckians may have been waiting for the Confederates to prove that they were in Kentucky to stay.[33]

Bragg had the chance to provide that proof when his army collided with Buell's Army of the Ohio near Perryville on October 8. Only a portion of each army got involved in the fight, and the battle concluded as a tactical standoff. Despite Kirby Smith's urging to renew the fight, and much to the surprise of Buell, Bragg chose to retreat into eastern Tennessee, bringing an end to Confederate efforts to gain control of Kentucky.[34]

Jefferson Davis' failure to place Kirby Smith unequivocally under Bragg's command and the lack of cooperation between Bragg and Kirby Smith may well have prevented the Army of Tennessee from having a successful campaign in Kentucky.[35]

What if Bragg and Kirby Smith had coordinated their efforts better in the Kentucky Campaign?

RICHARD MCMURRY: All of the Confederate campaigns in the West were full of missed opportunities. The biggest problem facing the Confederates in the Perryville Campaign was the divided command structure. There were three Confederate columns that marched into Kentucky: Bragg, Kirby Smith and Humphrey Marshall. They were all separate commands and Davis refused to give Bragg command over Kirby Smith. If the two armies had come together, Bragg would have had the command owing to his higher grade. Kirby Smith realized that and was determined to stay out of Bragg's command. Marshall stayed away from Kirby Smith's army for the same reason. Unified command was the solution but Davis never could bring himself to issue the necessary orders.

Owing to logistics, the Confederates could do no more than raid across the Ohio. They would need to get in and get out quickly. The Confederates never had the capability of conducting an invasion of the North. They conducted raids. Gettysburg, Morgan's raid into Ohio, Early's raid in 1864 — these were raids and not invasions. There was no railroad across the Potomac or the Ohio that they could use, so the ability of the Confederates to operate across those rivers was extremely limited.

The Confederates had the chance to threaten Cincinnati or cross into Southern Indiana to try to have an impact on the fall elections of 1862. If the Republicans lost seats in the Congress, especially in Copperhead areas like Illinois, Indiana and Ohio, it would have made a big difference in what the Lincoln administration was able to do when it came to the war effort.

The Confederates would need to be very careful and get back to Kentucky before Union gunboats could arrive on the scene and cut them off. Those gunboats on the river gave the North a weapon the Confederates never had the capability of offsetting.

LARRY DANIEL: Bragg's campaign in Kentucky was essentially a raid, although it had invasion implications because Bragg wanted to reestablish a government in Kentucky that would have favored the Confederacy. When you attempt to do that, it's no longer a raid. Bragg himself was unsure as to whether he was on a raid or an invasion and was unclear as to what he was really attempting to accomplish. Bragg wanted to recruit in Kentucky, where he thought there were thousands of volunteers ready to assist his army. That obviously was not true. I don't believe the Confederates really had a chance to cross the Ohio River and move north into Ohio or Indiana. We should also note that within a span of about six weeks, the North was able to raise an entire new corps, which ultimately was amalgamated into the Army of the Cumberland. The North had a huge reserve of manpower that the South could never really compete against.

Some have criticized Bragg for retreating south without renewing battle after the battle of Perryville. I understand Bragg's position. His position was that he had to save his army. If you lose that army, you've lost the main Confederate army in the West. It's easy to say that Bragg should have stayed and fought, but if Bragg had lost a good portion of his army in Kentucky, that would have resulted in the end of Confederate resistance for the most part in the West. Under the circumstances, I can understand why he pulled out and headed south. Bragg was nervous; Kentuckians had not flocked to join his army and what other purpose was there for him to stay in Kentucky?

KENNETH NOE: The great "what if" of Perryville is what if Kirby Smith, instead of wandering up to Lexington, had come under Bragg's command in Tennessee? If the Confederates had stuck to the original plan of plugging Cumberland Gap and taking on Buell somewhere in Tennessee, it would have been to the Confederates' advantage. As it was, Buell was able to be resupplied in Louisville and was reinforced as well. If the Confederates had been able to fight a battle in Tennessee and win it, there was not much that Federal forces could have done to prevent them from moving into Kentucky. The Confederate occupation of Kentucky could have lasted longer. The real Confederate mistake in the Kentucky campaign was going to Kentucky in the first place.

Had Bragg and Kirby Smith been able to combine and move more quickly in Kentucky, it's also possible they might have been able to take

Louisville. If the Confederates could have taken Louisville, there's not much that could have stopped them from going across from the Ohio River into Indiana and eventually Illinois. I can't imagine they would have been able to stay there very long due to the requirements to maintain a supply line south. It was certainly possible for the Confederates to cross the Ohio in the fall of 1862 and cause some political excitement in the Midwest. Moving across the Ohio wouldn't have been that difficult because of the great drought that summer. People were able to walk across it in places, so fording the river wouldn't have been a problem for the Confederates. The political gains might have been significant. There was a lot of opposition to the Lincoln administration in the Midwest. In the November election of 1862, Democrats took over the state legislatures in Indiana and Illinois. Yet Bragg never really intended to cross the Ohio. He talked about it once or twice but his real goal was to link up with Kirby Smith, go to Kentucky and have Kentuckians rise up and hold the state themselves. If there had not been promises of roughly 20,000 Kentuckians rising up in support of the Confederacy, Bragg never would have gone to Kentucky in the first place.

Mediation

One of the reasons Robert E. Lee took the Army of Northern Virginia into Maryland was to improve the odds that Great Britain and France would officially recognize the Confederacy and intervene to bring the war to an end.[36] The American minister in London, Charles Francis Adams, had already warned his government that the British might be on the verge of offering to mediate the conflict. In fact, the British prime minister and foreign secretary were prepared to call for a cabinet meeting to approve a mediation proposal, if Lee's raid into Maryland had turned out to be a success.[37]

What if a foreign power had attempted to intervene on the Confederacy's behalf?

GEORGE RABLE: Great Britain and France getting involved was always a concern for Lincoln. Those two countries, in the fall of 1862, had been talking about offering mediation. Antietam, to a certain degree, scotched that plan when Lee's invasion was thrown back. The Confederates were hoping to win a significant victory on northern soil to convince other nations that the Confederacy was a viable and legitimate nation. Gladstone had already said the Confederates had made a nation but the British prime minister, Palmerston, and the British cabinet were much more skeptical.[38] The French were not about to take action without the cooperation of the British.

How close Great Britain and France actually were to getting involved as potential mediators remains a point of contention among diplomatic historians. Had the mediation effort been made and rejected, would Britain or France have used naval power to break the blockade of Southern ports? Both the North and South remembered how important foreign intervention had been in the Revolutionary War, when the alliance with France helped the colonies gain their freedom from Great Britain.

GERALD PROKOPOWICZ: An offer of mediation by a foreign power would not have made any difference because the North would never have accepted such an offer. However, a foreign country recognizing the Confederacy would have complicated matters for the Lincoln administration, in terms of enforcing the blockade and keeping strategic materials out of the Confederacy. On the other hand, recognition of the Confederacy would not necessarily have resulted in a war between the Union and those foreign powers. You can recognize a nation without becoming its ally. It's difficult to imagine Great Britain going to war with the North over the secession of the Southern states.

There were certain elements in England that would have been very happy to see the United States permanently divided. Whether they would have been willing to go to war to achieve that is less certain. We also have to consider Great Britain's war making capability. Great Britain tried to fight Russia in the Crimea in 1854 and had a tough time putting six divisions in the field and keeping them properly supplied. That was against a nation that had no substantial naval power to resist them and that was not fighting for its survival. If that was the best the British could do against Russia, what could they have done militarily against the North? I'm not sure Britain would have been able to send an expeditionary force across the Atlantic and keep it supplied in order to be in a position to strike at a meaningful target in the North. It would have been a distraction and a problem for Lincoln but it would not have been decisive.

Summary

There are two inescapable conclusions when looking at the war in the East in the summer of 1862. Robert E. Lee was the consummate gambler and the Union commanders, namely George McClellan and John Pope, missed golden opportunities to potentially wreck the Army of Northern Virginia.

Superior numbers don't mean much unless a commanding general takes advantage of his resources and properly coordinates his attacks. Second Manassas and Antietam were perfect examples of this. Robert E. L. Krick stated that John Pope could have heavily damaged Jackson's wing of the Army of Northern Virginia at Second Manassas, if Pope had launched a concentrated assault and blocked the passes of the Bull Run Mountains to prevent Longstreet's arrival. Steven Woodworth, Craig Symonds and Peter Carmichael all agreed that McClellan's piecemeal attacks on September 17 at Antietam might have prevented the Army of the Potomac from destroying a large portion of the Army of Northern Virginia.

At the same time that Pope and McClellan failed to properly utilize their superior numbers, Robert E. Lee proved to be the consummate gambler. He divided his army on several occasions, offered battle at Antietam on September 17 and remained on the battlefield on the 18th. Perhaps it all comes down to personalities and capabilities. John Hennessy concluded that John Pope had problems managing an army in the field and Ed Bearss described McClellan as lacking the killer instinct. The commander of the Army of Northern Virginia did not suffer from those limitations. The Army of the Potomac had the numbers and it had the opportunities. It just didn't have Robert E. Lee.

7

Stalemate: Fredericksburg, Chancellorsville and Stones River

George McClellan was in no hurry to pursue the Army of Northern Virginia following the horrific slaughter along Antietam Creek. Stationary for nearly six weeks, McClellan finally sent the Army of the Potomac after the Confederates in early November but by then it was too late. An exasperated Lincoln had seen enough of the overly cautious McClellan, replacing him with Major General Ambrose Burnside, who freely expressed his doubts about his ability to handle such a large army.[1]

In time, Burnside's concerns about replacing McClellan would turn out to be warranted; for now, he put aside his reservations and set his men in motion, making plans to cross the Rappahannock River, capture Fredericksburg and fight Robert E. Lee somewhere north of Richmond.[2] The plan appeared to be working when advance elements of the Union army reached the north bank of the Rappahannock across from Fredericksburg on November 17.[3]

Burnside had beaten the Confederates to the town but a critical element was missing: The pontoons needed to cross the river had been delayed due to transportation problems and would not arrive until November 25.[4] Lee's army was given the time it needed to prepare strong defensive works on the heights overlooking Fredericksburg. Despite the forbidding Confederate fortifications, Burnside directed his army to make several valiant and bloody assaults on the Confederate lines on December 13; by the end of the day, the Army of the Potomac had suffered 12,000 casualties and had withdrawn back across the Rappahannock.[5]

Burnside's aggressiveness had resulted in a major battle with horrendous losses and it would be the same story in the West that December. The Army of the Cumberland's new commander, Major General William Rosecrans, brought his 45,000 men to Murfreesboro, Tennessee, and on New Year's Eve collided with Braxton Bragg's 37,000 Confederates from the Army of Tennessee near the Stones River.[6] After several days of hard fighting, and with neither army making much progress, Bragg departed the scene, leaving Rosecrans in possession of the field.[7]

Back in Virginia, the carnage of Fredericksburg prompted Burnside to change tactics and try his hand at maneuvering the Army of the Potomac around Lee's left flank in January of 1863. The heavens, however, refused to cooperate. Several days of cold, wet weather turned the roads into muddy quagmires and Burnside's men wasted several days stumbling around in the muck, in what was later referred to as the Mud March.[8] After less than six months on the job, Burnside was finished. Joseph Hooker would now lead the Army of the Potomac.

A hard drinking, hard fighting division commander, Hooker toiled to get his men ready for a spring campaign.[9] Hooker had a brilliant plan. Leaving a small portion of his army near Fredericksburg, Hooker took the rest of his men on a lengthy march around Lee's left flank, and by May 2 the Federals were at Chancellorsville, in position to threaten the outnumbered Confederates. For whatever reason, the normally aggressive Hooker suddenly became passive and reversed his course, setting up defensive lines in a desolate, wooded area known as the Wilderness. Hooker had committed a cardinal sin: He had surrendered the initiative to Lee.

Caught between two forces, no one would have faulted Lee had he decided to retreat. Instead, he used Stonewall Jackson to carry out a devastating attack on Hooker's unsuspecting right flank. After several days of hard fighting, Hooker ordered his army back across the Rappahannock River and the Confederates had another stunning victory. This time, however, Lee's success came with a hefty price tag; Jackson was accidentally wounded by his own troops on May 2 and died eight days later. The daring of Robert E. Lee and Stonewall Jackson had ruined one of the Army of the Potomac's most promising campaigns, but the loss of Jackson made it a bittersweet triumph for the Confederacy.

Ambrose Burnside, who missed his pontoons at Fredericksburg. LIBRARY OF CONGRESS.

Missing Pontoons

Ambrose Burnside's plan to seize Fredericksburg should have worked. The Union general's designs were derailed when the pontoons necessary to cross the Rappahannock River were delayed several days; Confederate Edward Porter Alexander claimed, however, that Burnside could have crossed the river with enough men to capture the town by simply fording the Rappahannock or by building boats.[10] Thanks to the late arriving pontoons, Robert E. Lee received the time he needed to prepare formidable defensive positions along a wooded ridge behind Fredericksburg that stretched several miles, from the Rappahannock and Marye's Heights on the left to Hamilton's Crossing on the Confederate right.

Burnside would not shy away from testing Lee's lines. Crossing the river and occupying Fredericksburg on December 11, Burnside was ready to assault the Confederate lines two days later with nearly 120,000 soldiers at his disposal compared to Lee's 72,000.[11] On the Confederate right, Stonewall Jackson's troops desperately beat back attacks made by William Franklin's Grand Division. Meanwhile, James Longstreet remembered the lack of Confederate fieldworks at Sharpsburg and ordered the construction of trenches and abatis on the Confederate left.[12] Seven Federal divisions mounted charge after bloody charge on a sunken road and stone wall that ran along the base of Marye's Heights; not a single Union soldier reached the stone wall.[13] Burnside's offensive on December 13 had been a disaster, costing his army more than 12,000 casualties, compared to 5,000 Confederates lost. The Army of the Potomac had no choice but to withdraw back across the Rappahannock.[14]

What if Burnside's pontoons had arrived on schedule at Fredericksburg?

DONALD PFANZ: If Burnside's pontoons had arrived on time, he would have been able to seize the town and could have moved immediately south toward Richmond. I'm not sure the pontoons were really even necessary. Joe Hooker and others urged Burnside to cross the Rappahannock River at a ford below Fredericksburg, which would have allowed the Union army to move across without the pontoons. For whatever reason, Burnside rejected that plan and moved to Fredericksburg where pontoons were necessary to cross the river. When the pontoons were late arriving, the delay threw Burnside's entire plan into confusion.

Lee thought Burnside would be able to cross and capture Fredericksburg. Lee's army was a couple of days away from the town, near Culpeper, and Lee was prepared to fall back to the North Anna River and make a stand there. Perhaps the big battle then would have occurred at the North Anna and not at Fredericksburg. Lee actually preferred a battle at the North Anna. The terrain was such that Lee could defend the river but could also launch a counterattack if he were successful in fending off a Union attack. At Fredericksburg, Lee could readily defeat Burnside, as he wound up doing, but could not really launch a counterattack due to the bluffs on the Union side of the river. Burnside was able to post artillery on the bluffs overlooking the town. If Lee had tried to launch his own offensive, the artillery would have protected Burnside's army.

ROBERT E. L. KRICK: Burnside had an opportunity possibly to force Lee and the Army of Northern Virginia to retreat. If Burnside had received his pontoons on time or decided to find another way to cross the Rappahannock at Fredericksburg, Lee might have been forced to retreat south. Lee could have retreated to the North Anna River, about 25 miles north of Richmond. Lee already had engineers surveying the North Anna to check how strong a defensive position the North Anna might be. So if Burnside had been inventive and found a way to get around Lee's flank, Lee's only alternative may have been to fall back to the North Anna. Had that happened, the winter campaign, which featured the Mud March, and the spring campaign of 1863 would have been very different. If Lee had decided to retreat from Burnside, he wouldn't have gone past the North Anna. It's hard to picture Burnside displaying enough zeal and energy to push down that far south in December 1862 in order to challenge Lee.

Franklin's Opportunity

William Franklin's Left Grand Division was given the task of storming Stonewall Jackson's lines at Fredericksburg. Jackson held the Confederate right with 30,000 men but he also had a weak spot: a 600-yard gap in a wooded area that A.P. Hill had judged to be impassable, due to swampy ground and tangled underbrush.[15] Brigadier General George Meade's division stumbled upon the opening, momentarily penetrating Jackson's lines.[16] Lacking support, the Federals were forced to fall back, although more than a third of Meade's men would be unable to make it back to the Union lines.[17] Franklin decided against making any further assaults, even though a large portion of his division had not been engaged.[18]

What if Franklin had attacked Jackson's lines with greater strength?

GEORGE RABLE: The Federal troops were able to penetrate Stonewall Jackson's lines and while Meade's division gained a lot of ground, the attack was not properly supported. There's still debate about Burnside's intentions on that part of the battlefield. Did he really intend to have Meade attack where he did or was the goal instead to flank Jackson's line? The

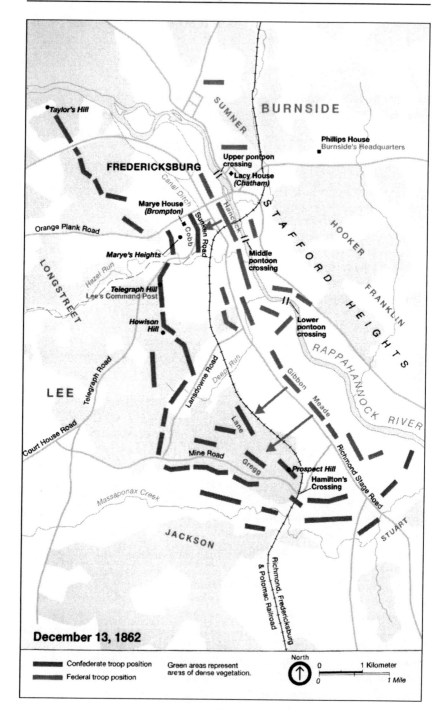

December 13, 1862

Confederate troop position   Green areas represent
                              areas of dense vegetation.
Federal troop position

difficulty on that part of the battlefield for the Union was that the Federals could penetrate Jackson's line but Jackson had a very deep formation. So even though Meade's attack was initially successful, Jackson was able to plug the gap and stop the breakthrough pretty handily, and even counterattack. Now if Meade's attack had been better supported by other units, say John Gibbon's division or Abner Doubleday's division, the Union success on the Confederate right might have been much greater. Burnside's defenders will tell you there was an opportunity lost there. I believe the Union success could have been greater but given the depth of Jackson's line, I'm not sure how much more ground the Union soldiers could have captured or held.

DONALD PFANZ: Burnside's actual plan of attack at Fredericksburg envisioned Sumner's forces, on the Union right, attacking Longstreet's wing on Marye's Heights, with the goal of holding it in place while Franklin's division, on the Union left, attempted to break Jackson's line. That plan fell through essentially because of personalities. Franklin was a very cautious man, much in the mold of his friend McClellan. Franklin decided to commit only a small portion of his army to the attack. Most of Franklin's men were left in the rear guarding bridges. So when Meade's men broke through part of Jackson's line, they simply didn't have enough men to hold the ground they were able to temporarily seize. Had Sumner been commanding on the Union left and been in charge of the attack on that part of the line, the attacks undoubtedly would have been much more successful and we would have seen a much bigger battle taking place south of Fredericksburg.

CRAIG SYMONDS: One problem with Burnside's plan was the way he organized his army into three cumbersome "Grand Divisions" rather than twice as many, more pliable, corps. Union corps in 1862–63 numbered between 10,000 and 13,000 men. Burnside re-organized them into three huge and unwieldy units of 22,000 men each. Because he couldn't really control them from headquarters, he left decisions on the field to the Grand Division commanders. William B. Franklin had responsibility for the Union left, below the town. When Meade's division in his command broke through Jackson's line, chain of command problems resulted in the failure to bring additional Federal forces in quickly to exploit the breakthrough. So in addition to the bull-headed stubbornness often attributed to Burnside at Fredericksburg, his command structure, too, was flawed.

Opposite: Fredericksburg, December 13, 1862.

Slaughter at Stones River

Murfreesboro, Tennessee, was the scene for a bloody three-day struggle between William Rosecrans' Army of the Cumberland and Braxton
Bragg's Army of Tennessee. On New Year's Eve, on the frozen fields surrounding the Stones River, the Confederates smashed into an undermanned and ill-prepared Federal right flank, forcing five Union brigades
to fall back to the Nashville Turnpike. As would happen on other Civil
War battlefields in the future, General George Thomas' Corps refused to
budge and the Federal line held.[19] Confederate attacks at a clump of cedars
known as the Round Forest, later referred to as "Hell's Half Acre," were
thrown back with terrible losses.[20]

Bragg thought he had won a major victory. When he arose on New
Year's Day, however, and discovered that Rosecrans' army had not retreated, Bragg failed to attack.[21] The Confederate commander waited until
late in the afternoon of the following day and then called for an assault on
an imposing ridge on the Union left, where Yankee artillery had a clear
field of fire. Major General John C. Breckinridge's division seized the high
ground but the Confederate success was short-lived, as a Federal counterattack recaptured the ridge. Bragg opted to withdraw from the field after
suffering over 9,200 casualties. This allowed Rosecrans, who had lost more
than 9,500 men, to lay claim to a victory that solidified the Union's hold
on Kentucky and central Tennessee.[22]

*What if Bragg had been able to employ more troops
in his attack on the Union lines December 31 at
Stones River?*

RICHARD MCMURRY: Bragg was operating with fewer men at Stones River.
Jefferson Davis sent Carter Stevenson's division from Bragg's army to
Vicksburg in December 1862. The division was in transit when the battle
at Stones River took place, and almost all of the division was in transit when
the Union assault took place at Walnut Hills (or Chickasaw Bluffs) near
Vicksburg. That's 8,000 to 10,000 Confederates who were not available for
either battle because they were moving from one army to the other. If
Bragg had those troops, it certainly could have made a big difference at
Stones River for the Confederates. Bragg would have needed to use those
troops wisely.

On the final day of battle, Bragg's decision to send Breckinridge's
division in an attack on the Union lines was a mistake. Had Bragg not
issued that order, he wouldn't have suffered the humiliating defeat he

suffered January 2, nor the casualties. His army still would have had to fall back because the army was so exhausted and its supply situation was so precarious. Once Bragg failed to crush Rosecrans and drive him back on the opening day of the battle, there was not much of an opportunity for a Confederate success at Stones River.

LARRY DANIEL: It's possible if Bragg had extra troops, the units that had been transferred to Vicksburg, and had used them that first day at Stones River, he might have been able to rout Rosecrans' army. Even if the Union army had been routed, it simply would have fallen back to Nashville, as the Federal army fell back to Chattanooga following its defeat at Chicka-mauga. I don't see that there would have been any different result in the long run. Short term, the extra troops could have made a difference on the battlefield if Bragg had used the extra manpower correctly, which is questionable. I don't believe Bragg's army would have been able to capture the numerically superior Federal army.

Bragg could have tried to fight a defensive battle at Stones River, if Rosecrans had cooperated. Once Rosecrans gained the high ground across the river, Bragg had to do something. He had to either pull back or he had to attack. Bragg chose to attack. In theory, it would have been better for Bragg to fight a defensive battle, although his offensive action on the first day was a clear victory even though it later fell apart. The attack routed a Union corps, McCook's Corps, which had been routed at Perryville and would wind up getting routed at Chickamauga.

ED BEARSS: The essential reason for the Confederate defeat at Stones River occurred in the second week of December when Jefferson Davis and Joe Johnston visited Murfreesboro. A decision was made by Davis to transfer four brigades from Tennessee to the Vicksburg theatre of operations. Both Bragg and Johnston opposed the move. If these troops had not been transferred to Vicksburg, Bragg would have had the necessary force, if he used it at the right time and place, to crush Rosecrans' army at Stones River December 31. By 8 o'clock that morning in the opening day of battle, the Confederates had crushed two of the three divisions in McCook's wing. By noon, the Confederates had seized the key ground at the intersection of what is now Van Cleve Lane and Manson Pike. The Union troops were forced to fall back to a new position along the Nashville Pike. The Union line, which had been in roughly a straight line extending from northeast to southwest, now constituted an acute angle. If the Confederates had used their available forces, namely Breckinridge's division, at the proper place or if Stevenson's division, sent by President Davis' orders, been available instead of in Mississippi, there's no way the Union Army could have escaped being closed up like a jackknife. The Confederates instead attacked piecemeal at the Union's strongest position at Round Forest. It was the same mistake made at the Hornet's Nest at Shiloh. The Confederates assailed that Union strongpoint again and again and frittered away their strength.

Hooker's Promising Campaign

It was a confident and aggressive Joe Hooker that initiated the Army of the Potomac's spring campaign against Robert E. Lee. Leaving a third of his army under Major General John Sedgwick to occupy the attention of the Confederates at Fredericksburg, Hooker took the rest of his men across the Rappahannock and Rapidan Rivers, in an effort to get around Lee's left flank. By May 1, some 70,000 Federals had gathered near Chancellorsville, a rural crossroads at the edge of the Wilderness, 10 miles west of the Army of Northern Virginia.[23] Logic dictated that Hooker would now advance and Lee would retreat. Chancellorsville would not be a logical battle.

With his cavalry raiding to the south, Hooker was operating blind.[24] As his infantry began to move into open country where Hooker's superior numbers and artillery would come into play, the Federal commander made an astounding decision: He ordered his men to pull back to Chancellorsville and prepare defensive works while awaiting Lee's next move. Rather than retreat in the face of a much stronger enemy, Lee kept a small portion of his army at Fredericksburg and took 45,000 men to Chancellorsville.[25] Hooker had allowed a master tactician to take control, a decision he would soon regret.

What if Hooker had continued to advance upon Lee's army, rather than falling back to Chancellorsville?

PETER CARMICHAEL: Hooker's maneuver around Lee's flank was masterful. He had Lee trapped between two opposing forces, the large portion of his army that made the flanking maneuver and the troops left back at Fredericksburg. At that crucial moment, Hooker lost his nerve and decided to pull back. If he had continued to advance, I don't believe Lee would have fought Hooker at Chancellorsville. I don't think Lee would have had any other choice but to fall back to the North Anna River. Hooker passed up one of the great opportunities of the war. You have to credit Hooker for placing his army in a position to heavily damage Lee. It shows a degree of imagination that not many of Hooker's predecessors had exhibited. For whatever reason though, Hooker lost his nerve. I suspect Hooker valued and appreciated the advantages of being on the defensive in a Civil War battle. So Hooker thought he would let Lee's army bloody itself attacking the Federals. What he failed to appreciate was that giving Lee the initiative was a big mistake.

JEFF WERT: Had Hooker not recoiled from the contact he made with Lee's troops near Chancellorsville May 1, Lee would have been in a bad situation. Many of Hooker's men had cleared the Wilderness and were heading out on open ground. I'm not sure Hooker lost his nerve per se. He never said he lost his nerve. However, by withdrawing from the contact with Lee's men and going back into the Wilderness, Hooker lost one of his big advantages over Lee, his artillery support.

Joseph Hooker, another Union general outmaneuvered by Lee. NATIONAL ARCHIVES.

Lee could not hope to match the federal artillery in open ground. By withdrawing into the Wilderness, Hooker's artillery advantage was negated. The bulk of Hooker's cavalry was also unavailable. They were off on a raid. So Stuart's horsemen controlled the roads, and the key to maneuvering in the Wilderness was holding the roads.

Hooker was expecting more assistance from Sedgwick's wing of the army near Fredericksburg, and he also expected Reynolds' Corps to rejoin him earlier in the day on May 2 to secure his right flank. Even with those elements taken into account, it made no sense for Hooker to withdraw into the Wilderness to fight a defensive battle. Hooker would have been better off to get clear of the Wilderness and push forward, at least to Salem Church, if he wanted to fight a defensive battle.

CRAIG SYMONDS: Hooker had a brilliant plan for maneuvering his army around the Rappahannock and Rapidan Rivers, to get into Lee's flank and rear. He did to Lee what Lee was used to doing to his opponents. Hooker's success in pulling off this maneuver surprised him. I think he got to the Chancellor mansion and looked around and was stunned by his success. So he waited for Lee to do the logical thing, retreat. When he heard a report from the front that troops were moving across Sickles' front heading south, Hooker thought Lee was retreating. Hooker, upon arriving at the Chancellor crossroads, needed to push out into open country and get out of the Wilderness. Grant in 1864 kept pushing after Lee. If Hooker had kept moving forward into open areas to exploit his initial move, he could have won an important victory, though not necessarily a decisive victory. I'm not sure Hooker had a plan beyond maneuvering to force Lee's retreat so we're not talking about a victory that threatened the destruction of Lee's army. If Lee had retreated as Hooker expected, it meant there might have been a battle eight to 10 miles further south, but not at Chancellorsville.

DONALD PFANZ: Hooker proved that while he was a great planner, when push came to shove, he just didn't have the self-confidence to stand up to Lee in battle. Hooker's defenders will tell you that it was all part of the grand scheme, to get to Chancellorsville and fall back on the defensive and make Lee attack him. That's simply an excuse after the fact. Had Hooker wanted to take a defensive position, he would have been better off assuming a defensive position two miles further east, away from the spot he chose. You would think if his goal had been to fight a defensive battle, he would have made sure his flanks were protected. If Hooker had chosen to move forward, there would have been a battle. Lee showed a disposition to fight. I don't believe Lee would have retreated south without a battle.

On May 1, Lee advanced toward Hooker and was preparing to fight. Hooker's numbers were greatly superior to Lee's and if Hooker had simply pushed his advantage, as his commanders urged him to do, it's difficult to see how Lee could have been successful. In fact, Hooker had the advantages in numbers and terrain and he had Union cavalry moving towards Lee's rear. Chancellorsville could have been a major Union victory. The Union had the advantage in nearly every area except in the area of commanding generals. If Hooker and his subordinates had performed even marginally up to par, Lee would have been hard pressed to extricate his army.

A year later for Grant, the key wasn't so much winning individual battles as it was maintaining the campaign, day after day, against Lee's army. Hooker would have gone after Lee's army in much the same way if he had been successful at Chancellorsville. Up until Chancellorsville, Hooker had always proven to be a very aggressive commander. Had he won at Chancellorsville, it would have boosted his confidence and Hooker would have remained aggressive in his pursuit of Lee.

Jackson's Flank Attack

Robert E. Lee had already taken a big risk by dividing his army and marching most of his men to Chancellorsville to confront Hooker. Now Lee gambled again. His cavalry reported that Hooker's right flank was in the air, not anchored to any natural terrain feature, and was thus vulnerable.[26] To take advantage of this opening, Lee decided to further subdivide his army on May 2, sending Stonewall Jackson and 26,000 men on a long, looping march to pounce upon the exposed Federal right flank.[27] Jackson, whose specialty was forced marches and flanking maneuvers, was just the man for the job.[28] His troops smashed into the Union flank late in the day, routing O.O. Howard's XI Corps.

The accidental wounding of Jackson that night by his own men would make it a costly Confederate victory but Lee's gamble had paid off. A badly shaken Joe Hooker would eventually retreat across the Rappahannock, after several days of hard fighting that cost the Federals 17,000 men and resulted in 13,000 casualties for Lee's army.[29]

What if Lee and Jackson had not attempted their
flank attack on Hooker on May 2?

MATT ATKINSON: Lee was a commander who liked to have the offensive initiative when he had the available resources. Lee correctly guessed Hooker's plan and he left part of his army to hold Sedgwick in place while the rest of his army went to confront Hooker. Upon finding that the Union right flank was up in the air, not sufficiently protected, Lee and Jackson decided to divide their forces. Jackson took his force on a long flank march and struck Hooker's right flank late in the day. Jackson surprised and routed the Union XI Corps. At the time of his wounding, Jackson was reconnoitering the Union lines in hopes of making a rare night assault. We'll never know if the proposed assault would have been successful.

The Confederates got a big break when Hooker was shaken up by a spent cannonball, while leaning up against a pillar at the Chancellor House. Hooker was knocked "silly" but would not relinquish command.[30] After Jackson was wounded by his own men, the Confederates decided to

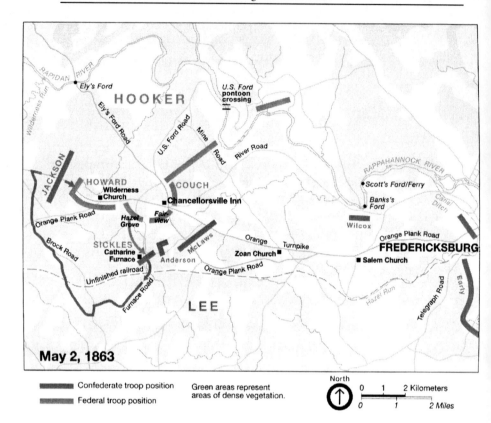

Jackson's flank attack, May 2, 1863

maintain the offensive the following day with a series of bloody assaults on Hooker's line. Even though the attacks weren't successful, the Union Army did retire across the Rapidan River. If Jackson had not executed the flank march, three alternatives were left to Lee. He could attack Hooker's forces with a frontal attack in the Wilderness, he could await Hooker's movements or he could retreat. None of these options suited Lee's style of generalship and therefore Jackson marched.

ROBERT E. L. KRICK: Lee might have been able to beat Hooker even without the flank march and Jackson's assault on the Union right flank. Jackson's flank attacked helped give the advantage to the Confederates but it didn't really decide the issue. If Lee hadn't decided to use Jackson in the flank attack, I don't see why the Confederates couldn't have defeated Hooker in a face to face confrontation in the Wilderness. As things turned out, the victory at Chancellorsville cost the Confederates the services of

Stonewall Jackson, who was shot and wounded by his own troops. Jackson died a week later. The loss of Jackson forced Lee to reorganize his army, switching from two corps under Jackson and Longstreet to a three corps arrangement. I agree with the conventional wisdom that Jackson's absence in later campaigns, not just Gettysburg, was a stiff blow to Robert E. Lee's command style.

JEFF WERT: If Lee had decided on a frontal assault instead of Jackson's flank attack, the Federals might have held. You have to assume the Federals would not have abandoned Hazel Grove, which gave the Confederates an artillery platform on May 3 that certainly helped Stuart's assault on Hooker's line.[31] You have to remember that Stuart's initial assaults on Hooker's line were pounded back May 3. Once Hazel Grove fell into Alexander's hands, the Confederates had an artillery advantage.

I believe Lee would not have hesitated to launch a frontal assault May 2. He certainly didn't shy away from it May 3. So if Lee had not found Hooker's vulnerable right flank May 2, Lee and Jackson would have instead worked out an assault plan that would have taken the Confederates directly at the federal line. If we had seen that frontal assault May 2, I'm not so confident of a Confederate victory. Lee may well have suffered a bloody repulse.

Lee Loses His Right Arm

Stonewall Jackson's flank attack on May 2 caught most of O.O. Howard's XI Corps totally off guard as several regiments fled for the rear without firing a shot.[32] Not one to rest on his laurels, Jackson rode forward that evening with his staff to search for a weak spot in the Union lines.[33] Returning from the reconnaissance mission around 9 P.M., Jackson's party was mistaken for Federal cavalry and fired upon by Confederate troops.[34] Jackson was hit several times; his medical director, Dr. Hunter McGuire, was forced to amputate Jackson's left arm just below the shoulder.[35] Transported to a small outbuilding near Guinea Station, the general's wounds began to heal but then Jackson contracted pneumonia, an illness for which there was no medical help.[36] The legendary Confederate commander passed away on Sunday, May 10.

Chancellorsville had been a stunning Confederate triumph that came with a hefty price tag. Robert E. Lee would be hard pressed to replace the veterans lost in the three-day battle. One of those veterans, Stonewall Jackson, would be irreplaceable.

What if Stonewall Jackson had survived the battle of Chancellorsville?

JEFF SHAARA: A lot of people assume that had Jackson survived Chancellorsville, the South would have won the war eventually. Jackson was certainly the finest field commander in Lee's army. When Grant took over in the East in 1864 and began to pursue Lee's army, Grant wanted Lee to come out and fight. Grant was trying to maneuver Lee into a full-scale battle because Grant knew he had the numbers advantage. Grant knew in a war of attrition that he was going to win. Lee knew that, and managed to fight defensive battles and maneuver away from Grant. I'm not sure Jackson would have done that in 1864. Had Jackson still been in the field in 1864, it's entirely possible that an impetuous Jackson would have done exactly what Grant wanted him to do—march out and fight in the open. So it's quite possible that had Jackson still been around in 1864, he would have been defeated soundly by Grant.

JACK WAUGH: In the final analysis, the Confederacy was doomed. Even with Jackson surviving until the end of the war, the South still would not have won. Jackson had led a charmed life the first two years of the war but he would have had setbacks, had he lived and fought, in 1864 and 1865. He was a great commander, one of the greatest of battlefield commanders, but he couldn't have coped with the overwhelming force the South was facing against Grant.

When Jackson died, the South not only lost a great commander but its morale suffered as well. It was a staggering, devastating emotional blow. Jackson was winning battles; that folded back into the South's perception of itself and its chances of winning the war. But with each battle and the loss of manpower, the South's chances for winning decreased and even with Jackson, Lee could not have won.

MATT ATKINSON: There are many areas where Jackson would have made a positive difference for the Confederacy beyond May 1863. In losing Jackson, Lee lost a commander who was adept at independent command. Lee had a habit of telling his subordinate commanders what he wanted done and would then leave it up to those commanders to decide how they would carry out the orders. Jackson had the ability to follow through on Lee's orders. The best example of this partnership was Chancellorsville. Lee formulated the plan and Jackson executed it. After the loss of Jackson, Lee really didn't have another commander who displayed that talent, and he

Opposite: VMI cadets gathered around Stonewall Jackson's grave in Lexington, Virginia. VIRGINIA MILITARY INSTITUTE ARCHIVES.

always had to be near his top lieutenants to make sure his objectives were being completed. With the loss of Jackson, the Army of Northern Virginia lost its mobility.

Summary

If Lincoln had been so inclined, he might have placed the following advertisement in one of the North's leading daily newspapers in 1862 and 1863: "Wanted: Intelligent and courageous individual to lead large army. The applicant must be energetic and a risk taker. Must be able to handle pressure and to deal with the unexpected." Lincoln had witnessed McClellan's excessive caution, Burnside's tactical ineptitude and Hooker's sudden loss of confidence, clear-cut evidence that the Army of the Potomac desperately needed a levelheaded commander who could maintain an aggressive pursuit of Robert E. Lee and the Army of Northern Virginia.

Both Burnside and Hooker had the resources to defeat Lee at Fredericksburg and Chancellorsville respectively. Donald Pfanz theorized that Burnside might have been able to cross the Rappahannock without pontoons and capture Fredericksburg, in all likelihood forcing Lee to retreat to the North Anna River. In May of 1863, Hooker had placed his army on Lee's left flank at Chancellorsville; several of the panelists agreed that had Hooker continued to move his army forward, Lee's best option might have been to retreat. Unfortunately for the Army of the Potomac, Burnside in 1862 repeatedly displayed his inability to cope with creeks and rivers, and Hooker discovered in the spring of 1863 how dangerous it was to surrender the initiative to an opponent like Lee.

Robert E. Lee never concerned himself with numbers. Burnside heavily outnumbered the Confederates at Fredericksburg; Hooker outweighed Lee at Chancellorsville. Very few commanders, outnumbered and caught between two forces, would have split their army, not once but twice, and then attack a vastly superior enemy. That's exactly what Lee did at Chancellorsville. Considering the risks Lee took at the Seven Days, at Second Manassas and in the Maryland Campaign, Hooker should not have been surprised.

Chancellorsville was truly the shining moment for Robert E. Lee and Stonewall Jackson. You get different opinions, however, when it comes to gauging the long-term impact of the loss of Jackson. Both Jeff Shaara and Jack Waugh questioned whether the Army of Northern Virginia would have been successful in the East, even with Jackson available beyond

1863. Matt Atkinson maintained that Lee's army was never quite as mobile once Jackson was taken out of the equation. Lee himself would have little time to dwell on Jackson's absence. The Army of Northern Virginia would soon make one more monumental effort to claim victory north of the Potomac.

8

Showdown
in Pennsylvania:
Gettysburg

Lee's impressive victory at Chancellorsville gave him several short-term options: His army could remain in Virginia or it could conduct another raid across the Potomac. Another possibility involved transferring two of Longstreet's divisions and troops from Joe Johnston in Mississippi to Braxton Bragg and the Army of Tennessee, to overwhelm Rosecrans' army and force Grant to abandon his campaign against Vicksburg.[1] At a meeting in Richmond on May 26, Jefferson Davis voiced his support for sending part of Lee's army to the West, while Lee and most of the cabinet members favored an invasion of the North.[2] The decision was made. The Army of Northern Virginia would raid Union territory in hopes of relieving the pressure on Vicksburg and fueling the peace movement in the North.[3]

Cavalry chief Jeb Stuart was assigned to keep tabs on the Union army on the march northward. With Lee's permission, Stuart decided to ride around the Army of the Potomac and wound up being out of touch with Lee for about a week.[4] Stuart would be sorely missed. Lee's army of 75,000 became widely dispersed in Pennsylvania while the 97,000 Federals in the Army of the Potomac, along with their new commander George Meade, closed in from the south.[5] A collision was inevitable and it occurred in Pennsylvania, at the little town of Gettysburg, resulting in the single greatest battle of the war.[6]

Entering Gettysburg from the west on July 1, the Confederates initially ran into Yankee cavalry under John Buford and then faced two corps of Union infantry. A.P. Hill's Corps and Richard Ewell's Corps finally overwhelmed the Federals, who retreated to high ground about a half mile south of the Gettysburg town square, an 80-foot rise called Cemetery Hill and a slightly higher eminence, Culp's Hill.[7] Ewell was told by Lee to attack the high ground if practicable. Ewell chose not to make any further attacks.

Even though July 1 had been another impressive day for the Army of Northern Virginia, the Army of the Potomac had been left with good ground to defend. The Union line resembled a fishhook, with the right flank at Culp's Hill, the left flank near two hills to the south, Little Round Top, and Big Round Top and the rest of Meade's army positioned along Cemetery Ridge, near the Taneytown Road. It would be up to Longstreet to pierce the fishhook on July 2. His assault against the Federal left and the lower end of Cemetery Ridge gained plenty of real estate; Meade's left flank was saved, however, when Union defenders on Little Round Top desperately staved off a late day Confederate attack. Lack of coordination had derailed the Confederate offensive, as Ewell's thrust against the Union right failed to get underway until the heaviest fighting on the Federal left had already died down.[8] In A.P. Hill's Corps, two brigades from Richard Anderson's division and all of the brigades from Dorsey Pender's division failed to advance on Meade's line.[9]

July 3 provided the battle's climactic end when 12,000 Confederates, led by a division under the command of Major General George Pickett, charged the Union center on Cemetery Ridge only to be blasted by Union artillery and small arms fire. Lee's Pennsylvania raid, so promising in the early stages of the campaign, had been turned back by the Army of the Potomac.

Stuart's Ride

Gathering information about the movements of the Army of the Potomac was never more important to the Confederates than it was in June and July of 1863. It was Jeb Stuart's responsibility to use his horsemen to protect the right flank of the Army of Northern Virginia as it moved northward and to keep Lee informed of the whereabouts of the Union army.

Stuart proposed to ride eastward, scout and harass the Federals, and reconnect with Lee north of the Potomac; the plan got sidetracked when Stuart's 4,800 cavalrymen encountered Winfield Scott Hancock's II Corps on June 25. Stuart opted to ride around Hancock's large force.[10] Stuart's three brigades would be out of touch with Lee for nearly a week, skirmishing with Union cavalry and plundering a Federal wagon train, before finally rejoining the Army of Northern Virginia at Gettysburg on July 2. Confederate Edward Porter Alexander questioned the value of the cavalry raid and argued that A.P. Hill's Corps would not have blundered into combat July 1 had Stuart been present.[11] Joe Hooker had sorely missed his cavalry at Chancellorsville; Robert E. Lee would regret not having Stuart close at hand in the days leading up to Gettysburg.

What if someone else had led the Confederate cavalry raid in June of 1863 and Stuart had remained near Lee's army?

ERIC WITTENBERG: There are really two issues to address. What were Lee's orders and did Stuart obey those orders? In paraphrasing Lee's orders, Stuart was charged with taking his cavalry and if possible passing around the Union army, keeping to the east of South Mountain. Lee told Stuart to feel the enemy's flank, damage the enemy and collect supplies for the Confederate army, and to operate in conjunction with Ewell's Corps operating between Harrisburg and York. Those were the basic operating orders for Stuart's expedition and Stuart obeyed those orders almost to the letter. Some folks castigate Stuart for the wagon train he picked up at Rockville, Maryland, and claim the wagon train prevented Stuart from arriving in Gettysburg in a timely fashion.[12] They don't bother to look at what the wagon train contained. The 150 wagons contained high-grade fodder, oats and barley, vitally needed by Lee's army.

Lee had three full cavalry brigades available to use between McConnellsburg, Pennsylvania, and Gettysburg. Lee himself made the decision not to use those commands. He had Imboden's brigade, which was a somewhat untried unit; subsequent events would show these were pretty good cavalrymen. The other two brigades were Robertson and Grumble Jones. Robertson was a difficult fellow to get along with but was fairly competent. Jones was as good as they came. I've often described Jones as the Confederate John Buford. Jones and Stuart hated each other, and that got in the way of the Confederates' ability to make effective use of Jones. Stuart respected Jones, however, and knew how good a soldier Jones was. Jones's brigade wasn't called to Gettysburg until the morning of July 3. Who made the call? Robert E. Lee.

SCOTT HARTWIG: When he left for a cavalry raid to the east, Stuart took the best part of Lee's cavalry with him. Stuart was absent when Lee really

Jeb Stuart. His ride around the Union army left him out of touch with Lee. (VIR-
GINIA MILITARY INSTITUTE ARCHIVES.

needed him to provide the Army of Northern Virginia with reconnaissance. One criticism of Stuart that is justified is that Stuart should have
left with Lee a competent cavalry commander who could have coordinated
the activities of the other cavalry brigades and served as Lee's intelligence

officer in Stuart's absence. Some have suggested that person should have been Wade Hampton. I can also understand where Stuart was coming from. If I'm going to undertake an expedition into enemy territory, I want my best team. I don't want one of my best players absent. Stuart had done this before, when he had left on a raid and had not really left anyone behind to be Lee's eyes and ears, and it had worked out in the past. It was a mistake on Stuart's part and it hurt Lee. Lee had other cavalry assets with him but they were not of the caliber of Stuart's men.

JEFF WERT: I don't think it crossed Stuart's mind to allow another cavalry commander to lead the raid to the east while Stuart stayed close to Lee to provide the Army of Northern Virginia with reconnaissance. Stuart had made his reputation with raids. Stuart's performance is one of the critical elements in the entire Gettysburg campaign. Some have been critical of Stuart. I think on the first day of his raid, when Stuart encountered the Union II Corps near Haymarket, he should have turned around. Lee's orders for the raid gave Stuart a lot of discretion, and in a major failure of judgment on Stuart's part, he used that discretion.

Another question is why Lee didn't use Jones's and Robertson's cavalry to scout for the enemy's movements. One answer may have been that Lee expected to get information from Stuart. He expected Stuart to be in a position to gain information on the disposition of the Union troops and to send that information back to Lee. Even without that information, Lee had to assume that the Federals were heading for Maryland. Lee well knew how concerned the Union government was with the protection of Washington. So Lee had to assume, with his men in northern Virginia, that the Federal army would be moving northward as well and were somewhere in Maryland. What surprised Lee, when he learned about the Union army's movements on June 28, was just how far north they were.

CLINT JOHNSON: Had Stuart stayed closer to Lee and had some other Confederate led the cavalry raid farther to the east, there still would have been a big fight somewhere in Maryland or Pennsylvania. Stuart gets a lot of unnecessary criticism in connection with the events of June and July 1863. To some degree, Stuart is to blame. I don't think he realized just how much Lee depended on him. Stuart left two brigades under Beverly Robertson and Grumble Jones to perform the task of screening Lee's movements. I'm not sure Lee really liked or completely trusted those two brigade commanders. So you have the combination of Stuart being away from Lee and leaving brigade commanders that Lee may not have been comfortable with. If Stuart realized that he was the only cavalry commander that Lee trusted implicitly, he may well have allowed another commander to lead the raid to the east while Stuart stayed close to Lee. Stuart would have been in a position to screen Lee and provide him with proper intelligence regarding the position of the Union forces. The main danger was the Army of Northern Virginia being attacked in Northern territory, so that should have been Stuart's main focus. Stuart would have been able to tell Lee that the Union forces were closing in on the Confederates. There was going to be a clash somewhere north of the Potomac, but Stuart might have been able to place the Confederates in a better position to initiate the contact.

If Practicable

Fighting began the morning of July 1 when A.P. Hill's Corps collided with Brigadier General John Buford's cavalry division west of Gettysburg. Buford's men held their ground for several hours before turning the fight over to Union infantry from John Reynolds' I Corps and then O.O. Howard's XI Corps.

Several hours of hard fighting followed but superior numbers won the day. With A.P. Hill attacking from the west and Ewell's troops striking from the north, the Federal lines collapsed. Union infantrymen fled through Gettysburg to Cemetery Hill where they were greeted by the assuring presence of Major General Winfield Scott Hancock, who immediately issued orders to strengthen the Cemetery Hill defenses and sent troops to occupy Culp's Hill.[13]

Lee instructed Ewell to attack Cemetery Hill, if such an assault was deemed to be practicable. With just a few hours of sunlight remaining and no guarantee of support from Hill's Corps, Ewell decided not to storm the Federal position. George Meade would have excellent ground to defend on July 2.

What if Ewell had attacked Cemetery Hill late in the day on July 1?

SCOTT HARTWIG: If Ewell had attacked Cemetery Hill on his own late in the day July 1, he would have been repulsed. If Lee had ordered A. P. Hill to support Ewell's attack, the Confederates may have been successful. If it's strictly Ewell, all of the Union artillery and infantry can concentrate against him. His troops would be attacking the steepest and most difficult part of Cemetery Hill. If Hill joins the attack, the Union defenders have to contend with a Confederate assault from two sides and the Confederates have superior numbers.

Richard Ewell. What if Ewell had found an attack on Cemetery Hill to be practicable on July 1? VIRGINIA MILITARY INSTITUTE ARCHIVE.

If Ewell had been successful in seizing Cemetery Hill on July 1, the Union army would have implemented the Pipe Creek circular and withdrawn to northern Maryland.[14] The Union army suffered heavy losses on July 1 but so did the Confederates. Proportionally, losses were about equal. In the strategic picture, taking Cemetery Hill did not accrue the Confederates any significant advantage unless the rest of the Union army had decided to keep marching on to the field, piece by piece, in an effort to retake the ground.

CRAIG SYMONDS: Part of the mythology of the Lost Cause is explaining Southern defeat in terms of overwhelming Union numbers and resources. At Gettysburg, however, the numbers were more or less even, so it became important to find some other explanation. Reluctant to accept the notion that Lee himself might have mismanaged the battle, many Southerners instead sought to find an explanation in the errors of his subordinates. They generally focus on three culprits: J.E.B. Stuart, who left Lee "blind" in Pennsylvania while he went "joyriding"; Dick Ewell, who refused to attack Cemetery Hill late on July 1; and James Longstreet for failing to obey orders quickly enough on July 2. So an assessment of Ewell's decision-making on July 1 is all tied up in this complex war of myth, history, and ideology.

Though Dick Ewell inherited Jackson's command, he was certainly no Jackson; on the other hand, Lee surely knew that about him. While operating under Jackson, Ewell never got the kind of discretionary orders that Lee routinely gave to his corps commanders. Such orders gave the subordinate in receipt of them a clear notion of the objective, without tying his hands as to the means he should use to achieve it. This allowed the subordinate commander sufficient flexibility to take advantage of opportunities as they arose. In a mature and self-aware command team, such orders generally work well. But at Gettysburg, the critics say, Lee's style of giving discretionary orders seemed to freeze Ewell into indecision. When Lee ordered him to take the high ground in front of him "if practicable," Ewell decided that it was not.

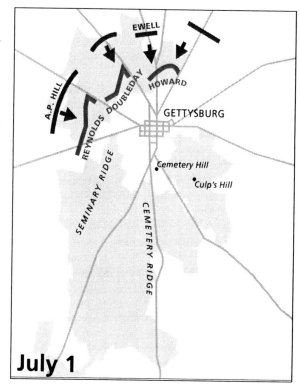

To begin with, it wasn't quite as simple as that. Ewell asked Lee if A.P. Hill's Corps could cooperate, and (based on Hill's assessment) Lee told him no. Then, too, there was a lot about the battlefield in front of him that Ewell did not know. For one thing, he didn't know where all the Union forces were. (Remember, Stuart was not there yet.) He knew that seven Union corps

Gettysburg, July 1, 1863

were converging on Gettysburg from the south and east along various roads, and when he looked up at Cemetery Hill, he was aware that the York Road ran into town behind his left flank. Rumor had it that Union troops were advancing along that road. If he attacked, arriving Union troops might outflank and destroy him. In addition, two of his divisions had been badly bloodied in the fighting earlier that afternoon, and his third division, that of Edward "Allegheny" Johnson, was still en route. Ewell, therefore, had good reason to pause and consider his circumstances when he got Lee's discretionary order.

There is also some uncertainly about exactly when Ewell got the order, and how long his "window of opportunity" was open. An attack at 3:00 might have gained much and perhaps made unnecessary much of the bloodshed of the next two days. On the other hand, it is not quite clear that a Confederate assault could have been mounted by 3:00, and by 4:00 the circumstances had changed. By then, the Union had some 40 cannon in place on Cemetery Hill backed by a fresh brigade of infantry, and more troops filing into line by the minute. At about 4:30, Winfield Scott Hancock arrived and surveyed the ground, and a half hour later he sent Meade a message saying that he did not think the position could be taken.

DONALD PFANZ: Ewell has been unfairly criticized over the years. He was an excellent commander. At Winchester in 1863, Ewell captured the town and was as effective in carrying out the attack as Jackson could hope to be. Jackson would have probably made frontal assaults and would have taken more casualties then Ewell did. Ewell also did a solid job in Pennsylvania in the days leading up to Gettysburg, getting his men to the town on time. If you look at the facts surrounding Cemetery Hill late in the day July 1, there was really no way for the Confederates to attack and take the high ground. When you consider the number of Union troops on the hill, how tired Ewell's men were and the problem of dealing with Union prisoners, you realize that had Ewell attacked, he would have suffered a very bloody defeat. Many people after the war, like Confederate general Richard Taylor and others, were looking for moments in the war where the Confederates missed an opportunity. Most Gettysburg scholars agree that Ewell was actually quite wise in not attacking Cemetery Hill.

PETER CARMICHAEL: There's plenty of evidence that Ewell was inclined to make the attack, but he needed support from A.P. Hill. He expressed that to both Hill and Lee. Lee was the overall commander on the field. If he thought Cemetery Hill could be taken, it was Lee and not Ewell who should have issued the order to advance. For whatever reason, Lee has always been exonerated of this tactical blunder. A.P. Hill had a fresh division available whereas Ewell's two divisions were pretty spent. Ewell's third division, Johnson's division, was still a mile away from the field. Throw in the chaos in the town of Gettysburg around Ewell's Corps, from the retreating Federals, and Ewell would be hard pressed to make the attack without help. Ewell needed Hill's support in making the attack. Hill never fulfilled Ewell's request for support. Lee was with A.P. Hill and he could have ordered a coordinated assault.

Stonewall

Stonewall Jackson at Gettysburg. It's the ultimate "what if." If Jackson had been available in June and July of 1863, would we have seen an epic struggle at Gettysburg and how would the battle have transpired? Was Jackson's absence more keenly felt on July 1 or July 2? Would Jackson have found it practicable to attack Cemetery Hill late in the day on July 1?

What if Stonewall Jackson had been present at Gettysburg?

JEFF WERT: If Jackson were present July 1 and were pressing the attack after the Union I Corps and the XI Corps fled the field toward Cemetery Hill, Jackson would have continued and at least tested the Union line on the hill. There was certainly some confusion and disorganization. The Confederates had just won a great victory pushing the Union troops through Gettysburg. Jackson would have found a way to gather together as many men as he could to test the Federal line on Cemetery Hill. There's no guarantee Jackson's assault would have carried the hill. The Union V Corps was coming up and was close at hand. There were probably about 20,000 Federal troops backed by artillery on Cemetery Hill.

Lee missed Jackson more on July 2 than July 1 at Gettysburg. Even if the Confederates had not carried Cemetery Hill late in the day July 1, Lee would have changed his tactics at Gettysburg had Jackson been there. Remember that Ewell didn't want to attack early on July 2. Ewell wanted Longstreet's wing to do the fighting July 2. I don't think Jackson would have done that. The Confederate assault on July 2 would have looked much different with better coordination.

STEVEN WOODWORTH: If Jackson were alive on the evening of July 1 or July 2 at Gettysburg, it's hard to say definitively that the South would have won the battle. It wasn't going to be easy, no matter who was in command, to take Cemetery Hill. Union forces had rallied in a strong position and were getting reinforcements, and you would expect any battle for Cemetery Hill to be a stout fight. You're talking about a 50-50 chance of the Confederates driving the Federals from Cemetery and Culp's Hills and forcing a retreat. The best case scenario for Lee's army would have been driving the Union troops off the high ground, gaining possession of the road network near Gettysburg and preventing Meade's army from concentrating at the Pipe Creek line. Perhaps then the Confederates could have followed up their victory at Gettysburg and defeated Meade's army a day or two later.

ED BEARSS: The big question regarding Jackson is whether he would be the Stonewall of the Valley in 1862 or the Jackson of the Seven Days around Richmond. I think he would be the Jackson of the Valley. Jackson would have made the decision to attack the Union troops either on or taking position upon Cemetery and Culp's Hills. If Jackson made the effort and committed enough troops to the attack, it had a chance to succeed. Many people who point to the lack of an attack on July 1 as being one of the reasons the South lost the war fail to remember that the Union troops on the high ground were there in force and had the advantage of position. By the time the attack would have been launched, Hancock was on the scene to lead the Union forces. He would have had at least the First Division of the I Corps on Culp's Hill. Granted, they got the daylights kicked of them earlier in the day, but the First Division fought hard all day and I don't think they were just going to roll over in any Confederate attack. Knowing Jackson and his personality, he would have made the attack. The odds of success were about 50–50 for the Confederates. A success by Jackson, attacking the Union high ground, would have turned the Battle of Gettysburg into a one-day battle rather than a three-day battle and would have meant another battle would be likely in the coming week elsewhere north of the Potomac.

Longstreet's Plan

With the Army of the Potomac now firmly established on Cemetery Ridge, Robert E. Lee felt inclined to renew the battle on July 2. James Longstreet would later claim that he urged Lee to pull out of Gettysburg and march the Army of Northern Virginia southward, in order to get between Meade's army and Washington and force the Army of the Potomac to attack.[15] Lacking information on the exact location of all of the Federal units, Lee rejected Longstreet's proposal and continued the fight at Gettysburg.

What if Lee had tried to move his army to the south after the fight at Gettysburg on July 1?

CRAIG SYMONDS: Exactly what it was that Longstreet recommended to Lee at Gettysburg is unknowable. I suspect that it is widely misunderstood, partly because of the implication in Michael Shaara's novel *The Killer Angels* that what Longstreet wanted to do was send John Bell Hood's division on a wider swing around the Round Tops. Most evidence suggests that this is not what Longstreet had in mind. His idea was to disengage from the battle altogether, leaving Meade in command of the battlefield, and move the entire Southern army southward and eastward to take up a blocking position between Meade's army and Washington. There he would invite the Federals to attack. His assumption was that pressure from Washington would compel Meade to attack at once, and the Army of Northern Virginia could win another Fredericksburg-type victory.

Like many counter-factual scenarios, this one depends on Meade doing exactly what Longstreet expected him to do. Keep in mind that if Lee took Longstreet's advice and put his own army between Meade and Washington, that move would also have put Meade between Lee and his only line of supply. Moving in enemy territory, an army can supply itself by living off the land (with food, if not ammunition) but only as long as it is moving. Once Lee took up a stationary blocking position, if Meade did not attack right away, Lee could not remain there indefinitely. He would have to leave his blocking position, and while on the move he would be vulnerable and without a supply line to replace ammunition.

I think Lee appreciated that Longstreet's alternative carried with it as many dangers as opportunities, and meanwhile he had the enemy here in front of him, un-entrenched and in more or less equal numbers, with the momentum on his side. He had a bird in the hand, and to him it seemed more promising than Longstreet's bird in the bush.

PETER CARMICHAEL: Longstreet's idea of pulling out of Gettysburg after July 1 and relocating the army to a defensive position south of Gettysburg, between Meade and Washington, was a terrible idea. I suspect he never really offered the idea to Lee in the first place. It's hard to say because Longstreet in his memoirs was so determined to defend himself, often at the expense of Lee. We do know there was confusion at Lee's headquarters, and Lee did not act at Gettysburg with the decisiveness that we are accustomed to seeing from Lee. There was a tentativeness and a degree of confusion we haven't seen before. Lee's victory on July 1 was one of the most spectacular victories for the Army of Northern Virginia. It's almost impossible for any Civil War general who won such a victory as the Confederates did July 1 to give up the tactical initiative and retreat. That's why I have a hard time believing that's what Longstreet suggested. Longstreet certainly preferred to fight a defensive battle and he must have had a lot of reservations about what was transpiring at Gettysburg. The idea that an attacking army could disengage and slip around the Union army to the south, without in some way being obstructed in that movement, is hard for me to imagine. If you had taken a poll of Lee's prominent officers and staff officers on July 2 or July 3 and asked them their thoughts on Lee's plan to attack the Union army at Gettysburg, I will bet about 90 percent of them would have supported Lee's plans. Most of the dissension or disagreement over the tactical moves was more or less Monday morning quarterbacking. It occurred after the war, as opposed to actually during the battle of Gettysburg.

SCOTT HARTWIG: Longstreet's proposal looks good on paper but really wasn't feasible for Lee to attempt without Stuart's cavalry to lead the way.

The cavalry force that Lee did have was good for guarding wagon trains and protecting lines of communication but wasn't very good for scouting and reconnoitering, which would have been critical to carry out such a move. I don't believe the Confederates could have gotten away with the move even if they had tried it. Meade was too good a general and his cavalry was much too active to have allowed a strategic turning movement like this to go undetected.

Sickles' Move

Operations on July 2 were greatly affected by the decision of one Union corps commander. Major General Dan Sickles, the leader of the III Corps, was instructed by Meade to take up a position on the far left of the Union line and to eventually occupy Little Round Top.[16] Sickles didn't like those orders at all. He believed that higher ground to the west would dominate the terrain assigned to his corps, so, without orders, Sickles marched his men a half-mile westward to a new position near the Emmittsburg Road and a peach orchard.[17] Sickles' Corps and two of Longstreet's divisions struggled for several hours for possession of the Peach Orchard, the Wheat Field and Devil's Den. The Wheat Field itself changed hands six times that afternoon.[18] The Confederates ultimately captured all of Sickles' advanced positions, devastating the Union III Corps.[19]

What if Sickles had remained in the original position assigned to him?

CRAIG SYMONDS: Despite all the efforts he made after the war to make it sound otherwise, the move that Dan Sickles made away from the main Union line on Cemetery Ridge and out to the Wheat Field and the Peach Orchard worked greatly to the Confederates' advantage and the Union's disadvantage. To be sure, the ground Sickles chose was better—for his command—than the ground chosen for him by Meade's staff. It was slightly higher and had a clearer field of fire. But it was also much wider. Sickles had to spread his 11,000 men out over a much broader front, and the result was that his brigades and divisions could not support one another effectively. They could be picked off one by one by Longstreet's echelon attack. And they were.

Longstreet's attack came late in the afternoon, but when it came it came like a thunderstorm, and it was one of the few occasions in the war when the side on the tactical offensive inflicted more casualties than it endured. One of the reasons for this was the fact that Sickles' men, spread out as they were, could be overwhelmed unit by unit and in detail.

SCOTT HARTWIG: If Sickles stayed put, it would have spared his corps many of the 4,000 casualties it suffered on July 2. Sickles was brave, but he did not work well as part of a command team and he did not read terrain very well. The line Meade wanted him on gave the III Corps a shorter, more compact line than the one Sickles ultimately took up, it allowed Meade to reinforce him more easily, and contrary to Sickles post-battle assertion, most of it was not on low ground. There were good fields of fire and importantly, Lee did not know Sickles was there. His orders to Longstreet were to attack up, or perpendicular to, the Emmitsburg Road, which also meant nearly perpendicular to the III Corps. If Sickles remained where Meade wanted him and Longstreet attempted to execute these orders, the III Corps would have been perfectly placed to hit Longstreet's flank. Even if Longstreet had discovered Sickles' position, it was a strong defensive position and I doubt that the Confederates could have carried it with only Longstreet's two divisions.

BRAD GOTTFRIED: Sickles has been cast as the scapegoat for tremendous losses on the Federal side July 2. The guy tried desperately to get Meade's permission to alter his position. Meade was more concerned about the northern portion of the battlefield, namely Cemetery and Culp's Hills. So while Sickles moved forward on his own to a new position, he did so reluctantly. He was very much concerned about his men suffering a repetition of the Chancellorsville debacle, due to the low marshy ground his men occupied initially at Gettysburg. Sickles wanted to be closer to the high ground at the Peach Orchard and Houck's Ridge, where he could post his guns. Sickles actually had a pretty nice area near the Peach Orchard where he posted 40 to 50 artillery pieces that wreaked havoc on the Confederates. No matter where Sickles was posted, he was going to be up against some very aggressive fighters that day, as he was facing Longstreet's Corps. I don't think there was much better fighting during the entire war than the efforts made by Longstreet's men July 2, even though they may not have captured all of their objectives. They took the Peach Orchard and the Wheat Field but could not take Little Round Top. Sickles' move forward to higher ground placed him out front of the rest of the Union line and there's no question that the salient was difficult for him to defend. Still, Devil's Den and Houck's Ridge were much better spots to defend than Sickles' original line.

Hood's Request

Lee's original attack plan on July 2 called for an assault up the Emmitsburg Road. One of Longstreet's division commanders, the hard charging John Bell Hood, realized that the advance of Sickles' Corps made Lee's plan outdated. Hood pleaded with Longstreet for permission to move his division around the southern edge of the Round Tops to strike the Union line on Cemetery Ridge from the left flank and the rear.[20] Even though Longstreet denied the request, the attack would wind up being directed against Little Round Top and Devil's Den. One of Hood's brigade commanders, Brigadier General Evander Law, recognized that an attack up the Emmitsburg Road would expose his flank and rear to destructive fire from Devil's Den. Law chose to ignore the original attack plan and instead launched a frontal assault on Devil's Den and Little Round Top.[21]

What if Longstreet had been allowed to come up with his own attack plan July 2? What if Hood had been allowed to move further around the Union left?

JEFF SHAARA: My father, Michael Shaara, was an advocate of Longstreet. A number of pro–Lee, anti–Longstreet folks believe Lee was essentially infallible and that Longstreet was the one making all of the mistakes. Longstreet understood the value of flank attacks. He wanted to get around the Union's left flank and into the rear of Meade's army to attack his supply train. John Bell Hood's division was capable of making that kind of an assault and Lee more or less put a clamp on Longstreet that day. That's not to excuse Longstreet from any wrongdoing. Longstreet did a lot of sulking at Gettysburg and it certainly took away from his effectiveness on July 2. Longstreet resented the fact that Lee did not allow Longstreet to plan his own battle that day. Longstreet became a little petulant about it. He realized the value of avoiding frontal attacks and the value of hitting the Union flank. We saw at Second Manassas and Chancellorsville how devastating flank attacks could be. As it was, on July 2 the Confederates nearly captured Little Round Top and nearly turned Meade's left flank.

JEFF WERT: If Lee had given Longstreet the discretion to put together his own battle plan for July 2, there may not have been an assault. Longstreet would have attempted some sort of broader turning maneuver. Longstreet wasn't looking at a flank march similar to Chancellorsville. Longstreet was talking about pulling the army out of Gettysburg and moving it about 10 to 15 miles south to good defensive ground in order to force Meade to be on the offensive. Hood wanted to go with a shorter tactical turning movement to try to get around the Union left flank. Longstreet sensed that Lee wanted no more delays in getting the attack underway. Could the Confederates have been more successful July 2 attempting a move around the Union left flank? That question is predicated on the idea that the Yankees were really stupid. I can't see how Hood could have attempted such a maneuver without being spotted. As it was, the Confederate attack gained a lot of ground. Longstreet later called it three hours of the best fighting ever turned in by any army. A critical factor that worked against the Con-

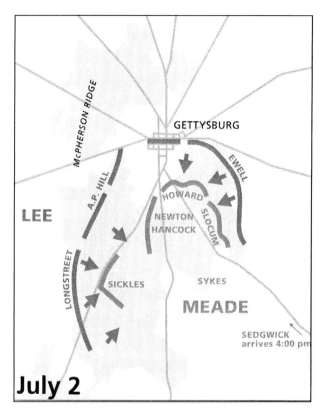

Gettysburg, July 2, 1863

federates was Hood being wounded in the first 20 minutes of the attack. Once Hood went down, Law led the division. Law wasn't up to the task. That's not a slap at Law, but it took about 30 minutes to find Law to bring him into command. His assaults were never coordinated particularly well against Little Round Top.

CLINT JOHNSON: Lee may have been better served to allow Longstreet to plan his own tactical maneuvers for the Confederate attack July 2. Lee usually let his subordinates plan the tactics for their battles. Longstreet was one for maneuvering and trying to get on the enemy's flank, so I believe we would have seen the Confederates attempting to angle around the Union left on July 2 if Longstreet had been allowed to come up with his own plan of attack. It would have been very interesting to see how Meade would have reacted had the Confederates been able to get around the Union left flank and into the Union rear, along Meade's lines of communication.

James Longstreet, Lee's old war-horse. LIBRARY OF CONGRESS.

Longstreet might have been able to capture Big Round Top, and Little Round Top and with cannons on those hills, the Confederates could have had enfilading fire on the Union line. We also might not have witnessed Pickett's Charge July 3. Instead, with the Confederates occupying the

Little Round Top, perhaps the most important position at Gettysburg July 2. LIBRARY OF CONGRESS.

Round Tops, the Union troops would have been forced to make the effort to retake those hills. If the Confederates had been successful July 2 taking the high ground near the Round Tops and perhaps Culp's Hill, then the Confederates would have been positioned on the high ground on both ends of the Union line. With enough troops available, that might have been the ideal time for Lee to attack the Union center. The Union forces might have been spread thin at the center at that point, and Lee might have been able to split Meade's line if Lee had enough men to carry out that kind of assault.

Saving Little Round Top

Meade had to hold certain parts of the battlefield in order to maintain the integrity of his fishhook. One of those areas was Little Round

Top. Meade's chief engineer, Brigadier General Gouverneur Warren, found Little Round Top essentially unoccupied on July 2. He also discovered evidence of an impending Confederate attack when a shot fired in the direction of the Rebels resulted in the gleam of reflected sunlight from bayonets.[22] Warren immediately sent Colonel Strong Vincent's brigade from Major General George Sykes's V Corps to defend the hill. The brigade's regiments from Maine, Michigan, New York and Pennsylvania had barely settled into their defensive positions when Hood's men attacked.[23]

At the very end of the Union line on Little Round Top, protecting the Federal left flank, were the 360 men of the 20th Maine and their commander, Joshua Lawrence Chamberlain. Chamberlain's regiment fought off several charges by the 15th Alabama and the 47th Alabama. With his ammunition nearly depleted, Chamberlain was left with two options: attack or retreat. Recalling Vincent's orders to hold the ground at all hazards, Chamberlain called for a bayonet charge and the 20th Maine sent the Alabamans fleeing in retreat.[24] The commander of the 15th Alabama, Colonel William C. Oates, would later claim that with just one more regiment, the Confederates could have turned the Union flank and captured Little Round Top.[25] Chamberlain's men, along with the rest of Vincent's brigade, had saved Little Round Top and preserved Meade's fishhook.

What if the Confederates had captured Little Round Top?

JEFF WERT: If the Confederates somehow had gained the ground, Meade might have been in a position where the rest of his line was untenable. You can credit the 20th Maine and a few other regiments with saving Little Round Top. What if the 20th Maine, out of ammunition, had decided to retreat? If you are in one of the other Union regiments on Little Round Top and the Alabamans are coming towards you from the flank and rear, how long are you going to hang around? Soldiers will stand frontal fire and some of the best soldiers can deal with flank fire but soldiers are not going to take frontal, flank and rear fire. How much Oates's Alabamans had left is another issue. I don't want to take away from the 20th Maine, but you can credit a number of regiments with saving Little Round Top, including the 83rd Pennsylvania, the 16th Michigan, the 44th New York and the 140th New York. When the 140th New York came over the crest, the Texans were coming right up the slope. The Texans were about three-quarters of the way up on the southwestern face and the 140th New York hadn't had a chance to load their rifles. They carried out a bayonet charge similar to the 20th Maine to push the Confederates down the hill. If the 20th

Maine hadn't held their ground, I think the Union troops would have lost Little Round Top because the Confederates coming from the rear of the Union troops would have unraveled the Federal line.

BRAD GOTTFRIED: Many folks have credited the 20th Maine with saving the Union left flank at Little Round Top. My feeling is that if the Confederates had been able to throw a few more regiments into the assault, the 20th Maine would have been pushed off Little Round Top along with the rest of Vincent's brigade.

It was so late in the day that even if the Confederates had taken Little Round Top, there wasn't much more they could accomplish July 2. The question then becomes what happens July 3. We may not have seen a Pickett's Charge. Remember that the Union VI Corps, the largest corps in the Federal army, had arrived around 3 P.M. on July 2. These guys weren't just going to sit around while the Confederates occupied Little Round Top. The operations July 3 might have focused instead on a Union counterattack to retake Little Round Top rather than a Confederate attack on the Union center. The Confederates would have brought as much artillery as possible up to Little Round Top the evening of July 2. At daylight July 3, the Confederates would have opened fire on the entire Union line and Meade's army would have suffered severe losses. You would have then seen the VI Corps attack Little Round Top and the Federals stood a good chance of retaking the ground. It would have been a numbers game. Longstreet's Corps was pretty badly beaten up and there were no fresh units available to defend and hold Little Round Top, except for Pickett's three brigades.

JEFF SHAARA: You can't underestimate the importance of Joshua Chamberlain and the 20th Maine and the role they played in saving the Union flank. Thanks to *Killer Angels* and the movie *Gettysburg*, Chamberlain has become such an iconic figure. Some people, as a result, are now attacking the idea that Chamberlain was a Union hero. No one disputes the fact that there were other Union heroes July 2 on Little Round Top. In my mind, if the 20th Maine didn't hold its position on Little Round Top that day, then the 15th Alabama could very easily have gone up and over Little Round Top and made its way into the rear of the Union army. It would have opened up a clear path between the two Round Tops. The Confederates could have simply marched right around Little Round Top and come in behind the Union line and Meade would have been in serious trouble.

SCOTT HARTWIG: The 20th Maine certainly performed heroically. It would have taken more than the collapse of the 20th Maine to lead to the destruction of the Union position on Little Round Top. The Union army could have recovered from one regiment giving way. Meade could have found some reinforcements to retake the ground. If more than the 20th Maine retreats, that's bad news for the Union Army. If the 15th Alabama forces the 20th Maine to retreat and then gets into the rear of the rest of Vincent's brigade on Little Round Top, it's certainly possible that Vincent's brigade retreats and the Confederates have a chance to take the ground.

When you consider the confusion of this type of battle, realize that with the smoke and the noise, you don't know how strong the enemy is. If one of your units breaks and retreats and it seems the enemy has superior numbers, some units might collapse if they think the enemy is on their flank or in their rear. If the Confederates take Little Round Top, that reshapes the entire south end of the battlefield. Union reinforcements that were directed elsewhere would instead have to go to Little Round Top to counterattack late in the day July 2. By sending reinforcement to Little Round Top, Meade doesn't have reinforcement to go to other sectors of the battlefield, like to the southern end of Cemetery Ridge. It was at that part of the battlefield late in the day that troops from Anderson's division of Hill's Corps attacked and nearly broke through. There were opportunities for the Confederates at that portion of the Union line.[26]

A.P. Hill is the mystery of Gettysburg. He exercised very little generalship at Gettysburg, and on July 2 Hill seemed to be unusually absent from the field when it came to giving orders to his corps. The Confederates also suffered the loss of one of their best division commanders July 2 when Dorsey Pender was mortally wounded by a shell fragment. We don't know what Pender might have done. Pender may well have put some of his brigades into the attack on the face of Cemetery Ridge, which may have prevented some Union troops being withdrawn from that area and being sent to the lower end of Cemetery Ridge. The Union reinforcements that would have been sent to Little Round Top would have been Crawford's division of Pennsylvania Reserves, two brigades of veteran troops. There was also a brigade of the VI Corps on the scene as well. Three full Union brigades could have led the counterattack to retake the ground. Unless the Confederates who had attacked Little Round Top received reinforcements, I don't think they could have held the ground.

If the Union forces weren't able to retake the ground at the end of July 2, Meade would have either withdrawn from the battlefield or he would have reshaped his line in some fashion. He could not have maintained his current position if the Confederates held Little Round Top. The Confederates would have had the night of July 2 to get artillery up on Little Round Top and would have had infantry forces close to the Taneytown Road, one of the routes Meade needed to get his army out of Gettysburg.

Charging the Union Center

Longstreet's offensive on July 2 had claimed the Peach Orchard, Wheat Field and Devil's Den and had nearly resulted in the taking of Little Round Top. For July 3, Lee planned simultaneous attacks by Ewell and Longstreet. Ewell's fight at Culp's Hill began prematurely in the early morning hours, however, when the Yankees recaptured trenches the Confederates had grabbed the night before. Longstreet would have to storm Cemetery Ridge on his own.

The 12,000-man charge would cover nearly a mile of open ground, with Major General George Pickett's division from Longstreet's Corps spearheading the attack. The attackers would guide on a clump of trees on Cemetery Ridge while 170 artillery pieces softened up Union defenders with a massive pre-assault barrage.[27] Despite stringent objections from Longstreet, Lee remained committed to the venture.

The cannonade started at 1 P.M. Two hours later, three Confederate divisions moved off in the direction of Cemetery Ridge. Exposed to long range artillery, small arms fire and murderous flanking fire, the charge died out near the copse of trees. Only 11 infantry brigades were involved in the attack; another 27 brigades had not been used.[28] Pickett's Charge had cost the Confederates 7,500 casualties.[29]

What if Pickett's Charge had been carried out differently?

CRAIG SYMONDS: Lee was really hoping that the artillery barrage July 3 would soften the Federal line and obscure the field with smoke to protect his advancing troops. He also planned for the artillery to move forward with those attacking. The artillery ran out of ammunition for the most part, and the artillery pieces north of Gettysburg, which were in an enfilading position, really were never used fully, so there was a breakdown in the artillery support. About 12,500 men went forward in Pickett's Charge, but it wasn't quite the hammerblow that Lee initially had hoped for. If more men had been used, and the artillery had properly supported the attack, it is possible the attack might have succeeded, but it was indeed a desperate gamble. Lee recognized it as a desperate effort, but put more faith in his men's superior morale than in the morale of the Union defenders. Lee thought the artillery barrage and the ensuing attack would be a psychological blow to the Federal troops, and that the Union troops would break. I think he underestimated the morale of the Union defenders.

CLINT JOHNSON: The Confederates made a mistake by not placing their artillery July 3 in enfilading position. It was also a mistake not to employ some easily moved mountain howitzers to blow down the fences along the Emmitsburg Road, which impeded the advancing Confederates. The fences could have been knocked down ahead of time. The attack failed when the Confederates had to climb over those fences. If the fences had been knocked down the night before, or perhaps by the 12 missing howitzers that Edward Porter Alexander had tried to save, the attack would have been carried out much more swiftly.

SCOTT HARTWIG: The attack could have succeeded and the Confederates could have taken Cemetery Ridge. A successful attack would have forced the Union army to pull back. Lee had envisioned, in making the attack, a Chancellorsville type victory, where Confederates hit the Union defenders with sledgehammer type blows and seize the ridge, causing the Union army to retreat from the field. The problem with Lee's tactics July 3 was that they were very expensive tactics in terms of the cost in manpower with very little return. Lee might have been able to drive the Union army from Cemetery Ridge and could have forced Meade to retreat from the battlefield. Strategically, what would Lee have accomplished? I understand why Lee made the attack but I don't think it was best option available to him.

Summary

The Confederate army that returned to Virginia in July was nothing like the army that had crossed the Potomac in June. Robert E. Lee had started the campaign with 60,000 supremely confident infantrymen led by a commander who had never lost a major battle to the Army of the Potomac.[30] The Army of Northern Virginia that returned to Virginia had just 35,000 soldiers able to fight.[31] While Meade's army had suffered losses of more than 23,000 at Gettysburg, the three-day battle had cost the Army of Northern Virginia roughly 28,000 casualties.[32] Gettysburg had also wreaked havoc with Lee's command structure; 17 generals and 18 colonels had been killed, captured or wounded during the campaign.[33]

Gettysburg had been an unplanned battle for the Confederates, largely due to faulty reconnaissance. Do we blame Robert E. Lee or Jeb Stuart? Even though Jeff Wert criticized Jeb Stuart for continuing to ride away from Lee's army on his cavalry raid after encountering Hancock's II Corps, Eric Wittenberg claimed Lee failed to properly use the three cavalry brigades he had on hand.

Richard Ewell has also received his fair share of criticism for failing to storm Cemetery Hill on July 1. Both Scott Hartwig and Donald Pfanz asserted that any attack by Ewell would have been repulsed. Although several of the panelists added that a Confederate attack might have succeeded if A.P. Hill's men had been added to the mix, as Peter Carmichael pointed out, Robert E. Lee never issued orders for a combined assault.

The most fascinating day at Gettysburg is day two. What if Lee had allowed Longstreet to come up with his own plan of battle? Jeff Shaara and Clint Johnson believed that Longstreet would have attempted to maneuver around Meade's left flank while Jeff Wert said there might not have been any fighting that day, due to Longstreet's desire to carry out a broader turning movement. And what if Longstreet's men had been able to gain control of Little Round Top on July 2? Jeff Shaara argued that the Confederates could have taken the hill and possibly gained access to the Union rear, if not for the efforts of the 20th Maine and the other regiments in Strong Vincent's brigade. Had the Confederates taken Little Round Top, there might not have been a Pickett's Charge on July 3, since the Federals might have spent the day trying to reclaim Little Round Top. Another possibility, as suggested by Scott Hartwig, is that the loss of Little Round Top may have forced Meade to withdraw from the battlefield.

Gettysburg was brought to a thunderous close on July 3 by the awe-inspiring spectacle of Pickett's Charge. Craig Symonds concluded that the attack would have had a better chance of succeeding if Lee had used more men in the assault and if the attack had received proper artillery support. Even if the charge had broken Meade's line, the cost may have outweighed the gain. Scott Hartwig declared that even though Pickett's Charge could have ended in a tactical victory for the Confederates, success on a strategic level would have been questionable, since the cost in manpower would be more than the South could afford.

Gettysburg had been the exact opposite of Antietam. At Antietam, Lee had been on the defensive with the ability to reinforce threatened sectors. At Gettysburg, Lee was forced to carry the battle to the Federals with very little coordination between the two Confederate wings. Lee's three corps commanders also turned in sub par performances at Gettysburg, as Ewell hesitated, A.P. Hill deferred and Longstreet sulked. Although the Army of Northern Virginia would still be a force to be reckoned with in the future, it would never fully recover from its losses at Gettysburg and would be facing a determined Union commander in 1864.

9

Mortal Wounds:
Vicksburg, Chickamauga
and Chattanooga

The year 1863 was truly monumental for Ulysses S. Grant and the Union effort to win the war in the West. Vicksburg fell in July, placing the Mississippi Valley firmly under Federal control and splitting the Confederacy in two.[1] Bragg's convincing victory at Chickamauga briefly lifted the South's spirits but by late November, Grant had driven the Confederates away from Chattanooga and was unquestionably the North's pre-eminent military leader.

Situated on high ground on the east bank of the Mississippi River, Vicksburg was defended by a Confederate army led by Lieutenant General John C. Pemberton. Initial attempts to capture the fortress had been abject failures but Grant remained persistent, transporting his army across the river from Louisiana in April and then fighting his way into Mississippi's capital city of Jackson on May 14. Pemberton and his immediate superior, Joseph Johnston, were unable to combine their forces against Grant, and the Federal commander scored additional victories at Champion Hill and the Big Black River. Grant finally settled on a siege that lasted nearly seven weeks and Pemberton surrendered Vicksburg on July 4.[2]

In Tennessee, William Rosecrans and the Army of the Cumberland had spent the first half of 1863 recovering from the Union's strategic victory at Stones River. By June, Rosecrans was finally ready to move against

Braxton Bragg and the Army of Tennessee; thanks to some slick maneuvering, Rosecrans forced the Confederates to evacuate Chattanooga without a fight and retreat into Georgia.[3] The Confederates would be back and back with a vengeance. Reinforced by units from the Army of Northern Virginia, Bragg pounced on Rosecrans on the banks of Chickamauga Creek on September 19; a Confederate assault the following day happened to strike an opening in Rosecrans' lines. Several Federal divisions broke and ran and only a staunch defense by Major General George Thomas allowed the Army of the Cumberland to escape to Chattanooga.[4]

As Bragg resorted to a siege to starve the Yankees into submission, the Army of the Cumberland slowly began to recover. Grant arrived in Chattanooga to take charge of operations, Thomas replaced Rosecrans as the new commander of the Army of the Cumberland and the Federals pieced together a new supply route over the Tennessee River, via Brown's Ferry.[5] By November, the hunter had become the hunted. Grant's army burst out of Chattanooga, captured Lookout Mountain on November 24 and then overran Missionary Ridge the following day, forcing Bragg's demoralized army to flee south into Georgia.

Grant's Gamble

One Union scheme after another to capture or bypass Vicksburg had failed during the first few months of 1863.[6] Grant finally decided to move his army south, along the west bank of the Mississippi, cross the river on transports and then head northeast, defeating any opposition that might stand in his way. It was a bold and risky plan. Outnumbered by the Confederates, Grant proposed to make an amphibious landing with no clear line of supply or retreat. Both Sherman and General James McPherson opposed the proposal.[7]

The crossing of the Mississippi went without a hitch; Grant secured his beachhead by defeating an enemy force at Port Gibson and by outflanking additional Confederates at Grand Gulf. Grant then made a radical decision. Rather than concerning himself with the protection of vulnerable supply lines, Grant gave up Grand Gulf as a base and opted to let his men forage for their supplies.[8]

After beating the Confederates at Raymond on May 12, Grant had a decision to make. He could advance directly on John C. Pemberton's Vicksburg garrison or move instead on the state capital of Jackson. Located approximately 50 miles to the east of Vicksburg, Jackson served as a supply base and a railroad center. Any Confederates seeking to reinforce Vicks-

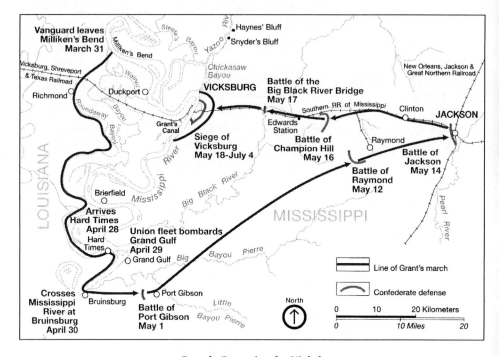

Grant's Campaign for Vicksburg

burg would have to come through Jackson.[9] Grant opted to go after Jackson and took the city on May 14.

Victories at Champion Hill on May 16 and at the Big Black River crossing a day later placed Vicksburg squarely in Grant's crosshairs. Repulsed in his first two attempts to storm Pemberton's fortifications, Grant settled for a siege. Vicksburg's fate was sealed and Pemberton was forced to surrender on July 4.

What if Grant had not taken the risk of approaching Vicksburg from the south?

ED BEARSS: Grant was the difference in the Vicksburg campaign. Grant fought five battles and the Confederates had superior numbers in the area each time. Grant always brought superior numbers to bear at the point of attack: the battles of Port Gibson, Raymond, Jackson, Champion Hill and Big Black. He possessed overwhelming numbers at four of the five battles and substantially larger numbers at the fifth, Champion Hill.

Grant was blessed by the fact that he was separated from Washington. It would take 10 days by the fastest means of communication to transmit messages to and from Mississippi. Grant's entire campaign, from the crossing of the Mississippi to his victory at Big Black Bridge, took 18 days. Grant's orders from Washington had been to cross the river, entrench at Port Gibson and send one corps of his army to General Banks to support the operation against Port Hudson. Grant knew that would take a lot of time. He realized he had the initiative and also understood that Washington wouldn't be in a position to interfere. He told Washington he had the initiative and would advance inland. After the battle of Big Black, he got a message from Washington disapproving of his move — after he had conducted this brilliant campaign.

GERALD PROKOPOWICZ: Grant's campaign against Vicksburg was truly remarkable. Grant was willing to go beyond what conventional wisdom called for. He disregarded those who warned him to be cautious and wait for other forces to arrive or wait to build up a traditional logistical operation. Winfield Scott had done this in the Mexican War — he had demonstrated that you could cut yourself off from your supply base and maneuver successfully — but no one had done it on the scale that Grant did. It required a great deal of courage on Grant's part to undertake such an operation.

It's worth remembering that Grant at this time had no one to depend on but himself. He knew that a single mistake could end his career, not to say what it could do to the Union war effort. He had won a battle at Shiloh, and been punished for it by having Halleck essentially remove him from command. If that was the consequence of victory, what would happen if he lost a battle?

Later on, Lincoln would become a strong supporter of Grant and would give him room to make mistakes, but in July 1863 the jury was still out. The War Department had Charles Dana tagging along at Grant's headquarters, spying on him and reporting back to Washington. Lincoln himself was skeptical of the plan to approach Vicksburg from the south, and thought Grant should have linked up with Banks at Port Hudson instead. When the campaign was over, Lincoln wrote a note to Grant in which he said, "You were right, and I was wrong." How often do you hear anyone, much less a powerful politician, say something like that? But the point is that Lincoln did not have any reason to put special trust in Grant before Vicksburg. If Grant had simply continued to batter at the fort from the north or the west, he would never have emerged as the Union's great general, and there would have been no one to direct the Overland campaign of 1864 with such tenacity, and perhaps no victory for Lincoln in the election that year.

LARRY DANIEL: Grant's campaign against Vicksburg was truly a brilliant campaign and I understand it is still studied today at West Point. I'm not sure it's entirely true to say that Grant cut loose from his supply line in approaching Vicksburg. Grant actually had a supply line and had roughly 500 wagons coming up in his rear. In fact, at one point, Pemberton wanted to attack Grant's supply line but the battle never materialized. Grant's successful campaign was actually a combination of Grant's brilliance and Pemberton's incompetence. Pemberton left too many troops to defend Vicksburg and once he was defeated at Champion Hill, he should have pulled out altogether.

Could Pemberton have attacked Grant's transports as they moved Grant's troops across the Mississippi? I don't believe such an attack would have been feasible; there were so many options available to Grant that Pemberton simply had no way of knowing for sure what Grant's plan would be. Had Pemberton attempted to contest the river crossing and then discovered it was only a diversion for a larger attack elsewhere, it would have been disastrous for the Confederates. Even if Pemberton had attempted to destroy Grant's army at the beachhead, I'm not sure how much damage Pemberton could have done because Grant had the backing of the Union ironclad fleet.

Richard McMurry proposed an interesting idea in his book *Two Great Rebel Armies*: to exchange land for time in the spring and summer of 1863. The idea was to send one corps from the Army of Tennessee to Lee's army in Virginia. You put all of your eggs in the basket of your best general and that of course is Robert E. Lee. Had that happened, the Confederates would have been pushed back south of the Tennessee River, but think about how useful an extra corps might have been for Lee at Gettysburg. Could an entire corps made the difference for Lee at Gettysburg? I don't know if it would have but that would have been the best gamble for the Confederates. The idea of taking good troops from Lee's army, sending them West and placing them under incompetent leadership was a bad idea.

Combining against Grant

Directed by the Richmond government to take command of all Confederate forces in the West, Joseph Johnston's dilemma was to find a way to combine his troops with Pemberton's men at Vicksburg. Pemberton received mixed signals from his superiors. Johnston, his immediate boss, told him to leave Vicksburg and combine with Johnston's men against Grant while Pemberton's ultimate superior, Confederate president Jefferson

Davis, instructed Pemberton to hold Vicksburg at all costs.[10] Pemberton attempted to satisfy both men and the result was a Confederate disaster.

What if Pemberton and Johnston had been able to combine their forces against Grant?

RICHARD MCMURRY: Joe Johnston didn't function well in many situations and this was one of them. Davis had sent Johnston west initially in a supervisory command over Bragg in Tennessee and Pemberton in Mississippi. Johnston didn't think the arrangement could work and in May 1863, Davis sent Johnston to Mississippi. Johnston didn't have the kind of personality to take an ambiguous situation and shape it the way he thought it should be shaped. Johnston was telling Pemberton that he thought it would be a good idea if Pemberton left Vicksburg and joined Johnston to fight Grant. I often wonder how things might have gone had Johnston sent Pemberton an order like this: Paragraph #1: Obey either Paragraph #2 or Paragraph #3, your choice. Paragraph #2: Get your army out of Vicksburg and meet me at such and such a point. Paragraph #3: Turn your command over to your next in command, consider yourself under arrest and report to my headquarters for trial. What would that have done? Johnston would not issue an order like that because he thought his authority over Pemberton was not clear, which it wasn't. Johnston could have tried to do a lot more than he did in terms of telling Pemberton to obey orders or else. Johnston could have also gone to Davis and told him either you take command here or I'll take command but we both can't do it. In the early stages of the Vicksburg campaign, there were more Confederates in the area than Federals but the Confederates were divided and the problem was to get them together under one commander. Johnston made no serious effort to do that. Whether Johnston would have actually fought Grant if he had been able to combine all of the Confederate forces is another matter entirely.

ED BEARSS: Pemberton was operating under a divided command. On paper, the chain of command went from Davis, the Confederate president, to his secretary of war to Joseph Johnston, the commander of the military division. Johnston lacked self-confidence in his authority. Both Bragg and Pemberton had a habit of corresponding directly with Davis and his secretary of war without sending copies of their correspondence to Johnston.

As soon as Grant crossed the river and won at Port Gibson, Davis informed Pemberton to hold Vicksburg. Davis felt the Confederates needed to hold Vicksburg and Port Hudson to maintain a connection with the

Trans-Mississippi. This message had important ramifications for Pemberton that dated back to his experiences in South Carolina. In the spring and
summer of 1862, Pemberton had suggested the idea of evacuating
Charleston once Union forces had started to close on the city. The South
Carolinians were upset by the suggestion and protested to Davis. Davis
decided to transfer Pemberton to command the newly constituted Department of Mississippi and East Louisiana. The transfer was dictated by political pressure from South Carolina.

Johnston directed Pemberton to evacuate Vicksburg and combine their
two armies with reinforcements coming from several points in the South,
including Charleston and Savannah as well as Bragg's army in Middle Tennessee. Johnston's plan was to unite those forces, beat Grant and recover
lost territory. So Pemberton was being told by Davis to hold on to Vicksburg and he was being told by Johnston to evacuate the city. If I were Pemberton and received those orders from Davis and had already been moved
once out of a choice assignment, I would do what the president said.

Following Grant's victory at Raymond, Grant decided to turn his back
on Pemberton and move toward Jackson. Johnston arrived in Jackson May
13 and told the Confederate War Department that Union forces had inter-
posed between Pemberton and Johnston. Johnston directed Pemberton to
combine with him farther north to engage Grant. On the 14th, Grant drove
Johnston out of Jackson and made it difficult for Confederate reinforcements to get to the scene. Pemberton told Johnston that he couldn't reach
Johnston, and instead he marched southeast preparatory to attacking and
interdicting Grant's supply and communication lines.

I don't believe a Johnston-Pemberton linkup was possible. Davis had
issued orders to Pemberton against the evacuation of Vicksburg. Pemberton had his choice of obeying his commander-in-chief or Johnston. Johnston's heart was not in combining with Pemberton or to aggressively press
Grant. Johnston did not make any move to cooperate with Pemberton
until July 1. By that time, Grant had been reinforced and had an iron ring
forged around Pemberton at Vicksburg. Grant also had Sherman with
30,000 men on the Big Black in case Johnston tried to come to the relief
of Vicksburg.

KENNETH NOE: Vicksburg was a lot more important symbolically, in terms
of morale, than it was in reality. Certainly there were supplies coming in
from the Trans-Mississippi but not as many as people often think. I think
Joe Johnston was absolutely right when he said Pemberton should never
have allowed his army to be trapped inside Vicksburg. Pemberton should
have come out, combined with Johnston and fought it out with Grant.

Vicksburg might have fallen but what was important was defeating Grant. There was a brief period when the Confederates would have had a numerical advantage over Grant. That disappeared pretty quickly once Grant was reinforced. A battle between the combined Confederate forces would have happened in northeastern Mississippi, somewhere between Jackson and Vicksburg, perhaps near Champion Hill. What would have happened is hard to say. Grant would still have been the superior general. Of course, with a few more men and better leadership on his part, Pemberton might have defeated Grant at Champion Hill. So with Johnston's men combining with Pemberton's, it's entirely possible that Grant could have suffered a significant defeat. Johnston would have been in overall command, so then you have to ask yourself whether Johnston have fought such a battle or retreated all over the place.

Rosecrans' Gap

Chickamauga Creek in northern Georgia was the scene for a brutal two-day battle between Braxton Bragg's Army of Tennessee and William Rosecrans' Army of the Cumberland. The two armies fought to a standstill on September 19; on the 20th, Bragg proposed to strike the Union left, with other attacks to follow in echelon across the entire length of Rosecrans' line.[11] The Federals drove back each Confederate charge with heavy casualties, until Rosecrans committed a fatal error. Under the mistaken impression that a gap existed near the center of his line, he ordered General Thomas Wood to pull his division out of line to fill the alleged opening. A hole was created where none previously existed. Confederates from Longstreet's wing had the good fortune to direct their attack at the vacant area and the panic-stricken Union line quickly disintegrated.[12]

What if Rosecrans hadn't mistakenly created a gap
in his lines at Chickamauga on September 20?

RICHARD MCMURRY: If a gap had not opened in Rosecrans' lines owing to a misunderstanding of orders, Chickamauga would have wound up like many other Civil War battles. You would have had a large number of casualties on both sides and one army or the other would have fallen back after the battle. In this case, Bragg's army would have been the one to fall back if for no other reason than logistics. Longstreet was in Georgia with Bragg; the long-term significance might be that he would have stayed there. He might not have returned to Virginia for the 1864 campaign. The 1864 campaign in Georgia would not have started at Dalton but instead would have started farther south. Thomas would not have picked up his reputation as being "The Rock." He would have been viewed as a competent corps commander but I can't see him being put in command of the Army of the Cumberland. Rosecrans may well have become the great Union general. At least Rosecrans would have been on par with Grant. If Grant captured Vicksburg and if Rosecrans took Chattanooga, then the question would become whom do you pick as the overall commander of the Union army in 1864?

LARRY DANIEL: If Rosecrans had not mistakenly created a gap in his lines and had either won a minor victory or achieved a stalemate at Chickamauga to force the Confederates back to Dalton, it would have been Rosecrans and not Sherman leading the campaign against Atlanta in 1864. Rosecrans would have been one of the great Union heroes; the war would have turned out essentially the same way.

GERALD PROKOPOWICZ: The Confederate victory at Chickamauga was perhaps the closest thing to a decisive battlefield victory the Confederates were able to achieve in the West, and yet it had no impact on the outcome of the war. Had the gap not opened in Rosecrans' line, then you would simply have had a more indecisive struggle along the lines of Stones River or Perryville.

All Civil War battles seemed to follow the same pattern. One side would attack and nearly win, but a heroic stand would be made somewhere by the defenders and the attackers then would fail to pursue. Everybody on the attacking side would bemoan the lack of aggressive pursuit of the beaten enemy, but the fact that such pursuit was so rare suggests that it must have been almost impossible to accomplish. There was very little chance of a decisive victory at any of these battles.

There's more room to speculate about different outcomes when you look at things from the strategic rather than the tactical standpoint. For example, consider how things might have been different had the Union high command not dispersed its troops in 1862 after taking Corinth, Mississippi, and instead focused in one direction, whether it be Vicksburg or Chattanooga. It is conceivable that such a campaign could have led to decisive strategic results for the Union in 1862.

The Rock of Chickamauga

As Longstreet's men poured through the opening in Rosecrans' line and Union soldiers fled in disarray, Major General George Thomas main-

William Rosecrans, possibly a Union war hero, if not for erroneous orders at Chickamauga. LIBRARY OF CONGRESS.

tained a strong defensive position on Snodgrass Hill and allowed the Army
of the Cumberland to escape to Chattanooga. The "Rock of Chickamauga"
fought off a multitude of desperate Confederate attacks, with the help of
Union reserves led by Major General George Granger.[13] Thomas and his

beleaguered units finally slipped away at dusk and, despite being urged by his subordinates to pursue, Bragg refused to send his exhausted army after Rosecrans.[14] Confederate losses at Chickamauga totaled over 18,400 while the Federals suffered more than 16,000 casualties in the bloodiest two days of the war.[15]

What if Bragg had pursued Rosecrans more aggressively after the Confederate victory on September 20?

ED BEARSS: The Confederates had a great opportunity when they shattered the right and center of Rosecrans' army and sent several divisions of his army fleeing back toward Chattanooga. McCook's Corps was routed; his corps always seemed to be getting routed. Crittenden's Corps was embattled and Thomas forged a new line for Rosecrans' army along the Lafayette road and Snodgrass Ridge. The Confederates piecemealed their attacks and Thomas was able to resist those attacks. The Union army fell back and took position on Missionary Ridge the evening of the 20th.

The Confederates should have attacked again the following day, on the 21st. It's true that Bragg suffered heavy casualties on the 20th, but in relative terms the Confederate casualties were less severe than those suffered by the Federals. Forrest reconnoitered and reported that the Union forces didn't appear to be in strength. Bragg decided not to order attack. Union forces then abandoned Missionary Ridge as well as Lookout Mountain on the 24th and fell back into Chattanooga. The Confederates had a window of opportunity to attack Rosecrans between the 21st and the 24th. Instead Bragg decided to lay siege to the city.

RICHARD MCMURRY: Bragg's army was beaten up pretty well following Chickamauga and pursuing Rosecrans after the battle was not an easy task. It's similar to Meade's army after Gettysburg. Meade took a pretty good beating at Gettysburg and two of his corps, the I and III, were disbanded after the battle and never reassembled. Meade was running short on ammunition and pursuing Lee wasn't going to be easy. It was much the same situation for Bragg's army at Chickamauga. Bragg suffered more casualties at Chickamauga than Rosecrans did. Civil War armies, with very few exceptions, didn't have the capability to fight a knockdown-dragout battle and then pursue the enemy.

LARRY DANIEL: If you read the Federal accounts from the night of September 20, you read that Rosecrans' army had pulled back north of Rossville and you hear about how demoralized the Army of the Cumberland was. You read about how the Federal army was a mass of chaos. Several

George Thomas, "The Rock of Chickamauga." LIBRARY OF CONGRESS.

high-ranking officers wrote that if the Confederates had attacked that night, a segment of the Army of the Cumberland would have been destroyed. Even if Bragg had achieved a greater victory at Chickamauga and captured an entire Union corps, Rosecrans still would have been able to pull back north of Chattanooga and receive reinforcements, and the Army of the Cumberland ultimately would have advanced south again. Even if Thomas had not made his defensive stand, the Confederates would have been hard pressed to achieve a long-term victory in the West. The South lost an entire corps at Fort Donelson and they kept on fighting. The South lost an entire army at Vicksburg and kept on fighting. For some reason, people think that if a Northern army had been largely destroyed, that the North would have sued for peace. That would not have happened. The North would have been forced to add more recruits and it would have stretched the war out, but we probably would not have seen a different outcome to the war.

Davis Backs Bragg

At a terrible cost, the Confederates had won a convincing victory at Chickamauga, although Braxton Bragg's subordinates were not entirely convinced that their commander was the right man to lead the Army of Tennessee. Bragg had not ordered a full pursuit of Rosecrans' army until September 22, and both General D.H. Hill and cavalry leader Nathan Bedford Forrest criticized Bragg for his lack of aggressiveness following the battle.[16]

The issue of Bragg's competency to command came to a head in October, when James Longstreet and 11 other Confederate officers petitioned Jefferson Davis to relieve Bragg.[17] Davis decided to travel to Tennessee to personally investigate the matter. After meeting with Bragg and four of his generals, and listening to Bragg's subordinates criticize his abilities, Davis threw his support to Bragg and retained him as commander of the Army of Tennessee.[18]

What if Davis had replaced Bragg sooner as the commander of the Army of Tennessee?

KENNETH NOE: Following a council of war in which Bragg's subordinates expressed their lack of confidence in Bragg, Davis should have relieved Bragg, even if Davis still personally supported Bragg. It was obvious at that point that Bragg did not have the trust of his army. Who would replace Bragg? There were a couple of choices. Longstreet was one. Longstreet didn't do all that well in independent command at Knoxville. William J. Hardee was another possible choice to replace Bragg. Hardee never really had a large independent command so it's hard to say how he would have performed. Events don't suggest that either Hardee or Longstreet would have been better than Bragg, but at least they would have had the support of their subordinate commanders. With Hardee in command and if Longstreet wasn't detached to Knoxville, Grant would have had to defeat a much stronger Confederate army to break out of Chattanooga.

LARRY DANIEL: If you take Bragg out of the picture as the commander of the Army of Tennessee, the question becomes: who leads that army? Who is qualified and who is acceptable to Jefferson Davis? Could Albert Sidney Johnston, had he lived, developed throughout the war as did Robert E. Lee? The answer is of course he could have, but up through Shiloh we certainly saw no genius in him. It's true enough to say if the bullet that struck Johnston had traveled instead all the way to Virginia and killed Lee instead, Lee's picture would not be on Stone Mountain today. Lee, however, evolved as a commander. Johnston could have evolved as well, but up through April, 1862, we saw no evidence of a genius.

William Hardee was not going to be the man to lead the Army of Tennessee. He was too conservative and lacked aggressiveness. Joseph Johnston was tried in the West and I see him as a failure. The only one who could have been a viable choice was Beauregard. He had a lot of quirky ideas, but he understood the art of war and could be aggressive at times. I'm not sure Beauregard would have ever been acceptable to Jefferson Davis, but Beauregard seemed to be the best option for commanding the Army of Tennessee. The problem was that the South needed two Robert E. Lees and it only had one. I don't think Stonewall Jackson, had he survived Chancellorsville, would have been able to make any difference in the West if he had been sent to command the Army of Tennessee.

The Civil War was a war of wills. If every battle in the war had been the equivalent of the battle of Fredericksburg, if the North had taken that kind of hit in every single battle, the South still would have run out of men before the North did. If the North was willing to take those kinds of hits, there was simply no way the South was ever going to win the war. It's all about breaking the will of the North. I've always contended that the North had a stronger will to win than most people believe.

ED BEARSS: There had been internecine fighting within the Confederate Army, surrounding Bragg, since Perryville. Polk and Hardee had opposed Bragg for months and Davis should have removed Bragg. Davis gave Joe Johnston an opportunity to run the army in what I like to call the battle of women. Initially Johnston lacked the will to take command of the army. first he decided not to take command because Mrs. Bragg was ill in January of 1863 — as if a woman's illness should be a factor as to whether or not you should take command of an army. The second time, in April of 1863, he decided not to take command because Mrs. Johnston was ill. Johnston may have used the illnesses as an excuse not to take command of the army as directed by Davis. So Bragg kept his command.

If you say no to Bragg, who runs the army? One name that comes to mind, had he not died at Shiloh, was Albert Sidney Johnston. He possessed the president's confidence and I believe Davis would have preferred A.S. Johnston to Lee. Commanders needed to have a mutual understanding with their president, their commander in chief. Joe Johnston and Beauregard never seemed to understand that fact. A.S. Johnston and Lee realized it. Longstreet may have been another option to replace Bragg; I think Longstreet went west believing he would get the command. Longstreet became miffed when Davis sustained Bragg, and the Bragg-Longstreet relationship went from bad to worse.

RICHARD MCMURRY: Steve Woodworth, in his wonderful book *Jefferson Davis and His Generals*, made a very good point that the key to understanding the Confederate failures in the West is understanding the Confederate generals in the West. The key general was Leonidas Polk. Polk had been appointed major general in August 1861 by Jefferson Davis, who made Polk one of the senior military officers in the Confederacy. As long as Polk was with the Army of Tennessee, he was a bottleneck. It was impossible to promote younger men like Alexander P. Stewart and Patrick Cleburne, who might have developed into competent corps commanders, while Polk was present. Polk was the one who became the leader of the anti-Bragg cabal and Polk was the one who so often disobeyed Bragg's orders. Polk spent about half his time writing letters trying to get Bragg dismissed. Bragg in effect was walking around with about a dozen knives sticking in his back, and 10 or 11 of them had Polk's fingerprints on them. The ultimate responsibility lies though with Jefferson Davis. Davis had the authority to remove Polk. Bragg tried to get Davis to do so on several occasions. Davis always took the attitude that his generals could work out their problems and that they would cooperate for the good of the cause.

Lifting the Siege

With the Army of the Cumberland holed up inside Chattanooga and Bragg besieging the city, Union leaders replaced Rosecrans with George Thomas and ordered Grant to travel to Chattanooga to assume overall command of operations.[19] Fortune soon smiled on the Federals. A new supply line, "The Cracker Line," was opened across the Tennessee River and Union reinforcements were on the way. Meade detached two army corps from Virginia under Joe Hooker and William T. Sherman was ordered to move east from Memphis to Chattanooga.[20] Union forces in Chattanooga were increasing their strength at the same time that the Confederates were getting weaker. Bragg detached Longstreet and 12,000 men to recapture Knoxville, leaving the Army of Tennessee with just 40,000 men stretched out along an eight-mile front trying to contain some 60,000 Federals.[21]

Grant was now ready to tackle Bragg on the towering heights overlooking Chattanooga. On November 24, Hooker's men captured Lookout Mountain; on November 25, Thomas' Army of the Cumberland moved against the Confederate rifle pits at the base of Missionary Ridge. Tactical blunders cost the Confederates. Bragg's main defensive line along the top of Missionary Ridge had been laid out incorrectly and was placed at the highest elevation, the geographical crest, rather than at the military crest, which would have given the Confederates the best field of fire down the slope. Bragg had also ordered his advance units to fire a single volley and then withdraw up the hill. When Thomas' men overran the rifle pits and saw the Confederates dashing up the ridge, the attacking Federals gained confidence and proceeded to shock the Union commanders by surging up the steep slope of Missionary Ridge and shattering Bragg's line.[22] Grant had won the Battle of Chattanooga and the Army of Tennessee was in full retreat to the south.[23]

What if Bragg had kept his entire army together at Chattanooga?

STEVEN WOODWORTH: Once Grant arrived in Chattanooga and opened The Cracker Line, all hope evaporated of starving the Yankees out of Chattanooga. The big question was what Bragg should have done next. His only viable option was a turning movement to the east and Longstreet was the first part of the movement. Had Longstreet been able to trap Burnside's force, or had he forced Burnside to retreat from Knoxville and opened up the possibility of a Confederate turning movement, then the question would have become whether Bragg could have repeated in late 1863 what he did in the Perryville campaign.[24] The Army of the Cumberland's draft animals were either dead or nearly skeletons from lack of feed. The Union army at Chattanooga would have been hard pressed to pursue Bragg.

GERALD PROKOPOWICZ: The Confederate defeat at Missionary Ridge was surprising from a tactical standpoint because it was unusual for any frontal assault to succeed. One can try to explain the Union success by stressing the psychological effect of Bragg's troops being able to see all of the Union troops advancing on the Confederate lines, creating the impression of an overwhelming force. Perhaps that was a factor, although the same conditions applied to Pickett's Charge at Gettysburg. Perhaps Bragg's personality and the dissension in the ranks and officers under Bragg may have been the factors that made his army so brittle that day.

Had Bragg not detached Longstreet's men to Knoxville, you would have had more Confederate troops retreating from Missionary Ridge. By conventional Civil War standards, the Confederates shouldn't have lost the ridge in the first place. So the conventional solution of adding more troops seems unlikely to have made any difference.

Had the Army of Tennessee had a different commander, perhaps a Joe Johnston or a Longstreet, the army presumably would not have been as demoralized at the command level as Bragg's army was. I don't think you can criticize Bragg's tactical moves at Missionary Ridge because he didn't make any significant tactical decisions. The Confederate troops were simply in place and when the attack came, it broke their will and they retreated.

Summary

The Confederate States of America didn't officially expire until 1865, but it's fair to say that the Confederacy received plenty of notification of its impending demise from defeats suffered in the West in 1863. In a four-month span between July and November, Federal forces captured Vicksburg and ejected Braxton Bragg's army from Tennessee. Ulysses S. Grant was instrumental in directing both operations. Vicksburg's loss split the Confederacy in half and opened the entire length of the Mississippi River to Union shipping; Grant's victory at Missionary Ridge further fueled his drive to the general-in-chief's position and set the stage for Sherman's march into Georgia in 1864.

In the campaign for Vicksburg, Grant acted boldly; Confederate military leaders were indecisive and disorganized. Richard McMurry maintained that Joseph Johnston should have been more direct in calling on Pemberton to unite their forces against Grant. Kenneth Noe also speculated that a combined army under Johnston might have been able to register a significant victory, although he noted that the cautious Johnston might never have launched a major assault against Grant's army.

Thanks largely to miscommunication and faulty orders that resulted in a gap in Rosecrans' lines at Chickamauga, a potential two-day stalemate instead became a major Confederate victory. Richard McMurry claimed that a drawn battle at Chickamauga might have changed the complexion of the 1864 campaign in the West. A minor Union victory at Chickamauga might have also redirected the careers of William Rosecrans and William T. Sherman. Perhaps, as Larry Daniel stated, it would have been Rosecrans, and not Sherman, who would have led the campaign against Atlanta in 1864.

Could the Confederates have reaped greater rewards from their victory at Chickamauga with a more aggressive pursuit of Rosecrans' beaten army? Ed Bearss declared that Bragg should have attacked Rosecrans the day after the Army of the Cumberland fell back to Chattanooga, although

Larry Daniel concluded that even if Bragg had inflicted more damage, Rosecrans eventually would have been able to renew the fight against the Army of Tennessee.

There's also that big question of who should have commanded the Army of Tennessee. According to Kenneth Noe, morale would have been much improved under Hardee or Longstreet and that would have made Grant's task of extricating his army from Chattanooga all the more difficult. Larry Daniel suggested that Beauregard might have been the best choice to lead the Army of Tennessee. Of course, as Daniel also mentioned, what the South really needed was a duplicate of Robert E. Lee. The Confederacy never could find one.

Union armies had made great strides in the West in 1863. In 1864, the Federals would turn up the heat on the Confederacy, with simultaneous offensives aimed at both the Army of Northern Virginia and the Army of Tennessee.

10

Grant against Lee: The Overland Campaign

The course of the Civil War took an important turn in March of 1864: Ulysses S. Grant was promoted to lieutenant general and received command of all Federal armies.[1] In the past, mighty Union armies had been broken up and scattered about in an effort to occupy territory. Now there was a new focus. As general-in-chief, Grant's top priority would be to seek out and engage the principal Confederate armies.[2]

Grant decided to accompany the Army of the Potomac to confront Robert E. Lee's heavily outnumbered Army of Northern Virginia. When the Federals moved into the densely wooded area known as the Wilderness, near the Chancellorsville battlefield of 1863, fighting broke out on May 5. Two days of savage combat cost the Federals more than 17,000 men while Lee suffered 7,500 casualties.[3] Many expected Grant to reverse his course and retreat across the Rapidan River to lick his wounds, but this was a new commander and a new era for the Union army. Grant's men moved south, aiming for the important crossroads at Spotsylvania Court House; Lee got there first and the two armies grappled for nearly two weeks before Grant recognized that the slaughter at Spotsylvania was getting him nowhere and decided to make another effort to sidle around Lee's right flank. Each time Grant maneuvered for an opening to get between the Confederates and Richmond, Lee was right there to meet him. Additional battles followed along the North Anna River, near Totopotomoy Creek and also at Cold Harbor on June 3, just miles from Richmond, when Grant launched a frontal assault that resulted in frightful losses for the Federals. Grant's attempts to constantly engage Lee's army during the Overland Campaign had proven costly to both sides, with the Army of the Potomac suffering 50,000 casualties and the Army of Northern Virginia losing approximately 30,000 men.[4]

Grant in the Field

As general-in-chief of all of the armies, Ulysses S. Grant could have easily directed the war effort from a desk in Washington but instead chose to keep his headquarters in the field with the Army of the Potomac. Even though George Meade would remain the army's commander, Grant would exert plenty of influence during the Overland Campaign against Robert E. Lee and the Army of Northern Virginia.[5]

Grant's plan actually called for several Union armies to be active in Virginia in the spring of 1864. Ben Butler's Army of the James would advance up the south bank of the James River toward Richmond. Another Federal force in the Shenandoah Valley, under Franz Sigel, was to march on Staunton and then head east, in the direction of the Confederate capital.[6]

The Army of the Potomac did its job, hammering away at the Army of Northern Virginia for more than five weeks during the Overland Campaign. Any hopes Grant may have harbored about receiving assistance from Butler and Sigel were soon shattered. Sigel's army was routed in the Valley at New Market on May 15, while Butler's advance up the James River came to an abrupt halt when his army was beaten at Bermuda Hundred, just 15 miles southeast of Richmond.

***What if Grant had not accompanied the Army
of the Potomac in the spring of 1864 and instead
had gone with Butler or Sigel?***

GORDON RHEA: What if Meade had maintained command of the Army of the Potomac? Meade was good at fighting defensive battles, as Gettysburg revealed, but 10 months had passed since Gettysburg without a major offensive in the East. This frustrated Lincoln and it was crucial to have a major offensive before the election of 1864. Lincoln needed victories, especially in Virginia. Meade was not the man to bring victories. I've often made jokes that if Meade was left in charge of the Army of the Potomac when it moved out in May of 1864, we'd be reading in today's papers that Meade's grandson was still maneuvering for good position.

Ulysses S. Grant. Could Grant have taken
Richmond in 1864 by leading the Army of the
James? LIBRARY OF CONGRESS.

None of the Eastern generals showed the same type of tenacity displayed by Grant. Grant never seemed to harbor any doubt about gaining the ultimate victory or how he would achieve it. His main goal was to defeat Lee's army and he fought a series of battles over a 40-day campaign, some of the most grinding battles of the Civil War. Grant realized that he could not allow the Confederate army to have any rest following a major battle, he had to start battles and keep them going. He realized campaigns had to be active on all fronts so the South couldn't shift troops as they did at Chickamauga. So Grant tried to coordinate his moves with Sherman and other commanders, up the James River and in the Valley.

If Butler and the Valley commanders had been more effective, it's possible the South may not have survived 1864. Sigel and Butler were political generals. If Grant had decided to go with one of the other armies, like Butler's Army of the James, and if Grant had been able to take Richmond in Lee's rear while coordinating a successful campaign in the Valley, the whole campaign could have been successfully concluded in 1864. Grant might have been better served had he traveled with either the Army of the James or the forces in the Valley, forces with weak commanders.

PETER CARMICHAEL: Great generals have to have the capacity and willingness to take risks and suffer casualties. Many people condemn Grant for fighting that kind of war due to the huge loss of life. Grant certainly made a number of tactical mistakes in 1864 but he also brought a unity of purpose to the war in Virginia and to the entire Union war effort. He had a perfect understanding of what it was going to take to bring the Confederacy to its knees, that is, taking the war to the Confederacy's armies and its infrastructure.

If Grant had been with Butler's army along the James, rather than with Meade's, perhaps Grant might have been able to capture Richmond. Then again, with Meade in sole command of the Army of the Potomac near Fredericksburg and meeting the kind of resistance that Grant eventually met, I think Meade would have responded in a very defensive, passive manner. I have great admiration for both Grant and Lee. They were both very skillful in handling their armies and were innovative and creative tacticians, although Grant doesn't get credit for that.

JEFF WERT: If Meade had led operations in the East rather than Grant, we would not have seen the tremendous casualties we saw in Grant's Overland Campaign. I'm not sure Meade would have maintained the constant offensive movement against Lee. A critical moment was the night of May 7 at the Wilderness, when the Federal army was starting to march away from the Wilderness after two savage days of fighting. The army came to a crossroads, the Orange Plank Road and the Brock Road. You can either head east back across the Rappahannock or turn south. I don't think Meade would have turned the army south as Grant did. Meade deserved a lot of credit for winning at Gettysburg. No other commander in our nation's history faced a greater burden or bigger challenge than Meade did at Gettysburg. I just don't believe Meade would have turned the army south to continue the campaign against Lee after those two days of battle at the Wilderness.

Grant always looked ahead. The other Union commanders in the East, like Hooker, Burnside and Meade, would have a short-term focus after a battle. The Wilderness was at best a tactical draw for the Federals and perhaps could be viewed a Confederate victory since Lee held the ground. After that battle, Meade would have moved back across the river. Maintaining the campaign and maintaining the drive against the Confederates was all the more important in 1864 because of the upcoming presidential election that year. To win the war, the North had to reelect Lincoln.

DONALD PFANZ: Grant brought something new and fresh to the East in 1864, and that was aggressiveness and sheer determination. In some ways, Meade was a superior battlefield commander to Grant, as far as maneuvering troops and so forth. Meade didn't have Grant's dogged determination and aggression. So if Meade had been left in charge strategically and tactically of the Army of the Potomac, we still would have seen some big battles in 1864, quite possibly in the same region as Grant's battles. Meade might have managed the Wilderness battle better than Grant. Grant made a lot of mistakes in the Wilderness and Spotsylvania. His brilliance wasn't so much in the tactical area as it was strategically, in conducting the overall campaign. He saw the big picture. He realized that while he might be losing battles, he had the luxury of bringing up more troops and would be successful in the end.

The Union war effort would have been much better off if Grant had been leading Butler's Army of the James while Meade led the Army of the Potomac. Butler simply wasn't a capable commander and his subordinates, Quincy A. Gillmore and William F. Smith, were quarrelsome. Between the three of them, they were like the three stooges at Bermuda Hundred. If Grant had been leading that Army in 1864, it's quite possible he would have captured Petersburg and Richmond in May while Meade applied pressure against Lee's army farther north.

More Friendly Fire

Grant's Overland Campaign got underway on May 5 in the heavily wooded region known as the Wilderness, a foreboding area 12 miles wide and six miles deep that was a loathsome mix of stunted pines, briers and dense undergrowth that restricted movement and reduced visibility in all directions.[7] The terrain offset Grant's numerical superiority and fighting raged on the main roads traversing the Wilderness, namely the Orange Turnpike, the Orange Plank Road and the Brock Road.

Winfield Scott Hancock's troops appeared to be on the verge of breaking through the Confederate lines on the Orange Plank Road on May 6 when Longstreet's First Corps, including two divisions just back from Tennessee, arrived on the scene to help bring the Union advance to a halt. Longstreet then learned about an unfinished railroad bed that led directly into Hancock's left flank. Four Confederate brigades were sent up the railroad cut on a surprise assault that threatened to collapse the Union flank. As the attack began to lose steam, Longstreet was knocked out of action, accidentally wounded by his own men while riding on the Orange Plank Road in an incident hauntingly similar to the fatal wounding of Stonewall Jackson almost a year earlier in nearly the same location. Struck in the throat by a bullet that passed through his shoulder; Longstreet nearly choked to death on his own blood.[8] Confederate Edward Porter Alexander would later claim that the loss of Longstreet seemed to paralyze the First Corps.[9] Longstreet would survive his wounds but would be out of action for nearly five months.

What if Longstreet had not been accidentally wounded at the Wilderness on May 6?

GORDON RHEA: Longstreet's flank attack was very successful and rolled up one of the Union flanks. Longstreet said he was ready to push the Federals back across the Rapidan River. My feeling is the Confederate attack was running out of steam when Longstreet was shot and the Confederates were about as mixed up as the Union troops. It did not seem likely that the Confederates would have been able to exploit the successful attack if Longstreet had not been wounded. I believe Longstreet's idea of what he had accomplished grew as the years passed.

DONALD PFANZ: Longstreet's wounding while leading a flank attack against Union forces may have prevented the Confederates from obtaining a larger success in the battle. Longstreet's plan was to send troops down the unfinished railroad and flank the fallback position the Union army had taken. It is quite possible that Longstreet's plan might have worked. Had it worked, you might have seen the left flank of the Union army crumbling just about the time that Ewell was turning the Union right flank. Had that happened, panic may have taken hold and you might have seen, at the very least, the Union army falling back to Fredericksburg.

ROBERT E. L. KRICK: Longstreet's accidental wounding, like Jackson's the year before, is best viewed for its long-term consequences. Some Confederate sources argue that Longstreet was struck down at the zenith of his triumph, having just rolled up the flank of the Union army. That much is true, but the attack had petered out, and despite what historians have claimed, the Confederates were not close to ejecting Grant from the Wilderness and sending him back to the Culpeper side of the Rapidan River.

Longstreet was very capable at fighting on the defensive with limited tactical offensive moves and the war, as it evolved in the summer of 1864, fell right into that pattern. Longstreet would have been very effective in the fighting around Petersburg had he been available to counter Grant's initial probes at Petersburg. The absence of Longstreet was also felt at Cold Harbor and at the North Anna.

Grant at Spotsylvania

Just days after the vicious two-day battle in the Wilderness, Grant and Lee clashed again, this time at Spotsylvania Court House. Lee's defensive fortifications included a rugged salient known as the Mule Shoe that extended northward from the center of the Confederate line. Boasting plenty of artillery and sturdy trenches, the Mule Shoe was further protected by a heavy abatis of cut down trees, with additional defenses located a short distance to the rear.[10]

Union troops went right after the Mule Shoe. 5,000 men under Colonel Emory Upton crashed into the salient late in the day on May 11; the assault ran out of steam due to a lack of reinforcements.[11] Grant sent even more men the following day. In an early morning attack, 20,000 troops from Hancock's II Corps stormed the crest of the Mule Shoe while Burnside's IX Corps hit the Confederates from the east. A Rebel counterattack by John B. Gordon's division pushed the Federals back but on the western face of the salient, at a point in the line that would be known as the Bloody Angle, fighting became hand to hand and continued throughout the day. The Confederates eventually withdrew to their second defensive line as the struggle for the Mule Shoe ended in a bloody stalemate. Two days of combat had cost Grant nearly 11,000 casualties; Lee's losses were closer to 10,000. There would be sporadic fighting for another week at Spotsylvania before Grant headed south in another effort to get between Lee and Richmond.[12]

What if Grant had used different tactics at Spotsylvania?

GORDON RHEA: Lee was outnumbered two-to-one at Spotsylvania Court House. Lee was fighting a defensive battle and the Union army was blinded in that Sheridan was chasing Stuart. Grant launched a series of assaults, several of which nearly broke Lee's lines, including the attack on May 12 when Grant threw his entire II Corps at the Bloody Angle, at the head of a bulge in the Confederate line, the Mule Shoe. There was a breakthrough with the VI and IX Corps as roughly 60,000 Union troops poured into the breach. There was no plan for reinforcements to exploit the breach. It was almost as if the cat had caught the mouse and then didn't know what to do with it. Lee was able to seal his line due to some confusion in the Union ranks. If the Union planners had handled the Mule Shoe differently and given more thought to exploiting a breach, that could have been the end of the Army of Northern Virginia. It was one of the closest calls in the war for Lee.

DONALD PFANZ: At Spotsylvania, Grant had plenty of troops involved in the May 12 effort to break Lee's line at the Mule Shoe. He used the II Corps and soon thereafter used the VI Corps. So there's half of his army right there. Before the end of the day, he also brought in two divisions of the V Corps. Essentially he had about 60 to 70 percent of his army in a very

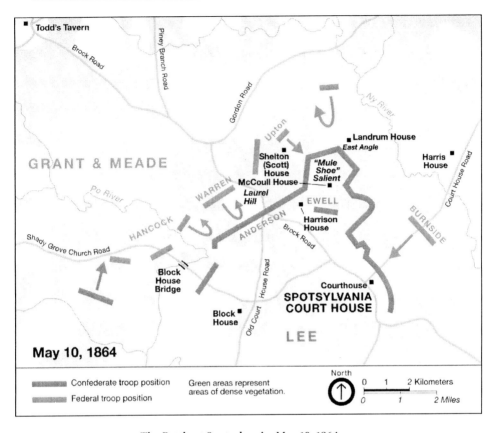

Todd's Tavern
Brock Road
Piney Branch Road
Gordon Road
Ny River
GRANT & MEADE
Upton
Landrum House
East Angle
Shelton
(Scott)
House
"Mule
Shoe"
Salient
Harris
House
Court House Road
McCoull House
Po River
WARREN
Laurel
Hill
EWELL
ANDERSON
HANCOCK
Harrison
House
Brock Road
BURNSIDE
Shady Grove Church Road
Block
House
Bridge
Old Court House Road
Courthouse
SPOTSYLVANIA
COURT HOUSE
Block
House
LEE
May 10, 1864

Confederate troop position   Green areas represent
Federal troop position   areas of dense vegetation.

North
0 1 2 Kilometers
0 1 2 Miles

The Battle at Spotsylvania, May 10, 1864

small sector. Grant actually hurt himself by having too many troops in too small an area. Only a limited number of troops could be effective in that kind of space and once you go beyond that number, troops get in each other's way and simply become targets for the enemy. At the Mule Shoe the problem wasn't having too few men, but too many.

CLINT JOHNSON: Grant had chances to do some serious damage to Lee's army at Spotsylvania, with Upton's attack, had he properly supported the assaults. Upton had an interesting idea for his attack on Lee's line at Spotsylvania. Instead of an attack on a broad front, Upton's idea was to attack on a very narrow front, much like an arrow, with a very long shank. The idea was to pierce Lee's line with a very narrow attack and spread the men out once through the enemy's line. Grant told Upton he would support the attack, but I don't think Grant really believed the plan had much chance for success so he didn't support the attack properly. Upton's attack was able to pierce Lee's line but Grant's lack of support prevented the attack from being a bigger success. Upton was left out on the field with his pants down and his men were essentially absorbed because of Grant's lack of confidence in the plan's success. Had Grant made plans to have the proper support on hand and at the key moment rushed forward the reinforcements, Lee's army at Spotsylvania would have been crushed.

Lee's Trap at North Anna

The North Anna River was the next stop for Lee and Grant after nearly two weeks of bloody combat at Spotsylvania. By May 23, Lee had a strong defensive line in place on the south bank of the North Anna, just 25 miles from Richmond. Grant decided to challenge the Confederate position and even though Hancock's troops made progress on the Union left, Warren's Corps was beaten back by A.P. Hill's men on the Confederate left. Still ailing from a recent illness, Hill failed to follow up on his success and received criticism from Lee, who himself was suffering from a severe case of diarrhea.[13]

Despite the fact that the two wings of his army could not readily reinforce each other, Grant tested Lee's lines again on May 24. After watching the Confederates repel two assaults, Grant gave up on the idea of attacking at North Anna and put his troops on the road again to maneuver around Lee's right flank.[14]

What if Lee had been able to reap more benefits from his strong defensive line at the North Anna?

GORDON RHEA: North Anna was a good chance for Lee to strike quite a blow against Grant. Some historians say it was a chance for Lee to defeat Grant's army but I wouldn't go that far. Lee had formed his army into a formation known as an inverted V. It looks something like a big A, with each wing on high ground and the apex touching the southern bank of the North Anna. When Grant crossed the river, half of his army ended up on one side of Lee's inverted V and the other half was on the other side of the wedge, so Lee had split the Union army in half. He could then hold either wing of his army with a few troops and shift men where he wanted for an offensive attack. It was an ingenious use of the ground by Lee. Lee was quite ill at the time as there was a dysentery epidemic sweeping through the army. There was really no one to replace Lee to run this complex offensive operation. Lee was not able to do it and therefore the trap wasn't sprung. Had Lee attacked, he would have damaged Grant's army badly. Union forces were strong in numbers, however, and Grant was able to reinforce his army, so I doubt Lee would have achieved an overwhelming victory.

ROBERT E. L. KRICK: Longstreet was sorely missed at the North Anna May 23 and May 24, especially on the 24th when Lee had Grant in a very awkward position and didn't have the offensive punch to take advantage of it. Lee himself was unwell at that time, and Longstreet could have taken over for Lee to lead military operations against Grant at the North Anna. Grant's army was divided into three sections at the North Anna and Lee had employed an inverted V formation with the point resting on the river. Clearly, with initiative and good leadership Lee could have concentrated his forces on one of the isolated sections. Lee might have been able to push one of the isolated segments of Grant's army into the river. I'm not sure the course of the war in Virginia would have been dramatically impacted. Grant's campaign wouldn't have been derailed because he simply wasn't the type of general to give up. Grant would have regrouped and pushed on, as he did following heavy losses at the Wilderness, Spotsylvania and Cold Harbor. On the map at least, the Confederates at the North Anna had one of their best opportunities in the east to crush a significant body of men, perhaps a third of Grant's army.

DONALD PFANZ: Lee showed his brilliance by taking a strong defensive position at the North Anna River. The ground favored the North but Lee was able to anchor his line on a high piece of ground and made an inverted V. Grant stumbled straight into the trap by crossing part of his army on one side of the V and another part on the other side. Lee then had the opportunity to potentially throw his army against a separated section of Grant's army. That plan never came to fruition as Lee, at the critical moment, fell ill and lay in his tent muttering the famous words, "we must strike them a blow, we must not let them pass us again, we must strike them a blow." At that moment, Lee was incapable of striking the blow. Remember the Union army heavily outnumbered the Army of Northern Virginia; Lee would still be looking at only even odds, more or less, if he had been able to attack one of Grant's wings by itself. If all went in Lee's favor, it's certainly possible to speculate that Lee could have destroyed a corps or two of Grant's army.

The Irreplaceable Lee

Robert E. Lee recognized the significance of Grant's spring campaign and repeatedly took extra risks to spur on his troops. When Hancock's early morning assault on May 6 sent Samuel McGowan's South Carolina brigade fleeing along the Orange Plank Road at the Wilderness, Lee emotionally ordered John Gregg's Texas brigade to drive away the Yankees.[15] Lee appeared to be ready to ride into battle with the Texans when several of the Confederates broke ranks to stop him.[16] Less than a week later at Spotsylvania, an early morning attack by the Federals overran Edward Johnson's division. Lee ordered John B. Gordon to counterattack with his division and gave every impression of leading the charge. Gordon's men gathered around

Robert E. Lee. Who could have replaced Lee as the head of the Army of Northern Virginia? LIBRARY OF CONGRESS.

Lee's horse, Traveller, and turned both horse and rider away from the danger.[17] With the Army of Northern Virginia desperately trying to fend off Grant's hammerblows, the South could ill afford to see Lee's name added to the growing list of casualties.

What if Lee had been killed, wounded or captured during the Overland Campaign?

ED BEARSS: You can see how desperate matters were becoming for the Confederates and for Lee in 1864. Once during the Wilderness and three times at Spotsylvania, Lee sought to lead charges, much as Albert Sidney Johnston did at Shiloh. If Lee had been shot or captured during these attempts to lead charges, the war would have ended much earlier than it did. By the summer and fall of 1864, it was Lee's army. The army was essentially fighting for Marse Robert.

The Army of Northern Virginia would have disintegrated much faster if Lee was killed, wounded or captured in the spring and summer of 1864. Even though Lee was best known as an aggressive, offensive leader, you could argue that as the army fell back on Richmond, Lee had his greatest days from June 15, 1864, until March 31, 1865, fighting on the defensive in and around Richmond and Petersburg.

GORDON RHEA: Lee was close to being killed or captured several times during the 1864 campaign. Lee's subordinate command structure had started to unravel. Longstreet was wounded, Ewell had started to fall apart, A.P. Hill was frequently sick and Jeb Stuart died during the Overland Campaign.[18] Lee was attempting to micro-manage his army. Lee was nearly captured by a Union breakthrough at the Wilderness on the Plank Road, and was saved in the nick of time by Longstreet's men. At Spotsylvania Court House, he tried several times to lead men into battle. There are stories of cannonballs traveling between Traveller's legs and of Lee nearly getting shot. During movements to the North Anna in the middle of May, Lee and his army unknowingly marched very close to Union encampments. Had Lee been killed or captured, it would have been a severe blow to the South. The Army of Northern Virginia would have been wrecked. Lee was a true symbol for the South. The psychological blow would have been tremendous.

As to who would have taken over for Lee, Longstreet was incapacitated, so Jeb Stuart would have been one possible choice, had he been available. He took over for Stonewall Jackson at Chancellorsville and did a very good job running the army. He had a very good sense about leading men and leading the infantry. I doubt Joe Johnston would have been brought East. Johnston had retreated in 1862 before Union forces advancing on Richmond, and I doubt Davis would have brought Johnston back to command the Army of Northern Virginia. Hood might have been an interesting choice. Some recent scholars have had more complimentary things to say about Hood's abilities as a general than earlier historians had. It's possible Hood could have brought the kind of aggressive nature needed to run the Army of Northern Virginia and kept up the Lee tradition, although Hood did not distinguish himself in command of large bodies of men. He was much more in the A.P. Hill style, good at handling a division and perhaps a corps, but not an army.

JEFF WERT: If Lee is removed, I can't see the Army of Northern Virginia being able to stay together. Who could have replaced Lee? Longstreet would have been the one to step up, but Longstreet was wounded at the Wilderness by his own troops. Longstreet was a fine defensive fighter and that was what the Confederates really needed in 1864 and 1865. He was sorely missed at Petersburg and the North Anna. He also launched some of the finest counterattacks of the entire war at Second Manassas and the Wilderness. I don't believe Longstreet, or even Stonewall Jackson, had the strategic and tactical acumen that Lee possessed or the vision that Lee had. Without Lee, Grant would have been able to place the Army of Northern Virginia in a situation where he would have inflicted serious, perhaps irreparable, damage on the Confederate army.

ROBERT E. L. KRICK: It would have been devastating to the Army of Northern Virginia to lose Lee in 1864. At least in 1862, had Lee's services been lost, Jackson and Longstreet were available. The capture of Lee at the Wilderness, combined with the injury to Longstreet and the death of Stuart May 12 following the battle at Yellow Tavern, would have placed the Confederates in an unimaginable bind in Virginia. There was no suitable replacement to lead the Army of Northern Virginia if Lee was killed, wounded or taken prisoner. It's possible that P.G.T. Beauregard would have been brought in to lead what surely would have been a demoralized Army of Northern Virginia. Even 140 years later, it is alarming to think of Beauregard dancing around Richmond, matched up against Grant. Grant would have clobbered Beauregard. Beauregard had done a fine job countering Butler at Bermuda Hundred and the trickle-down effect would have left perhaps W.H.C. Whiting commanding at Bermuda Hundred and Petersburg, a bleak prospect for the Confederates.

DONALD PFANZ: It's interesting to talk about potential replacements for Lee, had he been killed or taken prisoner, and what the impact might have been. Once Longstreet was wounded at the Wilderness, Ewell would have been the one to replace Lee, with A.P Hill following Ewell. I don't believe anyone could really adequately replace Lee or could have accomplished all that he did in the spring and summer of 1864 against Grant. In terms of strategy, administration, tactics and building morale, Lee was head and shoulders above the other Confederate generals—and the Union generals for that matter. I have a hunch that had Lee been incapacitated or captured, the Confederates would have decided to fall back to the Richmond defenses, resulting in a siege of the Confederate capital. Another possibility might have Joe Johnston returning to command the army in Lee's absence, although it's hard to picture Davis taking that action, considering how Davis and Johnston got along.

Summary

Grant's Overland Campaign took the war in the East to a whole new level. In the past, the Army of the Potomac had spent weeks recovering from major battles and commanders like McClellan and Hooker had retreated in the wake of Confederate offensives: McClellan after Gaines' Mill and Hooker after Chancellorsville. The Army of Northern Virginia had never seen the likes of Ulysses S. Grant before. Grant had proven at Shiloh that he wouldn't be fazed by enemy attacks and the unexpected; Grant had revealed at Vicksburg that he wouldn't allow temporary setbacks to deter him from his ultimate objective.

As general-in-chief, Grant could have accompanied any of the armies that were operating in Virginia in the spring of 1864. It was Jeff Wert's speculation that if Grant had not joined the Army of the Potomac, George Meade would have fallen back across the Rapidan River following the savage fighting at the Wilderness. Meanwhile, Gordon Rhea declared that a Union victory in Virginia might have actually occurred much sooner if Grant and not Ben Butler had been leading the Army of the James. Butler got bottled up at Bermuda Hundred, and both Donald Pfanz and Peter Carmichael agreed that Federal forces might have captured Richmond in 1864 if Grant had been leading the army approaching Richmond from the southeast.

As important as Grant was to the North, Robert E. Lee's presence was absolutely critical to the Army of Northern Virginia. Lee could have easily been shot or captured at the Wilderness or Spotsylvania; Ed Bearss, Gordon Rhea and Jeff Wert all concluded that a demoralized Army of Northern Virginia would have been hard pressed to oppose Grant without Lee at the helm. Who might have replaced Lee? Ewell and Beauregard were two of the names that the experts mentioned, but Lee was truly irreplaceable, as the Confederates discovered during the two days of operations along the North Anna River.

On a few occasions during the Overland Campaign, Grant came very close to crippling the Army of Northern Virginia. Perhaps his best opportunity was at Spotsylvania. Clint Johnson and Gordon Rhea claimed that Lee's army might have been wrecked if Union assaults had been carried out differently. Johnson criticized Grant for not properly supporting Emory Upton's attack on May 11; Rhea maintained that Grant should have been ready to exploit a breach of the Mule Shoe on May 12.

Grant's average daily loss, during the 40-day Overland Campaign, came to roughly 1,250 men. Under McClellan, Burnside, Hooker and even Meade, the Army of the Potomac had rested, refitted and reorganized after major battles and campaigns. That would not be the case under Ulysses S. Grant. His army would remain active and its next stop would be Petersburg.

11

Wearing Down the South: Atlanta, Petersburg and the Election of 1864

At the same time Grant was slugging it out with Lee in Virginia, the Union's new commander in the West, William Tecumseh Sherman, was focusing his attention on Atlanta, a key industrial hub with factories and arsenals that produced armaments for the Confederacy.[1] Sherman wielded plenty of resources, including James McPherson's Army of the Tennessee, George Thomas' Army of the Cumberland and a smaller unit, the Army of the Ohio, commanded by Major General John M. Schofield. All told, Sherman had 100,000 men at his disposal to confront Atlanta's guardians, Joseph Johnston and the 45,000 Confederates in the Army of Tennessee.[2]

Grant's Overland Campaign had turned into a bloodbath. Sherman tried a different tack, by employing wide flanking maneuvers to coax Johnston out of his strong defensive positions in north Georgia. On the one occasion Sherman tried to smash his way through the center of Johnston's line at Kennesaw Mountain, the Federals were beaten back with severe losses.[3] By the middle of July, however, Sherman's men had crossed the Chattahoochee River and were closing in on Atlanta. It was time for a change. Confederate leaders replaced Joseph Johnston, naming John Bell Hood the new commander of the Army of Tennessee.

Johnston and Hood were as different as night and day. Whereas Johnston rarely initiated combat, the always-aggressive Hood had never shied away from pitching into an opponent in the past. Now the leader of an entire army, Hood wasted little time in attacking the Federals, striking Thomas on July 20 at Peachtree Creek and McPherson two days later in the Battle of Atlanta. Hood's tactics produced plenty of casualties but his army made little headway and Union soldiers remained dangerously close to Atlanta.

Rather than storm the city or attack Hood's army, Sherman shifted his focus to severing Atlanta's connections with the outside world by cutting the Macon and Western line, the last rail line into the city not under Union control. Hood desperately tried to hold onto his last supply line by attacking at Ezra Church and Jonesboro; when those assaults proved unsuccessful, the Confederates evacuated Atlanta. On September 3, Sherman was finally able to inform his superiors in Washington that he had captured the city.[4]

In the East, Ulysses Grant's new target was the strategically important city of Petersburg. Most of the railroads that connected Richmond with the rest of the Confederacy came through Petersburg; the loss of the city could mean the loss of Richmond. Major General William F. Smith led advance elements of the Army of the Potomac to Petersburg on June 15, but Smith's chance to lay claim to a potential quick and easy victory was lost when he hesitated before the city's tiny Confederate garrison. Grant would have to lay siege to Petersburg.

Atlanta had been lost and Petersburg was now surrounded. The fall of 1864 brought even more bad news for the South, this time in the political arena, as Abraham Lincoln soundly trounced his Democratic opponent George McClellan in the presidential election of 1864. Lincoln's convincing victory at the polls guaranteed that the war would be won or lost on the battlefield.

Outmaneuvering Johnston

To get to Atlanta, Sherman first had to deal with Joseph Johnston's imposing defensive fortifications near Dalton and Rocky Face Ridge in northwestern Georgia. The rugged terrain was a natural fortress, a fact that Sherman knew all too well from having surveyed the area 20 years earlier as a young lieutenant.[5]

Rather than directly approaching the Army of Tennessee's lines, Sherman sent James McPherson and 24,000 men south and then east through Snake Creek Gap to smash the railroad depot at Resaca, 15 miles in the rear of Johnston's army. All that stood between the Federals and Resaca on

William T. Sherman, who outmaneuvered Johnston and outfought Hood. LIBRARY
OF CONGRESS.

May 9 was Lieutenant General Leonidas Polk's 4,000-man division. McPherson grew cautious, greatly overestimated the size of his opponent and
decided to delay his attack until the following day.[6] McPherson's decision
was a godsend to the Confederates. The delay gave Johnston time to rush
reinforcements to Polk; Johnston would eventually move his entire army

to Resaca. Although the Confederates had been forced to give up excellent ground at Dalton, McPherson had missed a golden opportunity at Resaca.

What if Sherman had been able to take Resaca in Johnston's rear?

LARRY DANIEL: Even if Sherman had been able to spring his trap successfully at Resaca, I don't that would have necessarily resulted in the destruction of the Army of Tennessee. Johnston would have been able to move his army off to the east in the mountains of Georgia. That would have placed Johnston's army in a rather embarrassing position in terms of supplies, but Johnston would have been able to slide around Chattanooga and go back into middle Tennessee again. Had Sherman taken Resaca and held a commanding position south of Johnston, I don't think that would have resulted in the destruction of the Army of Tennessee.

RICHARD MCMURRY: Johnston had prepared some elaborate fortifications around Dalton in northwestern Georgia and then left totally unguarded a crucial gap through the mountains 15 miles to the southwest. Sherman marched through the gap forcing Johnston to give up his lines at Dalton. Thomas told Sherman he wanted to take 40,000 or 50,000 men through the gap, to trap Johnston's army to the north. Sherman sent McPherson instead. McPherson went through the gap with just 8,000 men, not enough to do the job. Consequently, McPherson was uncertain when he realized that Johnston could assemble superior numbers, using the railroad, to attack McPherson while he was isolated. McPherson probably didn't have 8,000 when he got that far. Sherman didn't send enough cavalry with McPherson. Sherman had his own army spread out on an arc that was about 25 miles from end to end. Johnston was in the middle in impregnable fortifications, behind a mountain that could not be attacked. He had a railroad to move troops from one of his line to the other. If an enemy army got in that kind of situation in front of Lee or Grant, I could see either one of those two commanders striking the enemy at one end or the other, using the railroad to assemble superior numbers at the point of attack. In numerous places where Johnston received word that Sherman had a flanking column in motion, he simply fell back.

Johnston or Hood

McPherson's hesitation at Resaca forced Sherman to take another shot at outflanking the Army of Tennessee; Johnston's response was to withdraw

south along the Western and Atlantic Railroad, vacating Cassville and Alla-
toona Pass in order to block Sherman at New Hope Church on May 25.
Beginning to lose patience with how events were unfolding, a frustrated
Sherman called for an assault on Johnston's lines on the slopes of Kenne-
saw Mountain on June 27 and received 3,000 casualties for his trouble.[7]
Sherman would not make that mistake again. His men resumed their efforts
to outflank Johnston and on July 8 the Federals crossed the Chattahoochee
River, approximately 10 miles northwest of Atlanta.

Jefferson Davis decided it was time for a change. When Johnston
informed Davis that his plans for future operations would hinge on Sherman, the hard-hitting John Bell Hood was named the new commander of
the Army of Tennessee.[8] Hood immediately went on the offensive, assaulting Thomas' Army of the Cumberland on July 20 at Peachtree Creek. Two
days later, Hood struck the Union left wing under McPherson in the Battle of Atlanta. Although the fighting claimed the life of James McPherson,
Hood's men suffered horrendous casualties and were unable to push Sherman away from Atlanta.

Sherman's new priority became the last Confederate supply line leading into the city. McPherson's replacement, O.O. Howard, marched the
Army of the Tennessee west and then south to cut the Macon and Western Railroad; when Hood attempted to contest the Union advance on July
28 at Ezra Church, his men were slaughtered. In just nine days as the commander of the Army of Tennessee, Hood had lost 20,000 men.[9]

Sherman now sought to rupture the Macon and Western line once
and for all by targeting Jonesboro, 20 miles south of Atlanta. Hood was
out of options. To avoid being trapped in Atlanta without supplies, the
Confederates evacuated the city on September 1.[10] Sherman's troops entered
Atlanta the following day, depriving the Confederacy of a vital rail hub
and all but guaranteeing Lincoln's reelection.[11]

What if Johnston had commanded the Atlanta
Campaign from start to finish?

JEFF SHAARA: Atlanta was a key rail hub that was critical to supplying
nearly all of the Confederate armies in 1864. Sherman understood that if
you take Atlanta, you're essentially taking a knife and stabbing the Confederacy in the heart. The decision by Jefferson Davis to replace Joe Johnston with Hood hurt the Confederacy. In many ways, Hood lost Atlanta
more than Sherman won it. Hood overestimated the capabilities of his
own army and vastly underestimated Sherman's army. Hood proceeded
to beat up his army by attacking Sherman. Had Johnston been left in

Joseph Johnston. Should Davis have kept Johnston in command throughout the Atlanta Campaign? LIBRARY OF CONGRESS.

command, he might have been able to delay the capture of Atlanta. A lot of people will joke and say Johnston loved to retreat and would have continued to retreat south all the way to Cuba. Johnston was a fairly good defensive strategist and he, like Longstreet, understood the value of being on the defensive. Perhaps the man who could have saved Atlanta was lost two years earlier at Shiloh. Albert Sidney Johnston was probably the most capable Confederate general outside of Robert E. Lee. Had Johnston survived Shiloh, the war in the West might have been very different.

KENNETH NOE: I used to argue that keeping Johnston in command from start to finish at Atlanta would have helped the Confederates—that Johnston would have been able to hold onto Atlanta at least until the November presidential election. That might have had an effect on the political situation in the North. I don't know if Lincoln would have lost, but it certainly would have left the Republicans weaker than they were. The more I've studied Johnston, the more I suspect that Johnston at some point would have abandoned Atlanta and moved south. Johnston had been talking about falling back toward Macon. Even had he done that, at least Johnston would have kept his army intact. You wouldn't have had the tremendous casualties the army suffered under Hood in the various battles around Atlanta. The Army of Tennessee would have been a much more effective fighting force. Yet it's also important to note that some say Johnston was starting to lose the support of his enlisted men. We usually think Johnston was the popular commander and Hood was unpopular. In fact, a lot of men were starting to get annoyed with Johnston because he had retreated all the way from Dalton and really had not tried aggressively to stop Sherman at any point along the way. Davis always felt the Confederates would have been in a much better situation if Johnston had fought Sherman in northwestern Georgia.

CRAIG SYMONDS: The South's last opportunity to avoid total defeat was in the fall of 1864; the re-election of Lincoln was the death knell of the Confederacy. Lincoln was committed to a strategy of national union, and as long as he remained in office, the South had no hope of initiating any serious negotiations that might lead to a compromise. It is not certain that President McClellan would have opened negotiations in spite of the platform on which he ran, but he was nevertheless the South's best hope. Lincoln might well have won the election of 1864 even without the capture of Atlanta, but that achievement certainly influenced the final vote tally and gave Lincoln the mandate he wanted. Atlanta's fall proved that the administration's policy was making progress.

If the fall of Atlanta was so crucial, it begs the question: Was there some way the Confederacy could have delayed that event until after the election? The key player in this question is Joe Johnston. Some argue that if Johnston had not been fired in mid-July, he might at least have postponed Atlanta's fall, perhaps until after the election. Others argue that Atlanta fell when it did because Johnston had given up so much ground from Dalton to the Chattahoochee, leaving Hood with no viable option but to attack. So, which strategy was better: Johnston's or Hood's? Quite possibly, a deliberate strategy of delay that was supported by the administration would have worked. Or an offensive strategy employed from the outset by a commander who embraced it might have kept Sherman from Atlanta's door. What is clear is that the combination of Johnston's defensive strategy and Hood's offensive one was a dramatically unsuccessful combination for the South. Johnston should have been replaced sooner once it was clear that he and Davis had different strategic views, or else Davis should have stayed with him to the end. There is no certainty that either one would have been better, but either hardly could have been worse than switching desperately from one to the other.

ED BEARSS: I'm not sure it would have made any difference for the South if Davis had stuck with Joe Johnston all the way through or had gone to Hood from the start. The only thing that could have saved Atlanta for the Confederacy was having a duplicate of Robert E. Lee. Lee knew the value of being on the defensive but he also took advantage of Union mistakes by launching counterattacks constantly. Even in 1864, we saw Lee on the defensive at Wilderness and Spotsylvania but in both battles he launched counterattacks against Grant. Johnston never counterattacked. He lacked the self-confidence needed to go on the offensive, always looking to his rear, wondering if Davis was going to support him. Hood was the exact opposite. He was too reckless. The only person the Confederates had who could have saved Atlanta from falling was Robert E. Lee.

Opportunity at Petersburg

Just as Atlanta was an important rail hub for the Confederates to defend in the West, Petersburg served as the crucial rail junction for Lee's army in the East. Richmond was linked to the rest of the South by several railroads running through Petersburg, including the South Side Railroad from Lynchburg, the Weldon Railroad from North Carolina and the Norfolk and Petersburg line from the southeast.[12] Grant recognized that the loss of Petersburg could shorten the war by forcing Lee to abandon Richmond.

Approximately 16,000 Federals in three infantry divisions, under the command of General William F. "Baldy" Smith, approached Petersburg on June 15. Opposed by just 2,500 Confederates led by General P.G.T. Beauregard, Smith cautiously delayed his attack several hours to scout Petersburg's defenses and then brought offensive operations to a halt after capturing only a section of Beauregard's lines.[13] By the next morning, Beauregard had been reinforced; two days later, Lee brought the Army of Northern Virginia to Petersburg.[14] Grant would be forced to settle for a long and grueling siege.

What if Smith had gone after Petersburg more aggressively on June 15?

P.G.T. Beauregard. Beauregard's small force deterred Baldy Smith at Petersburg. VIRGINIA MILITARY INSTITUTE ARCHIVES.

ROBERT E. L. KRICK: The Army of the Potomac missed several opportunities at Petersburg. The first one was when Baldy Smith had a chance to take the city. It probably is fair to say that more aggressiveness by Smith during the opening phases of the campaign might have yielded war-winning rewards. Knowing what we do about the state of Confederate defenses and defenders, it is easy to view this as a squandered opportunity. As with so many other actions during the war, we have to be careful to balance hindsight with fair appraisal. Smith probably did not fail any worse than many others before and after, but given the potential for a sweeping triumph at Petersburg and remembering the 10 months that followed, his botched opportunity seems all the worse. You have to take into account how tired the Union soldiers were from the constant fighting. In hindsight, Smith should have taken the initiative and made a stronger push for the city. A really determined drive probably would have toppled the Petersburg defenses and the loss of Petersburg could have shortened the war considerably.

CHRIS CALKINS: Critics of Civil War commanders often fall into the trap of Monday morning quarterbacking, namely using information that the commanders lacked on the battlefield. Union General Baldy Smith led the initial assault on Petersburg June 15 with about 15,000 men. The Confederates defending the city were led by P.G.T. Beauregard who had a small force of 2,500 under the command of former Virginia governor General Henry A. Wise. They were behind earthworks and the Confederate position, featuring forts, batteries and connecting trenches, was a well-fortified position. Smith's men had seen their share of fighting and marching in the weeks immediately before Petersburg. They had learned an important lesson at Cold Harbor and that was assaulting a well entrenched enemy, behind earthworks, wasn't the smartest thing a soldier could do. One man behind earthworks could hold back three times his number.

When Smith and his men arrived at Petersburg, Smith made a few tactical errors. He spent precious time personally reconnoitering the position. Smith also wanted to bring up the artillery, but his artillery officers had taken the horses off the limbers to water them, so it was going to take time to get them hitched up again and move the artillery into position. It was late in the evening by the time the artillery was in position and Smith was ready to assault the Confederate line. Smith's men were supposed to be supported by members of Hancock's II Corps but Hancock's men didn't arrive until late in the evening. Smith's assault captured about a mile and a half of the Confederate entrenchments. It was a moonlit night but instead of trying to continue the advance into Petersburg, Smith decided to halt and await Hancock's arrival.

If Smith had captured Petersburg, it's debatable whether Lee would have retreated and given up Richmond. Lee was near Cold Harbor June 15 and was still under orders from Jefferson Davis. Richmond was Davis' top priority and the city had a formidable line of inner and outer earthworks. Had Smith captured Petersburg, Lee would have been ordered to fall into the trenches around Richmond and we would have had the siege of Richmond rather than the siege of Petersburg. Grant had targeted Petersburg because four rail lines entered Petersburg and were then funneled into one line leading north to Richmond. The two most important lines were the Weldon Railroad and the South Side Railroad. The Weldon brought in goods from the Deep South and the South Side connected Petersburg with Lynchburg. So if the Union army captured Petersburg and cut off rail traffic

leading into Richmond, the Confederates would have been facing a serious supply problem.

The Crater

To break the Petersburg siege, Grant turned to a unique and risky plan
that called for a regiment of Pennsylvania coal miners to plant 320 kegs
of black powder in a 500-foot tunnel that would be dug under a section
of the Confederate fortifications.[15] Once the mine was detonated, a division of black soldiers from Burnside's Corps would lead an infantry assault
against Lee's lines as regiments fanned out to the left and right of the
resulting crater to overwhelm the confused Confederates. Last minute
changes derailed the plan's execution. George Meade ordered white troops
to spearhead the assault rather than the black soldiers, and command of
the attack fell to Brigadier General James Ledlie.

Shortly before dawn on July 30, the mine was exploded. The result
was stunning: a huge gap in the Confederate entrenchments, a gigantic
hole estimated to be some 200 feet long, 50 feet wide and perhaps 30 feet
deep in the middle.[16] Problems quickly developed for the white soldiers
involved in the initial charge. Improperly briefed and confused by the
cloud of dust and dirt produced by the explosion, the men attacked into
the chasm rather than going around it and the attack soon bogged down,
giving the Confederate defenders time to gather themselves and successfully counterattack.[17] Union losses from the Battle of the Crater amounted
to 3,500 and Grant later admitted that his army had missed an opportunity to seize Petersburg.[18]

What if Union troops had gone around the Crater
in making their attack on July 30?

CHRIS CALKINS: The Union army's objective was to reach the high ground
called Cemetery Hill overlooking Petersburg. Had the Federals taken that
ground, they could have rained artillery fire on Petersburg and eventually
captured the city. They could have destroyed the rail bridge over the Appomattox River, which was the line that the Confederates used to carry supplies to Richmond. Some say if the colored troops had been allowed to
make the initial assault following the explosion, the assault would have
been successful. Some will also tell you that the war would have come to
an end nine months earlier than it did. There was a second Confederate
line behind the Crater called the Trench Cavalier. It had been built before

the explosion because the Confederates had suspicions that the Union army was tunneling beneath them. Due to the explosion, the exit from the crater was very steep and abrupt so as the Union soldiers went into the crater, rather than around it, they couldn't get out of it easily enough to continue the assault. So if the advancing Union troops had gone around the crater rather than into it, they could have taken advantage of the initial chaos in the Confederate line until Lee was able to arrive on the scene to order Mahone's men to counterattack. There was enough time between the explosion of the mine and the Confederate counterattack for the Union assault troops to win the battle. If the Union soldiers were successful at the Crater and had captured Petersburg, Lee's army would likely have been forced to move into the Richmond entrenchments, leading to a Union siege of Richmond.

MATT ATKINSON: The original Union battle plan called for the troops to circumvent the crater. The United States Colored Troops who were scheduled to make the attack were removed at the last minute, however, due to political considerations. In their place, white troops were slated to make the assault. These white troops had not been instructed to bypass the crater; as a result, they piled into the crater to escape the storm of iron being hurled at them.

Later in the day, when the assault faltered, the original black units were ordered to reinforce the crater area. To their credit, they bypassed the crater as instructed. Unfortunately, these units were too little, too late. The Confederates had recovered from their initial surprise and were quick to counterattack these Union reinforcements. If the United States Colored Troops had not been removed from the initial assault, the breach held by the Union troops would have been much wider.

ROBERT E. L. KRICK: The constant talk about the influence of the Crater itself on maneuvers during the Battle of the Crater is greatly exaggerated. It is more accurate to attribute that day's Union failure to the lack of tactical foresight by the Union commanders, and the fairly comprehensive response by the Confederates. The infantry that swarmed through the breach in the Confederate lines was not prepared to consolidate the immediate victory. Had they been well in hand, they would have turned either north or south, in a body, and widened the breach to such a degree that the Confederates would have labored mightily to plug it. Crowding into the crater itself made the Confederates' job easier, but the men who avoided the crater failed to expand the breakthrough and instead stood around waiting to be driven off. Furthermore, the Union high command failed to exert the necessary pressure elsewhere along the line to pin down

Confederate resources and prevent them from reinforcing the lines on the shoulder of the breakthrough. Likewise, the Confederate counterattacks were well managed, with excellent collaborative work by a half-dozen officers. Southern artillery also excelled in this fight.

Raid on Washington

Union military leaders must have had nightmares about Virginia's Shenandoah Valley. Stonewall Jackson had used the strategically fertile region in 1862 to tie up Federal troops that otherwise would have added their weight to McClellan's campaign against Richmond. In the spring of 1864, Grant had been hoping that a successful Union foray through the Valley would strengthen his campaign against Lee, but Grant's plans were temporarily sidetracked by Franz Sigel's loss at New Market on May 15.[19]

Sigel's replacement, Major General David Hunter, had better luck, at least initially, when he defeated a Confederate force at Piedmont, captured Staunton and then wreaked havoc in Lexington by burning the Virginia Military Institute on June 12. Robert E. Lee was forced to detach Jubal Early and 14,000 men from the Army of Northern Virginia, and that force wound up whipping Hunter at Lynchburg on June 18. Instead of retreating down the Shenandoah Valley toward Washington, Hunter chose to flee in the direction of West Virginia; the Valley was now open to Jubal Early and would once more become a Confederate invasion corridor aimed at the Union capital.

Driving north down the Valley, Early crossed into Maryland but had his timetable for reaching Washington momentarily delayed on July 9 by a small Union force guarding the Monocacy River crossing.[20] Two days later, Early's men were close enough to see Fort Stevens, at the northern edge of Washington's fortifications, and beyond it the dome of the U.S. Capitol.[21] With reinforcements from the Army of the Potomac filing into the Washington defensive lines, Early's hopes for entering the Union capital were dashed and he would soon be forced to fall back into Virginia.

What if Early had been able to temporarily enter Washington? What if Sigel or Hunter had been more successful in their campaigns in the Valley in the spring of 1864?

ED BEARSS: If Early had not been delayed at Monocacy, he might have been able to break into Washington. If Early had made it into the city, if only for a short time, it would have been much worse than it was when the British raided and burned the nation's capital in 1814. The Treasury Department alone employed about 5,000 people. If Early got into Washington, he wouldn't have been able to stay and hold the city but Early would have forced Lincoln to evacuate the capital. Even if Early didn't burn any buildings, he would have caused more consternation than the British did 50 years earlier. Undoubtedly, it would have also resulted in Lincoln writing an even stronger memo than he did, when he wrote while the Democrats were convening in Cincinnati for their national nominating convention in the fourth week in August. During the Democratic convention, Lincoln had written a memo that essentially stated that he was going to lose the election, based on the Union's current position in the war. Lincoln also stated that if he lost the election, the Democrat who won the election would have won under conditions that would not allow him to preserve the Union upon taking office. Lincoln further said in the memo that he would cooperate with the president-elect to try to save the Union by March 4. That indicates to me that by the fourth week in August, Lincoln felt his loss in the election was a possibility. If Early had raided Washington but was unable to stay in the city, the rest of his campaign likely would have played out as it did in 1864 with his eventual rout at Cedar Creek.[22] Combine that with the loss of Atlanta, and McClellan still would have lost the election of 1864.

JOHN HEATWOLE: The Valley Campaign of 1864 could have gone in several different directions. Had Franz Sigel won at New Market in May, Lee would have released Jubal Early and his Second Corps earlier than he did. Staunton would have fallen by May 17. The Federals would have destroyed Confederate supplies and warehouses and would have torn up the tracks of the Virginia Central Railroad as far as Waynesboro. When Sigel made contact with the regrouping Confederates, he would have started to doubt himself and would have withdrawn back down the Valley. Basically, Sigel would have thought he had done enough.

If Jubal Early had not been detached when he was to deal with Union General David Hunter at Lynchburg, Hunter would have faced only John C. Breckinridge at Lynchburg. Hunter had his limitations, the worst of which was a mercurial disposition that sometimes clouded his judgment. The thing that could have brought him victory at Lynchburg was that he was aggressive. A victory by Hunter over Breckinridge would most certainly have resulted in Lee's release of Early, and eventually Hunter would have been crushed or would have withdrawn as he did in reality. Hunter could have retreated back down the Shenandoah Valley, but only if he had been rested and resupplied. He also needed reliable scouting reports that he would not be flanked from the gaps in the Valley, such as Rockfish, Browns, Swift Run and Thorntons. Without these, Hunter would have run to the closest territory in Federal hands, directly into West Virginia. If Hunter had been able to retreat down the Valley, he might have delayed Jubal Early and there probably would not have been a Confederate move on Washington. Rear guard actions by Hunter against Early would have left more time for the Union VI Corps to secure the Washington line, or to move into the Valley to challenge Early.

Lincoln or McClellan?

A crucial political battle in the fall of 1864 would help to decide the fate of the Union war effort. Republican Abraham Lincoln and a familiar challenger, Democrat George McClellan, were vying for possession of the White House in a presidential election that would also serve as a referendum on the issue of whether the war should continue. The Copperhead wing of the Democratic Party had put together a platform that declared that the war was a failure and called for reunification based on the state of affairs before 1861.[23] With no apparent military victory in sight, Lincoln questioned whether he would be re-elected and expressed concerns that a McClellan victory would make it impossible for the North to win the war.[24]

Some Union soldiers were sent home to vote; others cast absentee ballots from their military camps. In the end, it was no contest. Lincoln received 78 percent of the soldier vote and beat McClellan by more than 400,000 votes overall, with an electoral advantage of 212–21.[25] Northern voters had sent a clear message of their determination to wage the war to a successful conclusion.[26]

What if McClellan had won the election of 1864?

GORDON RHEA: If Grant and Sherman had not been so successful, it's quite possible that McClellan would have defeated Lincoln in the election. Commanders on both sides were aware how crucial the spring and summer campaigns would be to the election. Editorials in newspapers recognized the importance: one in an Atlanta newspaper said bullets on the battlefields would be the balance in the 1864 election, that if the Confederates could win victories on the battlefields in 1864, Lincoln would not be re-elected. Lincoln himself was unsure whether he'd win. What won him the election were the fall of Atlanta and Grant's moves against Lee. There were no major victories and it was bloody, but Grant's campaign overall seemed to show the Union was making progress towards ending the war. The campaign blunted the offensive force of Lee's army.

The South was very interested in negotiating a peace. Had McClellan been elected, there would have been a major political offensive by the South to negotiate a peace. The South could not win by force of arms but it could wear down the Union and break down the North's will to fight. By the spring of 1864, the North certainly was war weary. Had there been major Confederate victories on battlefields, McClellan would have looked very attractive to voters and a negotiated peace was a realistic possibility.

PETER CARMICHAEL: There was not one great turning point of the war, not Gettysburg and not Vicksburg. People usually point to Gettysburg and Vicksburg as the war's major turning points and they believe from that point on the South could not win. In fact, the summer of 1864 marked the low point of northern morale. Both Grant's campaign in Virginia in 1864 and Sherman's campaign in Georgia had stalled, and frustration with the war effort had reached an all time high in the North. Lincoln had fears he wouldn't be re-elected. Had McClellan been able to win the 1864 election, it's difficult to say what might have happened to the northern war effort. There was actually a contradiction between the Democratic platform and what McClellan was offering in 1864. The Democratic platform called for an immediate armistice and it's hard to imagine that the war would have resumed following the armistice. McClellan was opposed to an armistice but he did favor some type of settlement. McClellan might have decided to concede slavery's existence if the South rejoined the Union. Jefferson Davis and his associates in Richmond, at this stage in the war, wanted independence at any cost. There were some in the South that would have preferred to settle and rejoin the Union with their slaves, but to many Southerners the idea of reunification, even with their slaves, was unthinkable. The brutality and destructiveness of the war turned many Southerners, who initially may have been ambivalent about the Confederacy, into hardened, loyal Confederates and rabid Union-haters.

DONALD PFANZ: Looking back, it appears that Lincoln's prospects for being re-elected were actually much more positive than it must have appeared at the time. Lincoln had written out a game plan for the Union war effort in case he lost to McClellan. The plan was to throw everything but the kitchen sink at the South in hopes of gaining victory before McClellan took office. Lincoln figured even the Democrats wouldn't sue for peace if they saw that victory was right around the corner. Lincoln's overwhelming victory in the election shows that perhaps Lincoln feared losing to McClellan for no good reason.

Had McClellan somehow won the election, it would have been interesting to see what action he would have taken. The Democrats were seeking an immediate negotiated peace although McClellan did not go quite that far. It's certainly possible McClellan might have agreed to a deal whereby the South returned to the Union while keeping their slaves. McClellan would have been interested in some sort of compromise with the South. Naturally, any compromise would have required the approval of the Congress, and McClellan would have had a tough time selling those kinds of deals to the Radical Republicans.

CRAIG SYMONDS: The platform on which McClellan ran called for the opening of negotiations that would lead to an end to the war. McClellan repudiated the platform, but he would have been under great pressure at least to open talks. Conceivably, those talks would have been preceded by an armistice. Once the shooting stopped, it would be politically difficult to start it up again. So it is at least possible that a McClellan victory would have changed the outcome of the war. On the other hand, by the time McClellan would have taken office (March 4, 1865) the war was virtually over, so that even the Copperheads might have appreciated that stopping to open negotiations would have been foolish. The more important consequence of a McClellan presidency would have been his lack of sympathy for the freedmen. But in that regard he was not any worse than Andrew Johnson.

Summary

The North's strategy in 1864 was simple: create unrelenting pressure on the main Confederate armies and eliminate two of the South's most important rail hubs. The Confederates fought desperately in defense of Petersburg and Atlanta but by the end of the year, Atlanta was gone, Petersburg was encircled, and with the re-election of Lincoln, the Confederacy's life expectancy could be numbered in months.

In the West, Sherman outmaneuvered Johnston and out-generaled Hood in the spring and summer of 1864. Who was the best choice to lead the Confederate defense of Atlanta? Jeff Shaara said Joe Johnston should have remained in command of the Army of Tennessee, although Kenneth Noe claimed that Johnston would have eventually abandoned Atlanta. According to Craig Symonds, Jefferson Davis made a mistake changing horses in mid-stream and should have either released Johnston sooner or retained him throughout the campaign. Ed Bearss aptly summarized the South's plight when he remarked that the Army of Tennessee needed a duplicate of Robert E. Lee.

Sherman had electrified the North with his victory at Atlanta. Grant, however, was forced to rely on a long and perhaps unnecessary siege at Petersburg. Robert E. L. Krick believed that Union general Baldy Smith could have overcome Beauregard's small defensive force and taken the city, obviating the need for a long siege and possibly shortening the war. Would the loss of Petersburg have spelled immediate disaster for the Confederates? Lee certainly could have retreated to Richmond but as Chris Calkins pointed out, the Confederates would have had a tough time receiving supplies if Grant had been in control of Petersburg.

In the spring of 1864, the South's watchword may have been stalemate. Most of the experts agreed, however, that the capture of Atlanta and Grant's tenacity in Virginia had improved Lincoln's re-election odds by the fall. If Lincoln had wound up losing the 1864 election, what action would McClellan have taken? Donald Pfanz and Peter Carmichael speculated that McClellan might have sought a settlement with the Confederacy that could have allowed the South to return to the Union with slavery intact. Pfanz was also quick to point out that, even as a lame duck president, Lincoln would have been able to accelerate the Union war effort even more than he actually did, to close out the Confederacy before McClellan assumed office in March of 1865.

Without question, by November of 1864 the handwriting was on the wall. Grant was grinding down the Army of Northern Virginia, Sherman was ready to devastate Georgia and Lincoln was assured of a second term in office. The outcome appeared certain. All that remained to be seen was how long the Confederacy could last and what a reunited country might look like.

12

A Just and
Lasting Peace:
Appomattox and
Assassination

As 1864 drew to a close, Grant's plan to apply relentless pressure to the main Southern armies had the Confederacy on the ropes. In the East, Lee's men were starving in the trenches of Petersburg; in the West, the misused and abused Army of Tennessee was still trying to recover from John Bell Hood's ill-advised attacks on Sherman's army in front of Atlanta.

The loss of Atlanta left Hood and the Army of Tennessee in desperate straits. Hood's solution was to lure Sherman out of Georgia by moving northward, in an effort to cut Federal supply lines. A frustrated Sherman pursued for a few months and then proposed a bold move. Thomas and Schofield would confront Hood in Tennessee while Sherman marched 300 miles from Atlanta to the coast, devastating the Confederacy's heartland and making Georgia howl.[1]Sherman's plan worked to perfection. At the same time his men sliced a 60-mile swath through Georgia, on a march aimed at crushing the spirit of the Confederacy, Hood's demoralized Army of Tennessee virtually ceased to exist as a legitimate fighting force after suffering disastrous defeats at Franklin and Nashville in November and December.[2]

Union fortunes in the East had never looked brighter as spring arrived in 1865. Grant's campaign against Petersburg was nearly nine months old when Robert E. Lee met with Jefferson Davis in late March to inform the Confederate president that Richmond and Petersburg were doomed. Lee's only viable option would be to take his starving, exhausted army into North Carolina to join forces with Joseph Johnston's small army.[3] Richmond and Petersburg were evacuated in early April and the Army of Northern Virginia marched westward, hoping to stay one step ahead of the Army of the Potomac. Hampered by a lack of rations, the weary Confederate column became strung out and an isolated segment fell prey to Federal forces at Sailor's Creek on April 6, with 6,000 Confederates taken prisoner.[4]

His men starving and surrounded by Union troops, Lee asked Grant for a suspension of hostilities to discuss surrender terms. The surrender document was signed on April 9 at Appomattox Court House; three days later, Lee's men stacked their muskets, laid down their flags and the Army of Northern Virginia passed into eternity.

More than 360,000 Union soldiers and approximately 258,000 Confederates had lost their lives during the Civil War.[5] Another victim would be added to the casualty list on April 14, when John Wilkes Booth assassinated Abraham Lincoln while Lincoln and his wife attended a play in Washington. Lincoln had promised to pursue a just and lasting peace but his replacement, Andrew Johnson, would incur the wrath of the Radical Republicans by supporting the gentler approach to reconstruction that Lincoln had favored.[6] It would be Johnson who would escape conviction on impeachment charges by a single vote in the Senate. It would be the reunited South that would suffer through the agony of Reconstruction.

Hood's Folly

With Atlanta now in Union hands, both Hood and Sherman attempted to carry out novel strategies in the final few months of 1864. Sherman had his men ravage the Georgia countryside, destroying railroad tracks, mills and Confederate morale. Meanwhile, Hood's grandiose plan called for the Army of Tennessee to defeat George Thomas' army, seize Nashville and force Sherman to give up his operations in Georgia to deal with a victorious Confederate army in Tennessee.[7] If Sherman failed to pursue, Hood proposed to take his army into Virginia and join with Lee against Grant. Sherman's plans worked to perfection. Jefferson Davis labeled Hood's idea ill-advised; events would prove him correct.[8]

Hood's tattered army ran into Schofield's 30,000 troops on November 27 at Spring Hill but the Federals slipped away at night and proceeded to prepare a strong defensive position at Franklin, 15 miles south of Nashville. Hood's men arrived on November 30, charged the Federal lines and were pushed back over the Union barricades. By the end of the day, Hood had collected 7,000 casualties and six Confederate generals had lost their lives. Despite the debacle, Hood wasn't finished yet. He marched his army to Nashville on December 15, only to be battered for two days by Thomas' 50,000 troops, thus eliminating the threat of the Army of Tennessee.[9] Five days later, Sherman entered Savannah, Georgia, and prepared for another march, this time into the Carolinas.

What if Hood had focused on Sherman rather than moving into Tennessee in late 1864?

RICHARD MCMURRY: If Joe Johnston were still in command of the Army of Tennessee after giving up Atlanta, Johnston probably would have retreated toward Augusta. The area below Atlanta was far less suitable than the area north of Atlanta for a small army to operate against a larger army. North of Atlanta, there are hills and mountains, and small armies can dodge around. South of Atlanta, the ground levels out and about 60 miles south of Atlanta the coastal plain is almost totally flat. I can't see Johnston doing anything but retreating in the face of Sherman's army, probably to the east toward Augusta rather than southeast toward Savannah. The place to defend Atlanta was north Georgia. Johnston would have retreated as Sherman advanced. Retreating toward Augusta and then to Columbia, South Carolina, was the direction to take to stay between Sherman and Lee's army in Virginia. Johnston might have been thinking about getting close enough to Lee that Lee might be able to send him reinforcements or vice versa. That kind of retreat would have been a logistical disaster for the Confederates. By 1864, the Confederacy's main sources of agricultural supplies were Mississippi, Alabama and Georgia, and to give up those states was fatal to the Confederacy. Selma was an industrial center that by 1864 rivaled Richmond, and Johnston would have given all of that up. Once the Confederates got south even of the Chattahoochee River, it was a logistical and political disaster for the South. Johnston bears primary responsibility for that.

KENNETH NOE: Sherman, when he discovered that Hood was moving north into Tennessee rather than pursuing Sherman, said that he would supply Hood with rations if he went all the way to Ohio. Sherman wanted Hood out of the way so he could march across Georgia. Thomas had enough men in Tennessee to handle Hood. Franklin and Nashville were unnecessary battles from the Confederates' standpoint. I suppose Hood felt he had to fight somewhere but those weren't the places to do it. Hood didn't have the numbers and he didn't have the supplies. The attack at Franklin was totally unnecessary. Some historians say Hood's best chance was at Spring Hill. If the Confederates had blocked that road and stopped Schofield from coming up the road, Hood might have won a significant victory south of Franklin. Yet the Confederates couldn't stop Schofield due to their exhaustion, low morale and the lack of supplies. The Army of Tennessee essentially let Schofield march right by them. When Schofield got past the Army of Tennessee, the fight at Franklin became a terribly bad idea. Pickett's Charge was a fight across a mile of open ground. The Confederate attack at Franklin was a charge across two miles of open ground down into a well-defended position. The Confederates would have been better off trying to flank their way around Franklin.

JOHN SIMON: There's been endless speculation about who would have made the best replacement as the Confederacy's top commander in the West after Albert Sidney Johnston fell at Shiloh. One of the problems was Jefferson Davis' persistent quarrel with Joe Johnston and Pierre Beauregard. Joe Johnston was one of the better Confederate generals. He had a better grasp of what the Confederates needed to do to win. Johnston conducted a brilliant campaign in 1864 defending Atlanta. He's the man who should have been left in command in the Atlanta campaign rather than being replaced by Hood. Perhaps Atlanta still would have fallen, but would Sherman have been able to march to the sea? I very much doubt that. Johnston would have maintained a stronger army and a better defense of Georgia and South Carolina. The march to the sea had a dramatic effect on Southern resources and on morale. The march from Savannah northward was a clear indication to the South that the jig was up. Johnston also should have had more authority with the Western armies earlier in the war. Even in the final days of the war in North Carolina, Johnston showed that he was absolutely top drawer as a Confederate commander.

Evacuating the Capital

Months of siege warfare at Petersburg had taken its toll on Lee's starving army, and losses at Five Forks on April 1 and on the following day in the trenches around Petersburg were the final straw. Lee elected to evacuate both Richmond and Petersburg, in hopes of giving Grant the slip and linking up with Joseph Johnston's small army in North Carolina. Less than a week later, however, hemmed in by Union infantry and cavalry at Appomattox Court House, Lee had no choice but to surrender his army to Grant. Johnston followed suit weeks later, surrendering to Sherman in North Carolina. When Confederates west of the Mississippi River capitulated in early June, the war was officially over.

What if Lee had evacuated Richmond and Petersburg sooner? What if Lee had been able to unite his army with Johnston's army?

ROBERT E. L. KRICK: Lee had very few options in the final few months of the war. If Lee had abandoned Richmond at some time after June 1864, but before April 1865, he certainly would have retained some strategic options that were not available to him when it actually happened in 1865. But the capture of Richmond would have buttressed flagging Union morale in 1864, and no matter when the city fell, its loss would have created a set of insurmountable challenges for the Confederates. Apart from the dire consequences of losing that portion of the South's supply network, the entire infrastructure of the country revolved around Richmond. Merely shutting all of the hospitals and prisons and removing their inmates would have crippled the South's railroad lines for many weeks.

Although Lee's army might well have won some important victories in central or southern Virginia after leaving Richmond, they would have been nothing more than final flailings. Unless one endorses the theory that the war could be won on a single battlefield, the strategy of abandoning Richmond and hopping around the state was unsound. Holding Richmond was more consistent with Lee's ambition of eroding the North's will to fight. Surrendering the soul of the Confederacy in favor of operational freedom for the Army of Northern Virginia only would have restored momentum to the Grant-Lincoln team.

MATT ATKINSON: It might have been better for the Confederates had Lee pulled out of Richmond earlier than he did, but Richmond was so symbolic for both sides. Grant's main objective in 1864 and 1865 after all wasn't Richmond but Lee's army. Lee desired to evacuate Richmond some months prior to the actual fall in April 1865. The Confederates could have pulled out of both Richmond and Atlanta sooner, but both cities were crucial to the Confederacy due to their industry. The main foundries, arsenals, supply depots and railroad hubs were in Atlanta and Richmond. The South didn't have a large industrial base to begin the war and it certainly would have been difficult for the Confederate armies to stay active in the field without those two cities.

The Confederates, as a last ditch effort, could have attempted to unite Lee's and Johnston's armies at an earlier date than they did. Although in early 1865, during the winter, it would have been an amazing feat if Lee had been able to evacuate his army from Richmond and Petersburg, get away from Grant's overwhelming force and march into the Carolinas to unite with Johnston. I'm not even sure the combined forces of Johnston and Lee could have defeated Sherman before Grant arrived on the scene.

CHRIS CALKINS: One of the key aspects of the nine-month siege of Petersburg was the wearing down of the Army of Northern Virginia. Lee knew that once Grant's army got to the James, it was only a matter of time before Grant took Richmond and Petersburg and wore down Lee's army. Lee wanted to avoid a siege but Jefferson Davis was micromanaging the strategic conduct of the war. Davis was adamant about Lee protecting Richmond. Lee had control only over the Army of Northern Virginia. Lee wanted to be free to maneuver on open ground and would have preferred to avoid a siege altogether, much as he did for the first month or so of Grant's Overland Campaign. Finally, in February 1865, Lee was given overall command of all Confederate forces, much too late to make any difference in the conflict.

As early as January or February, Lee was preparing to pull out of Petersburg. He was telling his corps commanders that they would be heading toward Burkeville Junction, at the crossing of the Richmond and Danville and Southside railroads. The Confederates planned to move to Danville and Lee wanted to hook up with Joe Johnston. If Lee could withdraw successfully from the Richmond-Petersburg front, he could then attempt to get to Danville. Work was already underway at Danville for building fortifications overlooking the Dan River. I doubt if Lee, even combined with Johnston, could have stopped Sherman. Naturally, Grant would also be in pursuit. At this point in the war, the Confederate soldier was fighting for one thing: Robert E. Lee. Lee had become the embodiment of the Confederacy.

Guerrilla Warfare

By the time Robert E. Lee arrived at Appomattox Court House, his options were extremely limited and he chose surrender. One proposal that a few of Lee's generals might have supported was guerrilla warfare. In a message composed on April 4, Jefferson Davis had urged his countrymen to continue to resist Federal troops, proposing partisan warfare on a large scale.[10] Rather than surrendering his army, Lee could have simply instructed his men to carry out bloody hit-and-run operations until Federal occupation of the South came to an end.[11] Lee recognized that such an order would have resulted in senseless bloodshed, and wisely discouraged guerrilla warfare tactics.[12]

What if Lee had advocated guerrilla warfare rather than surrendering at Appomattox?

MATT ATKINSON: If Lee had disbanded his army instead of surrendering, he would have plunged the already decimated South into anarchy. Bands of soldiers roving about the countryside without military order would have wreaked havoc. If Lee had issued an order to disband instead of surrendering, we might still have a Civil War occurring today. A good example of this scenario in the present day is Northern Ireland.

STEVEN WOODWORTH: The Confederates could certainly have prolonged the war considerably with guerrilla tactics. As Lee pointed out, that kind of warfare would have been very rough on the country. As we saw in Iraq, a war can be prolonged a good amount of time by guerrilla warfare but one has to have the willingness to destroy one's own society. Had the defenders of the Confederacy had the will to destroy their own society, the war could have gone on for quite some time and been very ugly indeed.

KENNETH NOE: Lee would have been a very different man had he been willing to advocate guerrilla warfare. But I would argue that a guerrilla war did take place anyway. Ku Klux Klan violence was, at a certain level, an organized guerrilla war fought for political reasons, and ultimately it helped undermine Republican governments in the South. Ironically, it might have been *less* successful with the sanction of an exiled Davis government. I suspect that the Northern people and Washington would have supported a stronger and longer effort to stamp out the Klan had Klan members been officially Confederates. More troops would have been involved in that guerrilla war. Instead, the North tired of its effort to "Americanize" the South and in 1877 gave Southern whites free rein to deal with African Americans as they saw fit.

Reconstructing with Lincoln

In his second inaugural address, Abraham Lincoln had promised to bind the nation's wounds to achieve a just and lasting peace. The events

Robert E. Lee, an opponent of guerrilla warfare and unnecessary bloodshed. LIBRARY OF CONGRESS.

of April 14, 1865, would change everything. John Wilkes Booth's assassination of Lincoln would have a dramatic impact on the way the reunification of the North and the South would unfold.

The new President, Andrew Johnson, quickly ran into problems with Radical Republicans in Congress who demanded stiff punishment for Southerners. Johnson had issued a proclamation granting pardons to almost all former Confederates who agreed to take the oath of allegiance to the Union. Johnson also took steps to offer Southerners more control over their state governments. When the Radical Republicans fought to pursue their own program, a harsh and violent Reconstruction period was guaranteed.[13]

What if Lincoln hadn't been assassinated and had served out his second term?

GEORGE RABLE: It was once assumed that Lincoln, had he lived, would have taken a much more conservative course toward Reconstruction than the path favored by the Radicals and even many moderate Republicans. Whatever the eventual shape of his own approach, I don't think Lincoln would have broken with the Republicans as Johnson did. Lincoln would have had the Republicans centered on a more cohesive policy in his second term. Lincoln would have also moved towards some kind of civil rights for freed blacks. I'm not sure how far he would have gone. I'm not sure if he would have favored unrestricted voting rights for blacks.

There are neo–Confederates today that view Lincoln as a horrible dictator who laid the groundwork for a leviathan federal government. Yet many defenders of the Lost Cause around the turn of the century saw Lincoln as a conservative who would have saved the Southern states from the so-called horrors of Reconstruction. Just look at the portrayal of Lincoln as the "Great Heart" in D.W. Griffith's classic film *Birth of a Nation*. The recent appearance of several strongly anti–Lincoln books that have sold well is the latest twist in the story. Given Lincoln's greatness as a political leader, much of this literature comes off as tendentious carping.

KEITH DICKSON: If Lincoln had survived to serve out his second term, he would have had a great deal of political difficulty. We know that his reconstruction efforts in Tennessee and Louisiana in 1862 and 1863, to return those states to the antebellum status quo, had only limited success. The South thought that once the war was over, things more or less would go back to the way they were before 1861. What we saw was that the Radical Republicans in the Congress were very much opposed to allowing the South to return to the status quo. So the Radicals would have bitterly opposed Lincoln's efforts to let the South up easy. They would have fought him every step of the way, and Lincoln would have been debilitated by this brutal, internal political battle. We would have seen some type of compromise between Lincoln's brand of reconstruction and the Radical's form of reconstruction. Lincoln's political capital would have been used up and he would have left office a broken, bitter and defeated man.

CRAIG SYMONDS: Lincoln's death was the greatest tragedy of the entire war. Some argue that Lincoln would have been kind to the South, letting them up easy. Some say he wouldn't have allowed the Radicals to force reconstruction on the South that led to bitterness and sectional rivalry. I don't agree with that assessment. I believe what made Lincoln great was his ability to pursue a specific and clear policy goal, and move toward it at the speed necessary to stay just barely ahead of public opinion. Lincoln knew how far he could go and where he could not go. Lincoln believed blacks should have citizenship and the right to vote. He knew how far and how fast he could go. Lincoln would have pursued the goals of the Radicals with a velvet

Abraham Lincoln. What would Reconstruction have looked like under Lincoln? LIBRARY OF CONGRESS.

glove. Lincoln would have made Reconstruction much less divisive and I believe civil rights would have come about 50 years earlier than they did.

CLINT JOHNSON: I don't believe Lincoln was planning to have a reconstruction period following the end of the war. He had planned to let the South up easy and also had thoughts of sending the freed slaves to Africa. Lincoln had told black ministers that he wondered if African-Americans and whites could live together in the United States. Lincoln had contemplated a massive repatriation of blacks to Africa. The plan would not have been feasible and most of the nation would have rejected the idea.

I do believe had Lincoln survived to serve out all or a larger portion of his second term, we wouldn't have seen the harsh Reconstruction we saw after 1865. We wouldn't have seen the postwar violence we saw with the birth of the Ku Klux Klan. The Klan was born because Reconstruction was harsh on the former white power structure in the south. I don't believe we saw, before Reconstruction, the type of violence against blacks we witnessed once Reconstruction started. In the reconstruction period, the whites were looking for scapegoats and the African Americans made perfect targets for them.

The South also gets blamed for Lincoln's assassination, but I believe in April 1865 Lincoln had more enemies in the North than in the South. The South was shocked by Lincoln's death at the hands of Booth. I don't believe it was a Southern assassination plot. Instead, I believe Lincoln had angered a lot of Northern bankers for refusing to finance the war the way they wanted. There are even theories that an Indiana beef dealer engineered Lincoln's assassination because Lincoln had interfered with a beef selling deal. The Radical Republicans stood to reap a lot of benefits from a tough Reconstruction on the South. Lincoln had nothing to gain himself from a harsh reconstruction period. So you had two warring forces in Lincoln's own cabinet. I'm just not positive that Booth wasn't a patsy. There's no doubt that Booth actually killed Lincoln, but whom Booth was working for when he killed Lincoln is another question. I think it's possible Booth may have been involved in a much deeper conspiracy to kill Lincoln. There were just too many bankers who had something to gain from Lincoln's death. I know Lawrence Baker, the head of the Secret Service in 1865, later supposedly wrote a secret confession where he intimated that Stanton was involved in Lincoln's death. We may never know who was involved and to what degree.

GERALD PROKOPOWICZ: Had Lincoln not been assassinated, American history would have been very different, but not in the way most people were taught in the 20th century. The traditional view, dating back over 100 years now, is that Johnson tried to be magnanimous toward the South, just as Lincoln would have done, but those evil Radical Republicans in Congress thwarted him with their vindictive schemes. That's the old view. Today, historians tend to look more closely at just what constituted Congress' "vindictive scheme" for the South, and it turns out that the things white Southerners considered most oppressive were civil rights and voting rights for the former slaves.

Johnson did oppose Congress on these issues, but not really out of tenderness for the South. He did it in part because he had no interest in racial justice, but more because as a Democrat, he was politically opposed to measures that would enfranchise a million black voters who were sure to be almost 100% Republican.

Lincoln, in contrast, had every political reason in the world to want the freedmen to be able to vote. Without them, there was no chance of establishing the Republican Party in the South, as the events of the next hundred years showed. Lincoln also felt a keen sense of obligation to African Americans who had fought for the Union, and considered it a matter of honor not to renege on his promise of emancipation, even though he was urged to do so at several points during the war.

For these reasons, had he lived, Lincoln surely would have done far more than Johnson did to defend the civil rights of the freedmen and to push for their right to vote. One possible result is that the Jim Crow segregation, which was not imposed until the 1890s, might never have come to pass. Imagine how different American history would have been with no *Plessy vs. Ferguson*, no "separate but equal," no Jim Crow.

At the same time, we would have no Lincoln Memorial, no Lincoln penny, no Lincoln on Mt. Rushmore. Lincoln was a controversial and in some quarters very unpopular politician during his presidency. It was only his assassination that made him a national icon. Had he lived, and had he taken the steps necessary to permanently dismantle the nation's racial hierarchy, he would have made enemies who would still not forgive him today.

MARK GRIMSLEY: How would Lincoln be viewed today had he lived? I don't believe any president would have had his reputation enhanced by dealing with Reconstruction. Grant's and Johnson's images were not brightened at all by Reconstruction. Lincoln actually had some experience with reconstruction during the war years. Reconstruction actually started in 1862. Postwar reconstruction started in 1865. Lincoln would have tried to handle the postwar reconstruction with the moderate course of action that he used throughout the war years. That would have meant fewer rights for African Americans than resulted from the actual Reconstruction under Johnson and Grant. In the historical Reconstruction, President Johnson blocked everything and it forced the Congress to perhaps go left of its intended policy. In addition to the 13th Amendment granting emancipation, several other constitutional amendments resulted, granting voting rights and other citizenship rights to African Americans. We may not have seen the 14th and 15th Amendments had Lincoln been around to serve out his second term. A Lincoln-led Reconstruction would have been more conservative than a Johnson-led Reconstruction.

African Americans in Uniform

Although the North didn't heavily recruit African Americans for military service until 1863, more than 180,000 had worn Union blue by the end of the war.[14] Many saw combat, performing admirably under horrible conditions, and 23 received the Congressional Medal of Honor.[15] In the South, the Confederate Congress waited until March of 1865 to approve the use of black slaves as soldiers. For the Confederacy, it was simply a case of too little, too late.

What if African Americans had not been allowed to serve in the Union army? What if they had been used as soldiers earlier in the war by the Confederacy?

MARK GRIMSLEY: It's possible the Union army still would have won the conflict without the service of African Americans in the army. You have to remember that African Americans made up about 10 percent of the Union army by the end of the war. They were fresh and highly motivated soldiers. The Confederates could have used African Americans as soldiers in their army without necessarily granting them political rights. The Confederates conceivably could have created a unit of African Americans who would have remained slaves despite their military service or received very limited rights, second class citizenship of some nature. Historically, minorities are attracted to military service as a way of trying to propel themselves toward society's mainstream. It's possible the Confederacy might have been able to make only limited concessions to African Americans in exchange for their support in joining the Confederate army. The problem was the North had upped the ante when it promised the slaves emancipation. Given the choice between serving the North or the South, it was a clear-cut choice in favor of freedom.

GERALD PROKOPOWICZ: Having some 180,000 African Americans serve in the Union military forces certainly was not insignificant. It changed the face of the war altogether. It made emancipation a fact, a done deal, by 1865. There were those in the North who were displeased when Lincoln issued the Emancipation Proclamation and wanted him to revoke it. Once African Americans were asked to fight for their country, it became totally unthinkable to reward them by returning them to slavery.

The issue of colonization, the idea of removing the freed slaves to some other part of the world, was also debated from time to time during the war. Lincoln proposed it to the Congress. Today Lincoln's supporters say it was a way to sweeten the deal so people would accept the Emancipation Proclamation. Lincoln's detractors say instead that it's evidence that Lincoln could not envision a multi-racial country. But once you begin arming the freedmen, colonization becomes a dead issue. It's simply out of the question to ask a person to fight for his country and then reward him by shipping him overseas, to Central America or Africa.

The arming of the African Americans changed the nature of the war and changed the goals of the war. It put emancipation at the center of the cause and created problems with prisoner exchanges, when the South refused to acknowledge African Americans as soldiers and treated them instead as escaped slaves. The Lincoln administration in turn promised harsh treatment of Confederate prisoners. Largely as a result of this, the exchange system broke down and the two sides rarely exchanged prisoners in the final years of the war.

Most people who are interested in the Civil War today are aware that the war was not fought solely by white Americans on behalf of black Americans. It was fought by both, and all Americans can take pride in the participation of all of those who were there. African American participation makes it impossible to argue that they were simply handed their freedom. They fought for their freedom as much as any other American did.

GEORGE RABLE: There was some talk late in the war about the South enlisting blacks to fight in the Confederate army. It's hard to speculate on the question of the South enlisting black soldiers and giving slaves their freedom at any point in the war. The South was a slave-holding society deeply committed to slavery. There had been a few calls for enlisting blacks in the Confederate army fairly early in the war. An aide to Jefferson Davis said the Confederacy could have enlisted large numbers of slaves into the Southern army early in the conflict. I think that's debatable. One of the problems the Confederates would have had in enlisting blacks into their army was their hesitation to promise freedom to those blacks willing to fight for the Confederacy. Even when the Confederate Congress decided to enlist blacks into the Southern army near the end of the war, the legislation specified that blacks would only be enlisted if their owners gave their consent and the states agreed as well. The document said nothing about freedom for blacks willing to fight for the South.

Paying for the War

At one point in the war, expenditures reached 2.5 million dollars a day in the North.[16] The Union relied heavily on war loans and Congress authorized the issuance of roughly 450 million dollars in paper money, Union greenbacks. A National Bank Act was also approved in 1863, giving the country a national currency for the first time, and wartime taxes brought in millions of dollars.[17]

While the North used a variety of methods to pay for the war effort, inflation slowly poisoned the South's economy. Lacking an adequate system of taxation, the value of Confederate paper currency rapidly declined.[18] In 1861, one gold dollar had been the equivalent of $1.03 in Confederate money; four years later, a dollar in gold equaled nearly 60 Confederate dollars.[19] By the spring of 1865, the South's economy had all but collapsed.[20]

What if the North had not come up with a unique approach to pay for the war or the South had adopted different fiscal policies?

GERALD PROKOPOWICZ: You can pay for a war by taxing your people today, or by borrowing money from your people and taxing the next generation to pay back over time the bonds you sold during the war. You can also print more money, which devalues your currency and thus takes money out of everybody's pockets simultaneously. The Union used all three methods while the Confederacy turned more and more to the indirect tax on citizens by printing more paper money. They had little choice. The Confederacy simply did not have the resources or infrastructure to support the war effort, no matter what they did financially. The South had plenty of food and plenty of cotton, but there was no way to get the food to the soldiers or the cities by the end of the war, and no way to get the cotton to the foreign markets. It wasn't so much a financial collapse as it was an economic collapse brought about by the North's military actions that made it impossible for the Confederate economy to continue to operate.

Certainly the North did a good job of mixing their methods for paying for the war while keeping the Union's economy stable. The inflation rate in the North was under 100 percent by the end of the war, which is not a bad record historically when you remember there were four years of war. Had the North only adopted one method for paying for the war, had they done nothing but print paper money or borrow, that would have sown economic trouble in the long run for the Union. But it was not financial strategy as much as it was the long-term design of the two economies that made the Union's economic success more likely.

MARK GRIMSLEY: If the North had not come up with a fiscal military revolution, a policy for paying for the war, then the North would have lost the war. The North came up with a nicely balanced program of taxation, greenbacks, interest bearing bonds and other options. The fiscal plans were so artfully balanced that the North was able to pay for the entire war with an inflation rate of only about 80 percent, which compares roughly with the inflation rate that the U.S. went through in World War 1 and in World

War II. By contrast, the Confederate fiscal policy was simply disastrous. The best thing the Confederates could have done was to send as much cotton as possible to Europe early on in the war. It would have created a surplus of cotton in Europe but at least the South would have had something to sell. This idea of trying to starve Europe of cotton, the self-imposed cotton embargo, to try to force the Europeans to intervene in the war was a terrible mistake on the part of the Confederacy. By the time the South realized its mistake, the blockade was becoming very effective and it was getting increasingly difficult for the South to get its goods across the Atlantic.

Another problem was that the Confederates were so conservative in their fiscal policies and so unimaginative that the South essentially waged a war according to the financial policies in use during the war of 1812. The Union blockade turned out to be very effective during the conflict. The blockade reduced Southern shipping dramatically and interdicted efforts by the Confederates to move goods along the coastal waterways. The South eventually became so dependent on the railroads for moving goods, placing a great strain on that part of the Confederate infrastructure, that it helped accelerate the wearing down of the rail lines in the South.

Victory for Dixie

Was Southern independence ever possible? At the beginning of the war, the North outweighed the South in several key categories. There were more than 18 million people in the North; the Confederacy had just 9 million people and more than a third of those were Negro slaves.[21] Northern farmers out-produced their counterparts in the South in corn, oats and wheat. The North controlled nearly all of the manufacturing capacity as well as two-thirds of the railway mileage.[22] Commercial shipping in the South was almost nonexistent, and at the outset of the conflict the new Confederate government possessed only about a million dollars in legal tender as a base for its currency.[23]

Given the North's advantages, could the South have won the Civil War?

JOHN SIMON: When the Constitution was written, white population numbers in the North and South were fairly similar. The white population in the North continued to grow. When you look at the numbers, the secession crisis of 1860–61 might have been the South's last chance to strike for independence with any hope for success, given the disparity of population between North and South. It's an important point to remember.

The North didn't start the war; it was the South that began the conflict at what, some people would say, was the last advantageous moment for the South to try to break away from the North. If the South had tried to break away from the North even earlier, in 1830 or 1850, it would have had better odds than in 1860. Not only was the Northern population increasing, but the Northern railroad network and industrial capacity were growing as well.

I would guess the C.S.A. would have lasted only a short period if the Confederates had been successful in the effort to gain independence. I suspect the achievement of independence would more likely have led to negotiation than to the permanent existence of two nations. There wasn't a strong sense of Confederate nationalism. Most people who supported the Confederacy viewed themselves as equally American as the people who lived north of them. I don't think it's hard to speculate that we would have seen a reunion, perhaps for economic reasons and perhaps for geopolitical reasons, probably not too long after Jefferson Davis left office. Davis was one of the very few who was so stubborn, so willful and so determined in support of the cause of the Confederacy that he'd have to be out of the way before any negotiation for reunion could take place.

GEORGE RABLE: If the Confederates fought skillfully on the defensive and inflicted enough casualties on the North, it was possible for the South to win. I'm not talking about the South surrendering a lot of territory or withdrawing constantly. I would say the idea of staying on the strategic defensive and going on the tactical offensive, when the opportunity arose, had a lot of merit. Hindsight is 20–20 and it's unfair for historians to dictate, after the fact, how the South should have conducted the war. I guess you could draw some parallels to the Pacific war in World War II. In World War II, as long as the Americans were willing to suffer losses and pay the price of casualties, then the U.S. was a good bet to defeat Japan. In the Civil War, as long as the North was willing to deal with its losses, it was a good bet to win, due to a much larger population and overwhelming industrial superiority.

JOHN HEATWOLE: For the Confederacy to have won the war, a number of variables would have to come into play. Because of the South's limited resources and manpower, the South could not have won without a series of circumstances coming to its aid first.

If Lee had scored a resounding victory at Antietam, Lincoln could not have put the Emancipation Proclamation into effect. This would have left the door open to a possible intervention by France or England to negotiate a peaceful settlement of hostilities, with the North being the big loser in the transaction; it could have at least begun a more vigorous and open shipping of supplies from Europe and England to the Confederacy.

If Fort Donelson had not fallen to the Union in February of 1862, Grant might not have continued to rise in the eyes of the chief executive. The strong hand needed to bring the war to a successful conclusion might never have been recognized, leaving Lee to wear down less aggressive Union commanders, inflicting horrific losses that would have brought out from the Northern citizenry a howl for cessation of hostilities.

If somehow the Confederates at Vicksburg had been able to go on the offensive against Grant and defeat his numerical superiority in detail, as Lee marched on Philadelphia or Washington after a victory at Gettysburg, the Federal government would have had to open some kind of truce talks.

How long could the Confederacy have lasted? Not long, and neither could have what was left of the United States. The financial depression that would have hit both sections would have crippled both, and opened the door for foreign investment that could have carried with it strings that would have been detrimental in the long run. A perceived victory by the South would have led other states in both the North and the South to take the road to secession if they had a difference of opinion with their respective government or neighboring states. What the eventual outcome would have been is hard to discern. Possibly the western or southwestern states and territories would have banded together to form a new country away from the eastern and southern centers of controversy, forever dashing the hope for a peaceful Confederate States of America or United States of America ever to co-exist.

A Fly on the Wall

Battles and campaigns shaped the Civil War, generals and politicians shaped the military actions. There's often plenty of documentation about what transpired at important gatherings but there are exceptions to that rule. We need to remember that even though a number of Northern and Southern military and political leaders wrote about the conflict, many wrote with political axes to grind or had to deal with faulty memories. Battlefield casualties also prevented some of the participants from telling their sides of the story. If we had the means to travel back in time to witness one of those crucial meetings, there would be no doubt as to what was said and how momentous decisions were reached, decisions that helped to decide the outcome of the war.

What meeting during the Civil War would you most like to attend?

KEITH DICKSON: The one moment in time I would have liked to have been present would be at the meeting of Lee and Jefferson Davis and the cabinet, right after the battle of Chancellorsville. It was at this meeting where the future of the Confederacy was largely decided, by tying the strategic goals of the Confederacy to a military campaign. Lee and Davis, at this meeting, decided how to take advantage of the initiative gained by the Southern victory at Chancellorsville. With a stalemate, for all intents and purposes, in the Western theatre, Lee and Davis met to decide how best to seize the initiative in the Eastern theatre, defeat the Army of the Potomac, and bring the North to a negotiated settlement. I would have liked to listen to the political discussions that went on as the Confederate leaders debated their options. We don't have a complete record of all that was said in this meeting, nor all the arguments that were raised both for and against the invasion of the North. We do not know what other options were raised and discarded. There has been talk over the years of Lee's influence on the policymakers, as well as the preconceived notions of Jefferson Davis that made the option to invade the only item for discussion.

ERIC WITTENBERG: If I could have been at one spot during the war to see what was discussed, it would be at the meeting of Buford and Reynolds at Gettysburg on July 1, 1863, to see what went into the decision for the Union forces to make a stand at Gettysburg. I've always felt Buford was the best cavalry commander the Union had to offer. He died in December 1863 of typhoid fever and is often overlooked. Historian Bruce Catton described Buford as being as plain as an old shoe. There was nothing flashy or flamboyant about him, unlike other cavalry commanders such as Jeb Stuart and George Custer. He was simply a quiet, competent commander who went about his business to the best of his ability. He avoided newspapers. In fact he hated newspapermen. The highest compliment I've ever seen paid to anyone, years after the war, was when Union General John Gibbon wrote that John Buford was the best cavalryman he ever saw.

DONALD PFANZ: From a political standpoint, it would have been very interesting to be at the meeting where Lincoln and his cabinet were discussing Fort Sumter. They needed to decide whether to re-supply the fort or to allow the South to starve out the garrison. There was a lot of politics involved as each side tried to make the other side look like the aggressor.

From a military standpoint, it would have been interesting to be in on the discussions July 2 at Gettysburg where Lee formulated his battle plan for the following day. Ultimately Lee decided to attack the Union center and the result was Pickett's Charge. There were very few witnesses able to speak about that meeting. It would have been interesting to see who spoke their opinions and what exactly they had to say about the plans for July 3.

JACK WAUGH: If I could be present at any decision in the war, it would be at a decision Lincoln was involved with. He was the central figure of the war and he was a genius. It would be fascinating to see how he was thinking during times of great stress, perhaps in battles and campaigns the North was losing, such as the Peninsula Campaign or Fredericksburg or Chancellorsville. It would be fascinating to see how he dealt with the stress and to see how he was able, despite it, to keep on keeping on and bring the country back together.

RICHARD BERINGER: What would be interesting to me would be to sit around a hot stove in Galena, Illinois, during the spring of 1861, listening to a fellow who had left the army under a cloud as a captain a few years before, had once sold wood on the streets of St. Louis, and who had finally gotten a job selling leather goods made in his father's tannery in Ohio. In this store in Galena, he discussed his fears about coming events, and decided to volunteer without pay to help the governor of Illinois train some of the early regiments that would be sent in response to Lincoln's call for troops. Who would have guessed that U.S. Grant, so far down on his luck in early 1861, would be a world acclaimed, victorious general just four years later? I would like to know what went through his mind, and how he came to his decision.

Summary

The final few months of the war were a living nightmare for the Confederacy. Lee's army wasted away in the trenches of Petersburg, Sherman ravaged Georgia and South Carolina, and Hood destroyed the Army of Tennessee at Franklin and Nashville. Could Sherman have marched to the sea with Joseph Johnston commanding the Army of Tennessee? John Simon claimed that with Johnston in charge, Sherman would have been unable to move through Georgia unmolested; Richard McMurry voiced his opinion that Johnston would have retreated in the face of Sherman's troops, in the direction of Lee's army in Virginia.

Could Lee and Johnston have united their armies in Virginia or North Carolina and kept the Confederacy alive, if only for a few extra months? Robert E. L. Krick noted that the Confederacy could not afford the loss of infrastructure that the evacuation of Richmond entailed, and Chris Calkins added his doubts that a combined Lee-Johnston force would have been able to overcome Sherman, let alone Grant's pursuing army.

The one point the experts could agree on was how much more smoothly postwar reunification efforts would have gone in the skillful hands of Abraham Lincoln. Craig Symonds called Lincoln's death the single greatest tragedy of the war, and predicted that the civil rights gains of the 20th century for African Americans might have been achieved 50 years earlier had Lincoln been at the helm. Gerald Prokopowicz suggested that the Jim Crow segregation laws of the 20th century might never have arisen if Lincoln had been in charge between 1865 and 1868. Prokopowicz added, however, that Lincoln's actions would have earned him additional enemies, to the point that Lincoln might be viewed in less glowing terms today.

The Civil War lasted four years. Reconstruction would linger for 12 agonizing and violent years as Radical Republicans attempted to punish the former Confederate states, and secret societies in the South used violence to intimidate recently freed black slaves and Northern carpetbaggers. Had Lincoln survived and served out his second term, we might have seen an enhanced civil rights package for African Americans and less vindictiveness toward Southerners. Perhaps a more constructive reunification period would have helped the nation avoid the 20th century nightmares of Ku Klux Klan violence and the "separate but equal" racial segregation policies of Jim Crow.

The Civil War eliminated slavery and brought together a divided nation, at the cost of hundreds of thousands of lives. Perhaps if Abraham Lincoln had been able to spend four more years in the White House, the sacrifice of the soldiers, both blue and gray, would have reaped even greater rewards for a nation attempting to bind its wounds.

Appendix:
Surveying the Experts

Several of the esteemed panelists agreed to provide responses to the following survey. It is my hope that they enjoyed it, despite the hardtack dinner for two, and that the reader is able to learn a bit more about the experts through their opinions.

Which general do you respect the most?

Robert E. Lee tops the list, with Grant a close second.

Robert E. Lee (8.5) Atkinson, Daniel, Dickson, Gottfried, Hennessy, Noe, Pfanz, Waugh, Wert

U.S. Grant (7.5) Bearss, Beringer, Carmichael, Calkins, Hennessy, Simon, Symonds, Woodworth

William Sherman (2) Prokopowicz, Rable

Patrick Cleburne (1) McMurry, **Nathan Bedford Forrest (1)** Johnson, **Wade Hampton (1)** Wittenberg

Which politician do you admire the most?

Much like the 1864 election, it was Abraham Lincoln in a landslide.

Abraham Lincoln (18) Bearss, Beringer, Calkins, Carmichael, Daniel, Gottfried, Hennessy, McMurry, Noe, Pfanz, Prokopowicz, Rable, Simon, Symonds, Waugh, Wert, Wittenberg, Woodworth

Judah Benjamin (2) Dickson, Johnson

John C. Breckinridge (1) Atkinson

Who is the most underrated general?

The Rock of Chickamauga refuses to be budged from the top spot.

George Thomas (4) Bearss, Prokopowicz, Symonds, Wert
Patrick Cleburne (2) Johnson, Waugh, A.P. Hill (2) Calkins, Carmichael,
    Joseph Johnston (2) Beringer, Simon, George Meade (2) Gottfried, Rable
P.G.T. Beauregard (1) Daniel, Braxton Bragg (1) McMurry, John S. Bowen (1)
    Atkinson, Richard Ewell (1) Pfanz, John Gibbon (1) Dickson, Wade Hamp-
    ton (1) Wittenberg, James Longstreet (1) Hennessy, William Rosecrans (1)
    Noe, William Sherman (1) Woodworth,

Who is the most overrated general?

Surprising—but remember, overrated can mean great but not perfect.

Stonewall Jackson (4) Beringer, Carmichael, Rable, Symonds
Albert Sidney Johnston (3) Daniel, Prokopowicz, Simon
Phil Sheridan (2) Wert, Wittenberg
Ben Butler (1) Calkins, Nathan Bedford Forrest (1) Noe, U.S. Grant (1) John-
    son, Winfield Hancock (1) Pfanz, A. P. Hill (1) Gottfried, Joseph Johnston
    (1) McMurry, George McClellan (1) Waugh, Alexander McCook (1) Daniel,
    James McPherson (1) Bearss, William Sherman (1) Atkinson, George
    Thomas (1) Woodworth, Joe Wheeler (1) Dickson

What was the turning point of the war?

Gettysburg was expected, Fort Donelson a bit unexpected.

Loss of Fort Donelson (4) Daniel, Noe, Simon, Woodworth, Gettysburg (4)
    Dickson, Johnson, Pfanz, Wittenberg
Vicksburg (3) Dickson, Johnson, Wert
Antietam (2) Gottfried, Waugh, The fall of Atlanta (2) Beringer, Symonds
Confederate occupation of Kentucky in September 1861 (1) McMurry, The
    three weeks between Antietam and Perryville (1) Bearss, The Emancipa-
    tion Proclamation (1) Prokopowicz, The Overland Campaign (1) Rable,
    Grant's crossing of the James River in 1864 (1) Atkinson, Lincoln's 1864
    election victory (1) Calkins

What was the best battlefield decision?

Lee and Jackson surprise Joe Hooker.

The decision by Lee and Jackson to launch a flank attack at Chancellorsville
    (5) Beringer, Dickson, Hennessy, Johnson, Noe
Grant's counterattack at Shiloh (2) Simon, Symonds, Grant's decision to
    attack Fort Donelson (2) Bearss, Woodworth, Meade's decision to hold his
    ground at Gettysburg (2) Gottfried, Wittenberg, The decision not to

attack Lee's defenses at Mine Run (2) Pfanz, Prokopowicz, **Grant's flank-ing movement below the James River after Cold Harbor** (2) Calkins, Carmichael

Bragg's decision to escape from Corinth and begin the Kentucky Campaign (1) Daniel, **Forrest at Brice's Crossroads** (1) Waugh, **Grant's decisions during the Vicksburg Campaign** (1) Atkinson, **Grant's decision May 7, 1864, to march south after the Battle of the Wilderness** (1) Wert

What was the worst battlefield decision?

A tossup between McClellan's cautiousness, Hood's aggressiveness and Pickett's Charge.

McClellan's failure to push his advantage at Antietam (3) Symonds, Waugh, Wert, **Pickett's Charge** (3) Gottfried, Pfanz, Wittenberg, **Hood's attack at Franklin** (3) Bearss, Dickson, Noe

Rosecrans' orders that produced a gap in his lines at Chickamauga (2) Johnson, Simon

Floyd and Pillow surrendering at Fort Donelson (1) Prokopowicz, **McDowell's decision to withdraw from Chinn Ridge at Second Manassas** (1) Hennessy, **McClellan's failure to attack at Antietam September 18** (1) Carmichael, **Sherman's attack at Chickasaw Bluffs in December 1862** (1) Beringer, **Hooker's hesitation at Chancellorsville** (1) Atkinson, **The Confederate retreat into the Vicksburg defenses after the defeat at Big Black River** (1) Daniel, **Rosecrans' decision to flee Chickamauga, abandon Rossville Gap and withdraw into Chattanooga** (1) Woodworth, **The Union decision not to call off the Battle of the Crater** (1) Calkins

If you could be a battlefield observer during the war, just like Arthur Fremantle, which battle would you wish to observe?

Antietam, an action-packed battle, was the single bloodiest day of the war.

Antietam (6) Bearss, Carmichael, Hennessy, Johnson, Pfanz, Waugh
Gettysburg (4) Gottfried, Prokopowicz, Symonds, Wert
Monitor vs. Merrimac (1) Beringer, **Shiloh** (1) Daniel, **Brawner's Farm** (1) Dickson, **Second Manassas** (1) Atkinson, **Perryville** (1) Noe, **Fredericksburg** (1) Rable, **Brandy Station** (1) Wittenberg, **Atlanta** (1) Woodworth, **Franklin** (1) McMurry, **Surrender parade at Appomattox** (1) Calkins

If you had a chance to speak with one individual from the war, over a hardtack dinner, who would it be?

Lincoln gets the nod, without Mary Todd.

Abraham Lincoln (6) Noe, Pfanz, Prokopowicz, Simon, Waugh, Wert
Robert E. Lee (4) Calkins, Carmichael, Dickson, Johnson

William T. Sherman (3) Daniel, McMurry, Rable

Jubal Early (2) Atkinson, Gottfried

John Buford (1) Wittenberg, **Ben Butler** (1) Hennessy, **Patrick Cleburne** (1) Symonds, **Jefferson Davis** (1) Beringer, **Nathan Bedford Forrest** (1) Bearss, **U.S. Grant** (1) Woodworth

Chapter Notes

Works cited and shortened titles can be found in full in the Bibliography. These abbreviations are used in the endnotes.

AH   *The American Heritage New History of the Civil War*

BAB   *Brother against Brother: Time-Life Books History of the Civil War*

B & L   *Battles and Leaders of the Civil War*

CWTI   Civil War Times Illustrated's *The Civil War: The Compact Edition, Fort Sumter to Gettysburg*

MA   *From Manassas to Appomattox*

1. On the Brink

1. Catton, *AH*, p. 6–7.
2. *Ibid.*, p. 2.
3. *Ibid.*, p. 18.
4. *Ibid.*, p. 27.
5. *CWTI*, p. 20.
6. Catton, *AH*, p.30, *CWTI*, p. 24.
7. *CWTI*, pp. 23–24.
8. *Ibid.*, p. 22.
9. Foote, *The Civil War,* I, p. 34.
10. *CWTI*, p. 24.
11. New York senator William Seward had hoped to be the Republican Party's presidential nominee in 1860. The Republicans nominated Lincoln, partly because he was considered less of an extremist than Seward and believed that the Federal government did not have the authority to interfere with slavery in the states. Catton, *AH*. pp. 27–30

12. Without additional slave states being added to the United States, the South's power in Congress would continue to shrink.
13. Davis, *Jefferson Davis*, p. 303.
14. Foote, *The Civil War,* I, p. 41.
15. Several delegates had favored Alexander H. Stephens of Georgia as the Confederacy's new president but Stephens' chances

may have been damaged by his statements that he would be unwilling to commit the first offensive act if it came to war with the North. Davis, *Jefferson Davis*, p. 303.

2. The Pinch Comes

1. *CWTI*, p. 27.
2. Catton, *AH*. p. 41.
3. *CWTI*, p. 27.
4. Catton, *AH*. p. 48.
5. *CWTI*, p. 25.
6. *Ibid.*, p. 27.
7. Dred Scott was a black slave whose master had kept him in Illinois and the Wisconsin territory for several years. Scott was brought back to Missouri but sued for his freedom, contending that his years in Illinois and Wisconsin had made him free. The U.S. Supreme Court rejected Scott's plea in 1857, ruling that the act by which Congress had forbidden slavery in the Northern territories was invalid because the Constitution gave slavery ironclad protection. Catton, *AH*, pp 27,30; *BAB*, p. 31.
8. *BAB*, p. 35.
9. *Ibid.*, p. 35.
10. Foote, *The Civil War*, I, p. 47.
11. *BAB*, p. 39.
12. Catton, *AH*, p. 53.
13. Pensacola was the location of another Union stronghold, Fort Pickens.
14. Catton, *AH*, p. 47.

3. Like a Stone Wall

1. Catton, *AH*, p. 78.
2. *Ibid.*, p. 78.
3. *Ibid.*, p. 81.
4. *CWTI*, p. 172.
5. While rallying his men on Henry House Hill, Bee was heard to shout, "There stands Jackson like a stone wall! Rally behind the Virginians!" *BAB*, p. 58
6. Davis, *Jefferson Davis*, p. 352.
7. Catton, *AH*, p. 92; *BAB*, p. 59.
8. Catton, *AH*, p. 92.
9. Longstreet, *MA*, pp. 52–53; Wert, *General James Longstreet*, pp. 76–77.
10. Gallagher, ed., *Fighting for the Confederacy*, p. 58.
11. Cub Run was a small stream that intersected the Warrenton Turnpike a few miles east of Henry House Hill, about a mile from Centreville.

4. Grant's Beginning, Johnston's End

1. Catton, *AH*, p. 115; *BAB*, p. 75.
2. Catton, *AH*, p. 116.
3. *BAB*, p. 75.
4. *Ibid.*, p. 80.
5. Catton, *AH*, p. 117.
6. *Ibid.*, p. 109.
7. Woodworth, *Jefferson Davis and His Generals*, p. 82.
8. Foote, *The Civil War*, I, p. 207.
9. Buckner became the ranking Confederate officer at Fort Donelson following the decision by Floyd and Pillow to flee the fort, to avoid capture.
10. *CWTI*, p. 268.
11. In the days following Grant's victory at Fort Donelson, the Confederates evacuated Nashville after spiriting away much needed supplies. The mayor of Nashville surrendered the city to Federal troops seven days after the loss of Fort Donelson. Foote, *The Civil War*, I, p. 217.
12. Catton, *AH*, p. 109.
13. *B & L*, I, p. 483.
14. Foote, *The Civil War*, I, p. 351.
15. *Ibid.*, p. 338.
16. Woodworth, *Jefferson Davis and His Generals*, p. 101.
17. *BAB*, pp. 84–85.
18. *CWTI*, p. 270.
19. One of Napoleon's greatest victories occurred at Austerlitz in Moravia on December 2, 1805, when the French army defeated a combined Russian-Austrian force.
20. Union forces took possession of New Orleans in late April.
21. *BAB*, p. 89.

5. Saving Richmond

1. Catton, *AH*, p. 97.
2. *Ibid.*, p. 99.
3. *Ibid.*, p. 119.
4. *BAB*, p. 105.
5. Catton, *AH*, p. 125.
6. *Ibid.*, p. 146.

7. *Ibid.*, p. 171.

8. Catton, *AH*, p. 178.

9. *BAB*, p. 90; Foote, *The Civil War*, I, p. 262.

10. Josiah Gorgas was the Chief of Ordnance for the Confederate government.

11. *CWTI*, p. 777.

12. Foote, *The Civil War*, I, p. 438.

13. *Ibid.*, p. 436.

14. Waugh, *Class of 1846*, p. 328.

15. *CWTI*, p. 784.

16. Catton, *AH*, p. 140.

17. Waugh, *Class of 1846*, p. 522; Young, *Around the World with General Grant*, vol. 2, pp. 210–211.

18. *BAB*, p. 105.

19. *B & L*, II, p. 171.

20. *BAB*, p. 109.

21. Catton, *AH*, p. 135.

22. Foote, *The Civil War*, I, p. 465.

23. Catton, *AH*, p. 146.

24. Sears, *To the Gates of Richmond*, p. 176.

25. *Ibid.*, p. 199.

26. *Ibid.*, p. 249.

27. Foote, *The Civil War*, I, p. 501.

28. *Ibid.*, p. 504.

29. *BAB*, p. 122.

30. *B & L*, II, pp. 381–382

31. Catton, *AH*, p. 148.

32. *BAB*, p. 123.

33. Gallagher, ed., *Fighting for the Confederacy*, p. 96.

34. McClellan attacked Lee's lines east of Richmond June 25, in what was to be the first of a series of partial attacks in McClellan's final campaign against Richmond. The Battle of Oak Grove instead turned out to be the opening battle of the Seven Days' Battles as McClellan surrendered the initiative to Lee following the Confederate attack at Beaver Dam Creek June 26. Sears, *To the Gates of Richmond*, p. 183.

6. Rebels on the Move

1. Catton, *AH*, p. 200.

2. *BAB*, p. 137.

3. Catton, *AH*, p. 219.

4. *Ibid.*, p. 230.

5. *BAB*, p. 132.

6. Foote, *The Civil War*, I, p. 621.

7. *CWTI*, p. 808.

8. *Ibid.*, p. 809.

9. *BAB*, p. 135.

10. Hennessy, *Return to Bull Run*, p. 458.

11. *BAB*, p. 136.

12. Hennessy, *Return to Bull Run*, p. 471.

13. At the Battle of Kettle Run August 27, Union troops from Joseph Hooker's division, including men from Col. Nelson Taylor's famed "Excelsior Brigade," tangled with three Confederate brigades. The battle cost the Federals 300 killed and wounded, and blunted Pope's advance on Manassas Junction. Hennessy, *Return to Bull Run*, p. 134.

14. *Ibid.*, p. 154.

15. Wert, *General James Longstreet*, p. 165.

16. Davis, *Jefferson Davis*, p. 468.

17. Catton, *AH*, p. 221.

18. Waugh, *Class of 1846*, p. 367.

19. November 4, 1862, was Election Day in most northern states. The number of Democratic congressmen increased from 44 to 75 although the Republicans would remain the majority party, thanks to the party's success in New England, the Border States and the Far West. Foote, *The Civil War*, I, pp. 753–754.

20. *BAB*, p. 139.

21. Johnson, *In the Footsteps of Stonewall Jackson*, p. 50.

22. One of the final shots fired by Confederate artillery September 15 at Harpers Ferry struck Dixon Miles. Miles died the following day. Catton, *AH*, p. 217.

23. *BAB*, p. 140.

24. Foote, *The Civil War*, I, p. 695; *CWTI*, p. 923.

25. Catton, *AH*, p. 225.

26. *Ibid.*, p. 226.

27. Gallagher, ed., *Fighting for the Confederacy*, p. 151.

28. *Ibid.*, p. 153.

29. Foote, *The Civil War*, I, p. 701.

30. Lincoln drew up the orders for McClellan's removal as the commander of the Army of the Potomac November 5, replacing him with Ambrose Burnside. McClellan received the orders November 7. Foote, *The Civil War*, I, p. 754.

31. Catton, *AH*, p. 217

32. *CWTI*, p. 275.

33. Woodworth, *Jefferson Davis and His Generals*, p. 147.

34. Foote, *The Civil War*, I. p. 739.
35. Woodworth, *Jefferson Davis and His Generals*, p. 160.
36. *BAB*, p. 137.
37. Catton, *AH*, p. 245.
38. William E. Gladstone was England's chancellor of the exchequer. Catton, *AH*, p. 245.

7. Stalemate

1. Catton, *AH*, p. 253; *BAB*, p. 190.
2. Catton, *AH*, p. 255.
3. *BAB*, p. 191.
4. *Ibid.*, p. 192.
5. Catton, *AH*, p. 255.
6. *Ibid.*, p. 255.
7. *Ibid.*, p. 263.
8. *Ibid.*, p. 263.
9. *Ibid.*, p. 268.
10. Gallagher, ed., *Fighting for the Confederacy*, p. 167.
11. *BAB*, p. 192.
12. Wert, *General James Longstreet*, p. 218.
13. *BAB*, p. 203
14. *Ibid.*, p. 203.
15. *Ibid.*, p. 194.
16. *Ibid.*, p. 194.
17. Foote, *The Civil War*, II. p. 37.
18. *CWTI*, p. 964.
19. Woodworth, *Jefferson Davis and His Generals*, p. 188.
20. *BAB*, p. 169.
21. *Ibid.*, p. 170.
22. *Ibid.*, p. 181.
23. Catton, *AH*, pp. 277–278.
24. Hooker had directed his cavalry chief, Major General George Stoneman, to carry out a raid south of Lee's army, in an effort to wreak havoc with Lee's supply lines and communications. Stoneman's raid was delayed several weeks by heavy rains; in the end, the raid resulted in only minor damage to Confederate installations and cost Hooker troops that could have provided him with much needed intelligence at Chancellorsville. Catton, *AH*, p. 283; Foote, *The Civil War*, II, p. 314.
25. Catton, *AH*, p. 281.
26. *BAB*, p. 212.
27. *Ibid.*, p. 213.
28. Waugh, *Class of 1846*, p. 417.

29. Catton, *AH*, p. 281; *BAB*, p. 219.
30. Hooker was leaning against one of the wooden pillars of the Chancellor mansion the morning of May 3 when an artillery shell hit the pillar. Part of the pillar struck Hooker, knocking him senseless. Foote, *The Civil War*, II, p. 304; *BAB*, p. 217.
31. Hazel Grove turned out to be one of the key positions on the Chancellorsville battlefield. When Hooker ordered Sickles to withdraw his corps from Hazel Grove, the Confederates claimed the ground. From Hazel Grove, Lee's artillery was able to enfilade the Union position at Fairview. Jeb Stuart, who had taken over command of Stonewall Jackson's Corps, organized the infantry assaults against the Army of the Potomac on May 3. *BAB*, pp. 216–217.
32. *BAB*, p. 215.
33. Johnson, *In the Footsteps of Stonewall Jackson*, p. 134.
34. Catton, *AH*, p. 286.
35. Foote, *The Civil War*, II, p. 302.
36. *BAB*, p. 219.

8. Showdown in Pennsylvania

1. Wert, *General James Longstreet*, pp. 243–245; Longstreet, *MA*, p. 327.
2. Davis, *Jefferson Davis*, p. 505.
3. Ibid, p. 504.
4. Catton, *AH*, p. 308.
5. *CWTI*, p. 1271.
6. Catton, *AH*, p. 314.
7. *BAB*, p. 272.
8. *CWTI*, p. 1278.
9. Wert, *General James Longstreet*, p. 278.
10. *BAB*, p. 272.
11. Gallagher, ed., *Fighting for the Confederacy*, p. 228, 232.
12. On June 28, Stuart's men happened upon a huge Federal wagon train packed with supplies at Rockville, Maryland. After a spirited chase, Stuart captured 900 mules, 400 prisoners of war and 125 wagons full of food and fodder. *BAB*, p. 272; Foote, *The Civil War*, II. p. 458.
13. Foote, *The Civil War*, II, p. 484.
14. In case of disaster, Meade planned to rally his army along the south bank of Pipe Creek, near Taneytown, Maryland. Foote, *The Civil War*, II, p. 466.

15. Longstreet, *MA*, p. 358.
16. *BAB*, p. 274.
17. *Ibid.*, p. 274.
18. *Ibid.*, p. 278.
19. *CWTI*, p. 1278.
20. *BAB*, p. 275.
21. Foote, *The Civil War*, II, p. 501.
22. *B & L*, III, p. 207.
23. *CWTI*, p. 1277.
24. Trulock, *In the Hands of Providence*, p. 147.
25. Oates, *The War between the Union and the Confederacy*, p. 216.
26. Following McLaws' assault of the Union lines at the Peach Orchard and the Wheat Field, three brigades from Richard Anderson's division launched an attack on the southern end of Cemetery Ridge. Brigadier General Cadmus Wilcox's Alabamans, Colonel David Lang's small brigade of three Florida regiments and Brigadier General Ambrose Wright's Georgians carried out an echelon attack around 6:30 p.m., but Brigadier General William Mahone's brigade and elements of Brigadier General Carnot Posey's brigade failed to take part in the attack. Wright's men briefly gained ground near the crest of Cemetery Ridge but were forced to withdraw due to a lack of support. Foote, *The Civil War*, II, pp 509–512.
27. *BAB*, p. 283.
28. Waugh, *Class of 1846*, p. 489.
29. Foote, *The Civil War*, II, p. 564.
30. *Ibid.*, p. 434.
31. *Ibid.*, p. 585.
32. *BAB*, p. 294.
33. Foote, *The Civil War*, II, pp. 577–578.

9. Mortal Wounds

1. Catton, *AH*, p. 328.
2. *Ibid.*, p. 294.
3. *Ibid.*, p. 393.
4. *Ibid.*, p. 393.
5. *Ibid.*, p. 398.
6. The failures included Sherman's disastrous assault on Chickasaw Bluffs in late December 1862 as well as several unsuccessful amphibious operations. *AH*, p. 294; *BAB*, p. 234–237.
7. *BAB*, p. 237.
8. *Ibid.*, p. 238.

9. Catton, *AH*, p. 290.
10. *Ibid.*, p. 293.
11. *BAB*, p. 304.
12. *Ibid.*, p. 305.
13. *Ibid.*, p. 309–310.
14. *Ibid.*, p. 311.
15. *Ibid.*, p. 311.
16. Wert, *General James Longstreet*, p. 319; *B & L*, III, p. 662; Foote, *The Civil War*, II, p. 760.
17. *BAB*, p. 317.
18. Woodworth, *Jefferson Davis and His Generals*, p. 242.
19. *Ibid.*, p. 317.
20. Catton, *AH*, p. 398.
21. *BAB*, p. 317.
22. *Ibid.*, pp. 323–328.
23. Catton, *AH*, p. 401.
24. Longstreet's assault on Burnside's army at Knoxville on November 29 was turned back, at a cost of 813 Confederate casualties. Foote, *The Civil War*, II, p. 865.

10. Grant against Lee

1. Catton, *AH*, p. 403
2. *Ibid.*, p. 407.
3. *BAB*, p. 344.
4. *Ibid.*, p. 355.
5. Catton, *AH*, p. 411.
6. *Ibid.*, p. 411.
7. *BAB*, p. 337.
8. Wert, *General James Longstreet*, p. 387.
9. Gallagher, ed., *Fighting for the Confederacy*, p. 362.
10. *BAB*, p. 346.
11. Foote, *The Civil War*, III, p. 209.
12. *BAB*, p. 349.
13. *Ibid.*, p. 350.
14. *Ibid.*, p. 352.
15. Foote, *The Civil War*, III, p. 169.
16. Rhea, *The Battle of the Wilderness*, p. 301.
17. Foote, *The Civil War*, III, p. 218.
18. Stuart was wounded at Yellow Tavern May 11 and died the following day in Richmond, six days after Lee had attempted to accompany Brigadier General John Gregg's Texas Brigade in a counterattack on Hancock's troops at the Wilderness. *BAB*, pp. 349–350.

11. Wearing down the South

1. *BAB*, p. 356.
2. *Ibid.*, p. 358.
3. Catton, *AH*, p. 431.
4. *BAB*, p. 368.
5. *Ibid.*, p. 359.
6. *Ibid.*, p. 360.
7. *Ibid.*, p. 364.
8. Foote, *The Civil War*, III. p. 419.
9. Woodworth, *Jefferson Davis and His Generals*, p. 288.
10. Davis, *Jefferson Davis*, p. 564.
11. *BAB*, p. 368.
12. *Ibid.*, p. 378.
13. Foote, *The Civil War*, III, pp. 428–431.
14. *BAB*, p. 380.
15. Foote, *The Civil War*, III, p. 532
16. *BAB*, p. 382.
17. Catton, *AH*, p. 434.
18. *BAB*, p. 384.
19. Confederate major general John Breckinridge defeated Sigel at New Market on May 15. Cadets from the Virginia Military Institute in Lexington were in the thick of the fighting and helped to repel Sigel's force. *BAB*, p. 385.
20. Early's men were delayed 24 hours at the Monocacy River by a small Union force commanded by Major General Lew Wallace. *BAB*, p. 387.
21. *BAB*, p. 387.
22. Union forces under Phil Sheridan defeated Jubal Early's Army of the Valley at Cedar Creek, Virginia, on October 19, 1864, in a battle that essentially finished Early's army as a fighting force. *BAB*, p. 391.
23. Catton, *AH*, pp. 471–472.
24. *Ibid.*, p. 472.
25. *Ibid.*, p. 512.
26. *Ibid.*, p. 513.

12. A Just and Lasting Peace

1. Woodworth, *Jefferson Davis and His Generals*, p. 294.
2. Catton, *AH*, p. 522.
3. *BAB*, p. 393.
4. *Ibid.*, p. 400.
5. *Ibid.*, p. 408.
6. *Ibid.*, p. 412.
7. Woodworth, *Jefferson Davis and His Generals*, p. 294.
8. Davis, *Jefferson Davis*, p. 575.
9. *BAB*, p. 371.
10. Davis, *Jefferson Davis*, p. 608.
11. Catton, *AH*, p. 571.
12. Gallagher, ed., *Fighting for the Confederacy*, p. 532.
13. *BAB*, p. 412.
14. Catton, *AH*, p. 383.
15. *BAB*, p. 399.
16. Catton, *AH*, p. 440–442
17. *Ibid.*, p. 446.
18. *Ibid.*, p. 455.
19. *BAB*, p. 392.
20. Catton, *AH*, p. 456.
21. *Ibid.*, p. 61.
22. *Ibid.*, p. 61.
23. *Ibid.*, p. 49, 455.

Bibliography

Buel, C. C., and R. Johnson, eds. *Battles and Leaders of the Civil War.* 4 vols. New York, Century, 1887–88; reprint, Edison, N.J.: Castle, 1956.

Catton, Bruce, and James M. McPherson. *The American Heritage New History of the Civil War.* New York: Viking, 1996.

Davis, William C., and Bell I. Wiley, eds. *Civil War Times Illustrated's The Civil War: The Compact Edition, Fort Sumter to Gettysburg.* New York: Black Dog and Leventhal, 1998.

Davis, William C. *Jefferson Davis: The Man and His Hour.* New York: Harper-Collins, 1991.

Foote, Shelby. *The Civil War: A Narrative, Fort Sumter to Perryville.* New York: Random House, 1958.

Foote, Shelby. *The Civil War: A Narrative, Fredericksburg to Meridian.* New York: Random House, 1963.

Foote, Shelby. *The Civil War: A Narrative, Red River to Appomattox.* New York: Random House, 1974.

Gallagher, Gary W., ed. *Fighting for the Confederacy: The Personal Recollections of General Edward Porter Alexander.* Chapel Hill: University of North Carolina Press, 1989.

Hennessy, John J. *Return to Bull Run: The Campaign and Battle of Second Manassas.* New York: Simon and Schuster, 1993

Johnson, Clint. *In the Footsteps of Stonewall Jackson.* Winston-Salem, N.C.: John F. Blair, 2002.

Longstreet, James. *From Manassas to Appomattox.* Philadelphia: Lippincott, 1896.

Oates, William C. *The War between the Union and the Confederacy and Its Lost Opportunities.* New York: 1905; reprint, with introduction by Robert K. Krick. Dayton, Oh.: Morningside, 1974.

Rhea, Gordon. *The Battle of the Wilderness May 5–6, 1864.* Baton Rouge: Louisiana State University Press, 1994.

Sears, Stephen. *To the Gates of Richmond: The Peninsula Campaign*. New York: Ticknor and Fields, 1992.

Time-Life, *Brother against Brother: Time-Life Books History of the Civil War*. New York: Prentice Hall, 1990.

Trulock, Alice Rains. *In the Hands of Providence: Joshua L. Chamberlain and the American Civil War*. Chapel Hill: University of North Carolina Press, 1992.

Waugh, John C. *Class of 1846*. New York: Warner Books, 1994.

Wert, Jeff D. *General James Longstreet: The Confederacy's Most Controversial Soldier*. New York: Simon and Schuster, 1993.

Woodworth, Steven E. *Jefferson Davis and His Generals: The Failure of Confederate Command in the West*. Lawrence: University Press of Kansas, 1990.

Young, John Russell. *Around the World with General Grant*. 2 vols. New York: American News Company, 1879.

Index

Numbers in **bold italics** refer to illustrations.